'Helen Zink provides a fascinating story that shows how team coaching not only transforms the team's relationship to itself but impacts the wider organisation and their stakeholders. She helps the reader look at the work through many different perspectives. A great addition to the team coaching literature'.

**Professor Peter Hawkins, Ph.D.**, *Chairman of Renewal Associates International, Emeritus Professor of Leadership and Global thought leader and author in* Systemic Team Coaching

'Helen Zink offers a unique insight into team coaching in this single case study. By diving deep into a single case, the book is able to offer insights as the team develops over time and also offers multiple perspectives, giving voice to different characters. This is team coaching under the microscope, which gives the reader a richer, deeper and fuller experience of the complexities and intricacies of coaching a team'.

**Professor Jonathan Passmore, Ph.D.**, *Director of Coaching and Behavioural Change, Henley Business School, UK, and Senior Vice President CoachHub*

'This book is courageous, unique, insightful and a must read for anyone interested in teams. It is fascinating to read five different and illuminating viewpoints, told in their own words and to pick up on some of the, at times, unspoken tensions. This "warts and all" story shows honesty, integrity and vulnerability of the author and other contributors, and I applaud, admire and respect the unique scope this affords us as readers'.

**Eve Turner**, *Master Executive Coach, coach supervisor, researcher and author, past chair APECS (Association for Professional Executive Coaching and Supervision), founder of the Global Supervisors' Network and co-founder Climate Coaching Alliance*

# Team Coaching for Organisational Development

Working with teams, leading teams and being a member of a team is part of everyday working life for most of us. Through the lens of a team coaching case study, this book considers the development journey of a team and system influences over a three-year period.

Readers are invited to walk in the shoes of the team, the team leader, the organisation, the team coach and the coach's supervision and support networks, providing a unique insight into team coaching and development that goes beyond the traditional focus on the coach's perspective. Helen Zink uses her considerable experience as a leadership and team growth coach, and leader to illustrate how team coaching interventions can be combined with other disciplines such as positive psychology, change management and strategic implementation in effective ways. The book takes a pracademic approach, showing how theories, models and best practice are applied to a real case and highlighting both the successes and challenges experienced to offer an example for all those involved in team, leadership and organisational development.

With it widely recognised that collective leadership and teamwork is needed to deal with the rapidly changing environment organisations find themselves in, this is a timely and important resource for coaches, team coaches, coach supervisors, team leaders, team members, organisational development specialists, change managers, academics and consultants.

**Helen Zink** is a growth coach, leadership coach and team coach, with significant hands-on business and leadership experience at a senior level.

Helen draws from a large toolkit, including coaching, team coaching, applied positive psychology, change management and many strategic tools and methodologies.

**David Clutterbuck** is one of the early pioneers of developmental coaching and mentoring and co-founder of the European Mentoring & Coaching Council. Author of more than 70 books, including the first evidence-based titles on coaching culture and team coaching, he is visiting professor at four business schools. David authored the Foreword.

**The Team Leader** is a senior executive with over 30 years' experience in various large organisations globally. While this is his first contribution to a published work, he is passionate about developing and supporting people, hence initiating and committing to the journey this book is based on. His hope is that, by sharing this journey, others undertaking a similar development path will gain from his insight, including other leaders, teams, organisations and coaches.

**Tammy Turner** is an EMCC and ICF Master Coach and Team Coach, and EMCC Accredited Supervisor. She has authored over 25 articles and textbooks on coaching, supervision and team coaching. Turner International creates organisations of the future through team, and teams of teams, coaching, supervision and team coaching training.

# Team Coaching for Organisational Development

## Team, Leader, Organisation, Coach and Supervision Perspectives

**HELEN ZINK**

With guest authors Tammy Turner and the Team Leader

*Foreword by David Clutterbuck*

Routledge
Taylor & Francis Group
LONDON AND NEW YORK

Designed cover image: © Getty Images

First published 2024
by Routledge
4 Park Square, Milton Park, Abingdon, Oxon OX14 4RN

and by Routledge
605 Third Avenue, New York, NY 10158

*Routledge is an imprint of the Taylor & Francis Group, an informa business*

© 2024 Helen Zink

*British Library Cataloguing-in-Publication Data*
A catalogue record for this book is available from the British Library

*Library of Congress Cataloging-in-Publication Data*
Names: Zink, Helen, author. | Clutterbuck, David, writer of foreword.
Title: Team coaching for organisational development : team, leader, organisation, coach and supervision perspectives / Helen Zink, with guest authors Tammy Turner and the Team Leader ; foreword by David Clutterbuck.
Description: Abingdon, Oxon ; New York, NY : Routledge, 2023. | Includes bibliographical references and index.
Identifiers: LCCN 2023006512 (print) | LCCN 2023006513 (ebook) | ISBN 9781032435343 (hardback) | ISBN 9781032435336 (paperback) | ISBN 9781003367789 (ebook)
Subjects: LCSH: Teams in the workplace. | Employees—Coaching of. | Personnel management.
Classification: LCC HD66.Z548 2023 (print) | LCC HD66 (ebook) | DDC 658.4/022—dc23/eng/20230223
LC record available at https://lccn.loc.gov/2023006512
LC ebook record available at https://lccn.loc.gov/2023006513

ISBN: 978-1-032-43534-3 (hbk)
ISBN: 978-1-032-43533-6 (pbk)
ISBN: 978-1-003-36778-9 (ebk)

DOI: 10.4324/9781003367789

Typeset in Dante and Avenir
by Apex CoVantage, LLC

# Contents

# List of figures

# List of tables

## Appendix tables

# List of theory breaks

# Biographies

**David Clutterbuck** is one of the early pioneers of developmental coaching and mentoring and co-founder of the European Mentoring & Coaching Council. Author of more than 70 books, including the first evidence-based titles on coaching culture and team coaching, he is visiting professor at four business schools. He leads a global network of specialist mentoring and coaching training consultants, Coaching and Mentoring International. www.clutterbuck-cmi.com. David authored the Foreword.

**Michael** (the Team Leader) is a senior executive with over 30 years' experience in various large organisations globally. While this is his first contribution to published work, he is passionate about developing and supporting people, hence initiating and committing to the journey this book is based on. His hope is that by sharing this journey, others undertaking a similar development path will gain from his insight, including other leaders, teams, organisations and coaches. Michael co-authored Chapter Five and part of Chapter Eleven.

**Tammy Turner** is an EMCC and ICF Master Coach and Team Coach, and EMCC Accredited Supervisor. She has authored over 25 articles and textbooks on coaching, supervision and team coaching. Turner International creates organisations of the future through team and teams of teams, coaching, supervision and team coaching training. www.turner. international. Tammy authored the supervision section of Chapter Six and part of Chapter Eleven.

**Helen Zink** is a growth coach, leadership coach and team coach, with significant hands-on business and leadership experience at a senior level. Helen draws from a large toolkit, including coaching, team coaching, applied positive psychology, change management and other strategic tools and methodologies. She holds many qualifications and certifications, including: Senior Practitioner Team and Individual Coach with EMCC, Advanced Certification in Team Coaching and Professional Certified Coach with ICF, MSc (Coaching Psychology), MBA, BMS (hons), and other certifications. Helen's business Grow to be Limited is how she shares her passion for growing leaders and teams with others. www.growtobe.co.nz.

# Foreword

*David Clutterbuck*

A team is a Complex Adaptive System (CAS) nested in other CAS's. An externally resourced team coach enters that system and – consciously or unconsciously – immediately becomes part of it. The external team coach is a catalyst, which means that they not only influence the team but are themselves changed. This dual internal and external perspective of the team coach is a valuable resource that amplifies the core role of coaching – to engender a clarity that supports insightful decision making through shifting perspectives.

When the team coach is a member of the team, however, the complexities multiply. The coach must manage the additional issues of relative power, engagement in the day-to-day work practices and avoidance of groupthink. The coach does not have hierarchical power, but does have other kinds of power – particularly, power of expertise and moral authority. He or she both takes part in the team's activities and helps the team step back from them and view them with a critical eye. To rise above the limiting assumptions of the team, he or she must constantly step into the role of external observer.

Team coaching is the fastest-growing aspect of coaching internationally. Among the reasons is the need for coaches, in an increasingly saturated market for coaching individuals, to expand their service offering. Equally, they wish to add greater value to their clients. The ability of a leader to perform is dependent to a large extent on their team, so creating a co-learning space that includes the leader and the team has a much wider and deeper impact. The team coach also helps the team see itself through the eyes of its stakeholders and influencers. In Systemic Team Coaching (STC), the interface between the team and its stakeholders becomes a driver of improved performance. In CAS team coaching, the team gains a greater understanding of its role in the system and how, for example, it can influence relationships between stakeholders – thus the whole system becomes more effective.

One way to look at coaching is as a Russian doll in which the innermost entity is one-to-one coaching. The next layer is coaching the leader to create a coaching culture in his or her team. Outside that is the layer of team coaching, directly supporting the learning conversations between the leader and the team and between the team members. Beyond this lies the embryonic world of coaching teams of teams, then organisational coaching and finally macro-systems coaching (for example, coaching multiple stakeholders and influencers in the context of addressing climate change or poverty from a CAS perspective). Each layer of the Russian doll requires greater systems awareness, a wider toolkit and the courage to help the systems see themselves.

The leader, the team and the coach form a dynamic and evolving system. In her role as an internal team coach in this case, Helen provides a perspective that the externally resourced coach cannot. In particular, she is able to feel and experience the learning journey of the team and its members from inside. As an external team coach, I experience the team only in short bursts, when interviewing them individually in the initial discovery stage, when observing team meetings and in the team coaching sessions. What happens in between is revealed only in the shadows. The clues people give about their evolving understanding and the conversations with colleagues are no substitute for being part of that evolving experience.

One area where this internal insight is particularly valuable is that of choices, explored in Chapter Ten. The core of coaching is to create clarity, to help teams and individuals better understand their internal and external worlds and link those understandings to make better decisions. As a team coach, I often observe the team appear to come to a firm consensus, then a few weeks later find that the commitment has faded in the light of other priorities. When we dig deeper, we often find that the team's unity on the issue was a superficial triumph of groupthink. Helen's narrative is, for me, a unique insight into the processes that enhance and detract from the impact of the team coaching intervention.

There is substantial learning here for team coaches, team members, team leaders and supervisors of team coaches. For the external team coach, it is a reminder of how limited our potential to bring about change is. You can persuade an elephant to move by goading it from behind or tempting it from the front. Pushing or pulling will not work! When you create a symbiosis or partnership with the elephant, however, you can ride its back and gently encourage it.

For team members and team leaders, the lessons include the importance of taking responsibility for outcomes and for collective learning, performance and well-being. Casting the team coach in any of the roles of the drama triangle (victim, persecutor or rescuer – covered in Chapters Seven and Eight) will hinder their ability to support you in bringing about change. There is much written about responsibility and accountability in teams, but little about why people – even in otherwise high performing teams – tend so often to avoid responsibility. The lack of role clarity creates a mist that settles around the feet of team members, and it often requires the tenacity and courage of a team coach to blow it away.

For supervisors, a lesson from this inspirational case study is that the boundaries we set around coaching and team coaching are contextual and open to challenge. When I asked a group of team coaches a while ago if they thought it would be possible to coach from within a team, the response from almost all of them was no. They cited in particular the difficulty of challenging. Could the internal coach hold up the mirror to the team leader as closely as an outsider, with less to lose? Would the need to maintain positive collegial relationships lead them to soft-pedal feedback? Read what happened and see what you think!

Another audience I believe will benefit from immersing in Helen's experiences is senior HR professionals, especially those at board or top-team level. In a recent study I conducted on the transition between senior Human Resources (HR) function head and Director (HRD), one of the themes identified was the emerging role of the HRD as internal coach to his or her peers. This not only enhances the prestige and reputation of HR, making it possible to have a greater influence over strategy and policy; it enables HR to make a much more significant contribution to company performance.

Many things make this a unique and valuable contribution to our understanding of team coaching. There are very few in-depth case studies of team coaching, and no others I am aware of with such a wealth of reflection over such a substantial period of time. The vast majority of published cases are written solely from the perspective of the coach or coach pair. This remarkable study offers no less than five perspectives – the coach, the team, the team leader, the organisation and those involved in supervision.

I have been delighted to play a small part in the system, through occasional supervision and mentoring for Helen. I have watched her grow in confidence over some of this journey and seen the impact of her increasing self-awareness on engaging with the systems of the team.

I hope this book encourages courageous leaders to build the coaching culture in their teams with the aid of an internal team coach. I also hope that internal coaches will see the personal and professional growth potential of embedding themselves, for at least part of their time, in the systems of a team in their organisations. It is already common practice to place agile coaches (although coach in this sense is more akin to instructor) in technology focused teams.

This book is a little like an advent calendar, with each chapter being another door, behind which is hidden a surprise. Thank you, Helen, for gifting the surprises to us.

Professor David Clutterbuck

# Preface

*Helen Zink*

I never intended to write this book; 1 suppose it evolved from forces within the system.

I had been working with the Consulting Services lead team (Team) for around three years when Michael (Team Leader) announced he was leaving Green Apple Co. I thought, "I had better get all the information I need about this case before he goes, just in case I want to write something about it in the future!" I had written short pieces about this case prior – focused on the first year I worked with the Team as an internal coach and as part of the Team. However, there was more of the story to tell as I transitioned to an external coach role and continued to work with the Team.

While gathering information from across Green Apple Co, I talked to Michael and Tammy (my team coach supervisor) about the richness of the story. Those conversations gradually evolved into the concept of this book, telling the same story from five different perspectives within the system. My perspective would be one of them, of course, but the perspectives of the Team, Michael, Green Apple Co and Tammy would be even more interesting.

I also thought it might be useful to compare all five perspectives and see what insight that provided. Michael was skeptical on this point. I recall him saying, "I'm not sure your concept will work – I'm not sure there will be enough difference in our points of view." I also recall laughing in response; given the tension in the system I experienced, I was confident there was meat on the bones of this story – and I was right!

I do not enjoy writing – I find it hard work. So why did I put myself through the pain of this project?

Helping others grow to be the best they can be drives me – so much so – I was willing to tolerate the pain of writing to cultivate growth! I hope this story will help other coaches and team coaches like me, and also other teams, leaders, coach supervisors, Human Resource professionals, academics and consultants. There is much insight to consider in the pages that follow.

I consider myself a pracademic in the field of team coaching, defined as someone who is both a practitioner and academic. This book is an excellent example of pracademia in that it shows the application of team coaching theories, models and best practice, resulting in successes and failure, and insight gained. In turn, insight gained from this case will, I hope, inform future practice, theories, models and best practice.

Figure (i) illustrates the way I see myself and this book within a cycle of both applying and contributing to team coaching and organisational development body of knowledge. Fortunately, in this case, the Team, Michael, and I, were all willing to experiment with many tools, models, modalities and approaches – facilitating high levels of individual and collective learning for all involved.

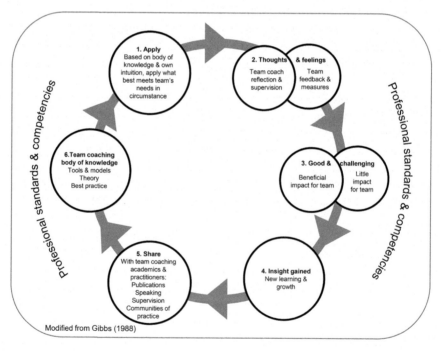

Figure (i): Pracademic cycle

I hope this book enables you to apply valuable new insights in your own circumstances. If one person or one team's experience is enhanced as a result of this book, the pain I experienced writing it has been worth it.

## Reference

Gibbs, G. (1988). *Learning by doing: A guide to teaching and learning methods*. Oxford: Oxford Polytechnic.

# Acknowledgements

It takes a village to pull a book together and I would like to specifically thank some of my villagers.

Thank you to Michael, the Team Leader, and chief scientist. Michael created the experiment that has become this book and the conditions conducive to the experiment playing out. I also acknowledge Michael's contribution to creating the book concept, including brainstorming the multidimensional nature of this case. I also appreciate the time he invested in co-authoring the Leader perspective chapter.

Thank you to the Team for being the perfect lab rats, and their willingness (eventually) to be part of the experiment.

Thank you to David Clutterbuck and Tammy Turner, who convinced me that team coaching was a valuable area to pursue, and their formal and informal support of my development. I appreciate their faith in me when I wavered, and for including me in moulding a discipline that is still evolving and developing rapidly. I also appreciate their time and contributions to this book and their belief that the story was worth sharing.

Thank you to my team coaching supervision group and professional network – my peers – whom I tapped into and still tap into for advice, support and shared learning experiences. I also appreciate peers who contributed directly to this book by providing content and also reviewing early versions of the manuscript.

Thank you to my publishers Routledge not only for agreeing to publish this book, but also answering my many questions and mentoring me through the publication process.

And to my family and friends, thank you for listening to me, the hugs, and for mopping up my tears when needed.

I love my village people!

# Abbreviations

| | |
|---|---|
| BAU | Business as Usual |
| CAS | Complex Adaptive System |
| CEO | Chief Executive Officer |
| CPO | Chief People Officer |
| DNA | Deoxyribonucleic Acid |
| EA | Executive Assistant |
| EMCC | European Mentoring and Couching Council |
| EQ | Emotional Quotient (or Emotional Intelligence) |
| HPT | High Performing Team |
| HR | Human Resources |
| HVT | High Value Team |
| ICF | International Coaching Federation |
| IQ | Intelligence Quotient |
| KPI | Key Performance Indicator |
| OD | Organisational Development |
| PERILL | Purpose, External processes, Relationships, Internal processes, Learning, Leadership (Clutterbuck, 2020) |
| SME | Subject Matter Expert |
| STC | Systemic Team Coaching (Hawkins, 2021, 2022) |
| Y1 | Year One |
| Y2 | Year Two |
| Y3 | Year Three |

# Terminology

| | |
|---|---|
| 360 | Performance evaluation approach that gathers feedback from stakeholders including people above, below and beside someone. In the context of an organisation this might be feedback from a person's: Manager, coworkers, direct reports, vendors, clients, customers, suppliers. |
| 90-day plan | Action plan covering a 90-day time period. |
| C-suite | Senior executive team typically comprising of: Chief Executive Officer, Chief Operations Officer, Chief People Officer, Chief Financial Officer, Chief Information Officer. |
| DNA | Fundamental and distinctive characteristics or qualities of someone or something. |
| Good endings | Work done to recognise the importance of the end of a phase or period of activity. It allows participants to process change – like a eulogy at a funeral. |
| Hailstorm(s) | A term used by the Team in this case to refer to a significant environmental event(s) damaging apple crops to the extent that stakeholder expectations were not met, and reputation suffered as a result. |
| Hard S's | Elements of McKinsey's 7 S's model that relate to tangible and process related rather than |

|  | people related: Strategy, systems and processes, structure (Peters & Waterman, 2006). |
|---|---|
| Leadership vacuum trap | A perceived void in leadership filled unconsciously by someone who is not the leader. |
| Leaf spot | Serious contagious virus, capable of destroying the global apple industry. |
| Level one learning | In the moment, "double loop learning" or "learning in action," where learning happens in real time and is considered as next steps are taken. |
| Level two learning | After the event, "single loop learning," "learning on action," where learning after the event either through informal or formal reflection is taken into consideration when planning future events. |
| Level three learning | Sometime after the event, "single loop learning," "learning on action" where reflection happens sometime later, and the benefit of distance and more experience provides more learning about the event to be applied sometime in the future. |
| Meta-reflection | Reflection going beyond initial reflection. A deeper journey of thought resulting in even more in-depth insight than the original layer of reflection. |
| One-to-one coaching | Coaching one person, or one person at a time. |
| PERILL Plus | PERILL model created by the Team in this case, which extends the six elements of the PERILL by adding a seventh – team resilience and wellbeing. |
| Siloed | Organisation operation characterised by the intentional or unintentional separation of resources, funds, talent and knowledge. |
| Soft S's | Elements of McKinsey's 7 S's model that are people and relationship related: Shared values, style, staff and skills (Peters & Waterman, 2006). |
| Systemic Team Coaching | Coaching that considers the wider context the client team is in, including internal and external stakeholders and the wider environment (Hawkins, 2021, 2022) |

| | |
|---|---|
| Team coaching | Coaching a team of people collectively, as if they are one entity or client. |
| Top-down | A leadership style characterised by the leader taking control and power, making decisions and directing staff on what to do. |
| Who's the boss | A term used by the Team in this case to refer to an event where they were not clear who was leading the Team. |
| Year One | The first 12 months of the three-year period this case covers. |
| Year Two | The second 12 months of the three-year period this case covers. |
| Year Three | The third 12 months of the three-year period this case covers. |
| Year Four | The time period after Year Three. |
| Year Two plan | Consulting Services strategic implementation plan for Year Two including, strategic goals, initiatives and measures. |

# Characters

Alias' have been used for all characters in this book, including the organisation and function, to protect confidentiality, with the exception of the Coach and Supervisor who use their real names.

**Team**
Consulting Services Lead Team

**Team members at beginning of Year One**
Drew
Greg
Jane (voice in Chapters Four and Eleven)
Rosa
Taylor

**Team members who joined later**
David
Diana
Ethan
Janet
Tom

**Team Leader or Leader**
Michael (voice in Chapters Five and Eleven)

**Organisation**
Green Apple Co

**Function**
Consulting Services

**C-suite**
Sally CPO (voice in Chapters Six and Eleven)

**Team Coach or Coach**
Helen (voice in Chapters One, Two, Three, Seven, Nine, Ten, Eleven and Twelve)

**Supervisor**
Tammy (voice in Chapters Eight and Eleven)

**Supervision Group**
Amy
Fred
Jim
John (voice in Chapter Eight)

**Professional Network, Family and Friends**
Anna
Heather
Keith
Kirsten
Rachael (voice in Chapters Eight and Eleven)
Robbie

# How to read this book

*Helen Zink*

I am Helen, the Team Coach in this case study, and this guide will help you navigate this book.

As the concept of this book was forming, my biggest concern was how readers would navigate the multidimensionality of it – five voices representing five system perspectives, over three years, all examining the same case, while highlighting learning that occurred at the time, as well as learning occurring now as this book is written.

To simplify, a movie analogy is helpful. A movie like *Babel* (González Iñárritu, 2006) where the same story is described by different characters in parallel plots. In *Babel* it is not clear the characters are telling the same story until the end of the movie, where a plot twist brings all parallel plots and characters together.

As this book is not intended to be a psychological drama like *Babel* – although some parts may seem like one– I am more helpful and tell you up front – "spoiler alert" – it is the same story throughout!

This book is written in several voices – the most frequent voice is mine, the Coach in this case. At the beginning of each chapter, I make it clear who the author(s) is/are, and which character is narrating that particular chapter, or parts of the chapter.

As a visual learner, I absorb and make best sense of information using images, diagrams and metaphors rather than words – so this book is filled with my learning bias. I also use "Theory Breaks" throughout the book to explain theories and models referred to in the main text, rather than breaking the flow of the story.

I rarely read books like this logically from beginning to end – I tend to flick through books when looking for something in particular. The following explanation will be especially valuable for those with similar habits to mine. Also note that each chapter begins with a few words on "How to read this chapter" linking back to this overall "how to" guide. You will need it – this book is a CAS in itself!

With parallel movie plots, multiple voices and authors, images/diagrams, Theory Breaks, and "how to" guides in mind, the following will help navigate the multidimensionality of this book.

## Chapter One – Introduction

(Written in my voice as Coach)

Chapter One introduces the premise of the book – a team coaching case study viewed from five different perspectives in the system over three years. Key concepts used throughout the story are also covered, such as: The notion of a team as a system and CAS, cognitive bias and perspective taking, and reflective learning. Using movie production as an analogy, the equivalent would be the "clapper board," providing basic information needed to set up the movie as "action" begins.

## Section A – Background

Section A consists of two chapters providing information needed for each of the parallel plots narrated in Section B. Without this section, Section B would be much longer and repetitive, as each character would need to repeat basic information.

## Chapter Two – Context

(Written in my voice as Coach)

Chapter Two describes the setting for the case by introducing system elements and their environment. In a movie, this aligns to introducing lead "characters" and the "eras" in which the movie is set. Characters are not fully brought to life until Section B, where they share their respective stories using their own words and emotions.

## Chapter Three – Approach

(Written in my voice as Coach)

Chapter Three describes the team development and coaching approach applied in this case, including interventions used and outcomes measured. The approach is described as neutrally as possible, as opinion on whether approaches and interventions used were successful or not is held until Section B. Using a movie production analogy, this would be a description of common "scenes" throughout the movie.

## Section B – Five perspectives

Section B comprises five chapters where five elements in the system describe their perspective of the experience in their own voice. This includes their thoughts on whether the approach and interventions

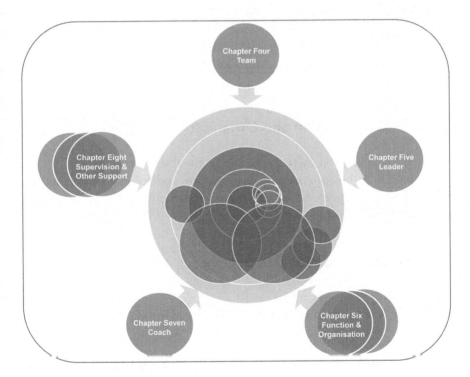

Figure (ii): Five system elements

described in Chapter Three were useful, what was good, what was challenging, and what they learnt from the experience. Each system element describes themselves as well as other elements in the system, as illustrated in Figure (ii). In the movie analogy, Section B is the "parallel plots" section, where the same story is narrated by different characters in their own voices, and each character talks about themselves as well as other main characters in the movie. This is where we get to understand characters better, including their quirks and emotions.

## Chapter Four – Team perspective

(Written in the voice of Jane, a member of the Team)
Chapter Four is the Team's perspective of their own development journey. Jane's character represents all members of the Team.

## Chapter Five – Leader perspective

(Written in the voice of Michael, the Leader)
Chapter Five is the Team Leader's perspective of the story, narrated in his own voice.

## Chapter Six – Function and Organisation perspective

(Written in the voice of Sally, a member of the C-suite and CPO)
Chapter Six is the Function and Organisation's perspective of the journey. Sally's character represents all the Team's stakeholders within Consulting Services and Green Apple Co.

## Chapter Seven – Coach perspective

(Written in my voice as Coach)
Chapter Seven is my perspective as Coach and my version of events.

## Chapter Eight – Supervisions and Other Support perspective

(Written in the voices of Tammy, John and Rachael)

My Supervision and Other Support networks represented by:

Tammy – Supervisors' perspective. Tammy was my primary supervisor throughout the period of the case.

John – a member of my team coaching supervision group, representing everyone in my supervision group.

Rachael – a professional peer and friend, speaking on behalf of all my professional networks, family and friends.

## Section C – Insights

Section C consists of three chapters which bring together perspectives in Section B, forming further insight, or meta-reflection. In a movie, this would be the "plot twist" and "climax" section of the story.

## Chapter Nine – Comparing perspectives – similarities

(Written in my voice as Coach)

Similarities of what was good, what was challenging and what was learnt from all five perspectives are combined in Chapter Nine, providing rich insight. This is the "plot twist" in the movie analogy, where it becomes clear that the parallel plots, described by five different characters in Section B, are in fact telling the same story with many similarities.

## Chapter Ten – Comparing perspectives – differences

(Written in my voice as Coach)

Taking a combined view of what was good, challenging and what was learnt also reveals some misalignment between perspectives. Using the movie example, this is the "climax," where the five characters compare notes and realise they have differing opinions.

Chapter Ten also considers how different things would have been if disagreements between perspectives had been shared and resolved earlier in the journey. Like the movie *Sliding Doors* (Howitt, 1998), this chapter considers the implications of different choices on the CAS.

## Chapter Eleven – The future

(Written in the voices of Jane, Michael, Sally, Helen, Tammy and Rachael)
   Chapter Eleven looks to the future, where the five system elements describe their intentions in applying learning and insight from this case to new situations. The movie is almost over at this stage. As characters describe their hopes for the future, there is also a sense their stories are not over – perhaps there will be another movie – a "sequel"?

## Chapter Twelve – Conclusion

(Written in my voice as Coach)
   The conclusion wraps content of the entire book together and summarises key take-outs. The equivalent in a movie would be the "epilogue" – a summary of key points to mull over after the movie.
   Figure (iii) depicts the same information described above as a diagram to aid those who, like me, prefer visual outlines. In a movie, this would be the "story board" – used to illustrate the flow in plot, and purpose of each part of the movie.
   Now grab your popcorn and take a seat . . . let the story begin . . .

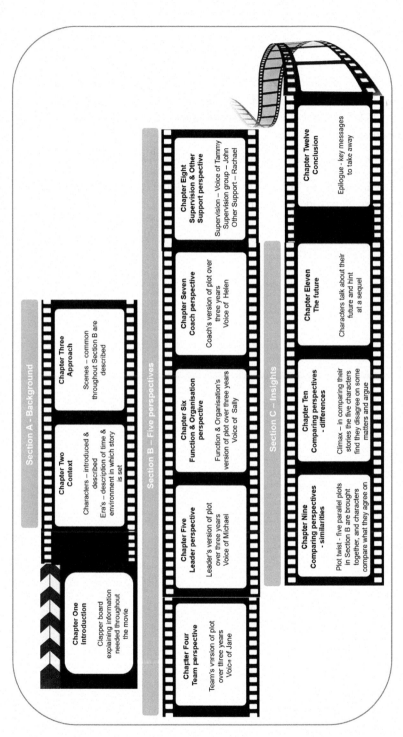

Figure (iii): Book structure – story board

## References

González Iñárritu, A. (Director). (2006). *Babel* [Film]. Paramount Vantage.

Hawkins, P. (2021). *Leadership team coaching: Developing collective transformational leadership*. London: Kogan Page. https://doi.org/10.1111/peps.12006_5.

Hawkins, P. (2022). *Leadership team coaching in practice: Case studies on creating highly effective teams*. London: Kogan Page.

Howitt, P. (Director). (1998). *Sliding Doors* [Film]. Intermedia Films, Mirage Enterprises, Miramax.

Peters, T. & Waterman, R. (2006). *In search of excellence: Lessons from America's best-run companies*. New York: Harper Business.

# Introduction

1

*Helen Zink*

---

## HOW TO READ CHAPTER ONE

I am Helen, the Team Coach in this case, and this is how this chapter fits into the overall book.

Chapter One, narrated by me, introduces the premise of the book – a team coaching case study viewed from five different perspectives within their system over three years. Key concepts used throughout the story are also covered in this chapter, such as: The notion of a team as a CAS, STC, cognitive bias and perspective taking, and reflective learning. It would be best to read this chapter first to frame up the rest. Section A follows – providing information needed for each of the parallel stories told in Section B. Once we hear all five perspectives, Section C combines and compares insight from each perspective for further learning.

Using a movie analogy, Chapter One is the equivalent of a "clapper board," providing the basic information needed to set up the movie just before "action" begins.

---

"We really don't know how and if this will work, but would you like to be part of our experiment?" Of course, I said yes, I could not resist an invitation like that. I accepted Michael's offer of a role in his Team, and the story begins. At the beginning, no one could have anticipated how challenging, crazy and messy, yet rewarding and transformational, the experiment and this case would be for all involved.

DOI: 10.4324/9781003367789-1

This book tells the story of a STC case study, told by five elements within a Team's system from their own perspectives over three years. Other coaching case studies are written solely from the perspective of the coach or team coach. Not this one! This book is all about the insight and power of taking multiple perspectives.

Warning – this book is not a comprehensive step-by-step "how to" guide for running a perfect team coaching process. It is not the application of a particular team coaching approach or body of knowledge. It is not a PhD or structured research project either. Other publications do that – written by far more experienced and qualified people than me. This story is real, involving the eclectic application of theory and approaches with a real team in a real system. The five versions of the story told in this book are complex, messy, exposing "warts and all" insight into the organic and demanding nature of STC.

In terms of content, Section A covers context and the overall team development and coaching approach used. In a movie this would be a description of "characters," "eras" and "scenes."

Section B is where the five system elements tell their version of the story in their own voices. The system elements are: The Team, Leader, Function and Organisation, Coach (me), and my Supervision and Other Support networks. This is the "parallel plots" section, where the same story is narrated by different characters in their own voice – like parallel plots in the movie *Babel* (González Iñárritu, 2006).

Section C combines and compares insight from each perspective for further learning – or meta-reflection of similarities and differences. The impact of choice within a CAS is also considered – like the movie *Sliding Doors* (Howitt, 1998), just one different choice made by one party could have changed the entire development trajectory. We also hear how the five characters intend to apply experiences from this case to their future life, work and development journeys.

Although the unique circumstances of this case will never repeat, real stories of learning and resilience are shared in the hope that insight gained will be applied in other circumstances by other teams, team leaders, organisations, HR professionals, OD specialists, coaches, team coaches, academics, consultants, change managers and anyone working with or in teams.

The remainder of this chapter explains concepts fundamental to the premise and remaining content of this book.

## Team as a system and Systemic Team Coaching

A CAS (Cavanagh, 2006) is a group of interdependent parts which, when combined, create something different and bigger than the sum of their individual parts. The strength of the CASs, and also their complexity, comes from the interaction and interrelationships between elements in the system, rather than the individual elements themselves. Using a science analogy consider the combination of oxygen and hydrogen – both gases. When their molecules combine, they create something quite different, with very different characteristics – water. A team is similar – when combined, people behave and act differently than when alone or in a paring. The more members in a team, the more complex the interaction between them is to understand.

This book takes a systemic stance, combining notions of a team as a CAS and STC (Hawkins, 2021, 2022). Complexity and uncertainty are appreciated rather than attempting to distil events into simple linear cause-and-effect relationships (Theory Break 1.1).

---

## THEORY BREAK 1.1: TEAM COACHING AND SYSTEMIC TEAM COACHING

According to Clutterbuck (2020) team coaching is defined as "partnering with an entire team in an ongoing relationship, for the purpose of collectively raising awareness and building better connections in the team's internal and external systems and enhancing the team's capability to cope with current and future challenges."

Hawkins and Turner (2020) describe systemic coaching as "coaching that focuses on creating value for the individual . . . and the teams they are part of in the organisation . . . they work for, as well as the organisation's stakeholders and the wider communities and ecology that organisation is part of."

By combining these definitions STC (Hawkins, 2021, 2022) focuses both on the internal and external workings of a team – there are multiple dynamics and stakeholders in play, and the coaching process needs to incorporate the complexity of these dynamics and involve stakeholders throughout the process. It is not a simple linear step-by-step process.

---

To illustrate, if the focus was on two team members, A and B, interacting with each other in isolation from anyone and anything else, the system would be relatively simple, as illustrated in Figure 1.1; interactions between team members would be linear and outcomes relatively predictable.

This simple closed system is also completely unrealistic – no one works in isolation like this. As we add more system elements, more team members,

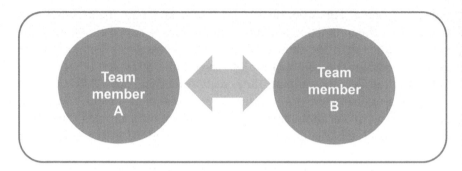

Figure 1.1: Simple closed system with two team members

stakeholders, suppliers, customers, and other teams within an organisation, the number of connections between elements increases exponentially. The interactions between elements are complex, and outcomes unpredictable. In a team coaching context, a coach may support a team with a particular intervention, in the hope that the intervention might create insight helpful for the team. However, in reality, the outcome is impossible to predict. Back to our science analogy, oxygen and hydrogen might be combined assuming water will be produced, but molecules may combine in a different way than hoped, resulting in hydrogen peroxide.

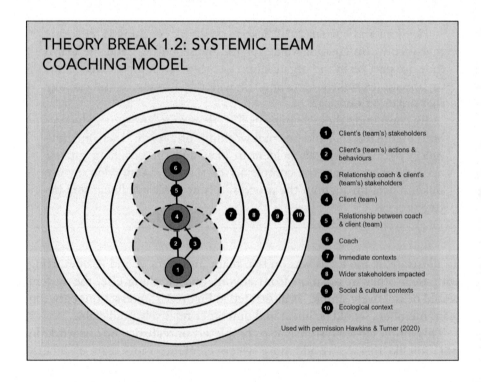

## THEORY BREAK 1.2: SYSTEMIC TEAM COACHING MODEL

1. Client's (team's) stakeholders
2. Client's (team's) actions & behaviours
3. Relationship coach & client's (team's) stakeholders
4. Client (team)
5. Relationship between coach & client (team)
6. Coach
7. Immediate contexts
8. Wider stakeholders impacted
9. Social & cultural contexts
10. Ecological context

Used with permission Hawkins & Turner (2020)

Hawkins and Turner (2020) have created a model to help conceptualise multiple elements in play in STC. If you are a coach, you will have come across the seven-eyed coaching model often used to understand the relationship between the coach and their client in a traditional one-to-one coaching scenario. In STC, the same model has many more eyes, at least ten, as many more system elements are included (Theory Break 1.2).

In this case, the Team has several members; they lead a Function; that Function sits within an Organisation; and that Organisation is part of a wider environment. Most of the Team's key stakeholders are within the Organisation, but some are outside. In addition, the Leader is also part of the C-suite. The Coach (me) is part of the Team as well, and I took advantage of Supervision and Other Support networks throughout the journey, which were also part of the system via me. There are many other elements in the system too and potential interactions between all system elements and dynamics of those interactions become very complex very quickly.

If I tried to draw the Team's full system, there would be an exponential number of circles and connection lines resulting in a diagram too complex to comprehend. Instead, I have opted to use a simplified system diagram, illustrated in Figure 1.2, drawn in a similar way to the Hawkins and

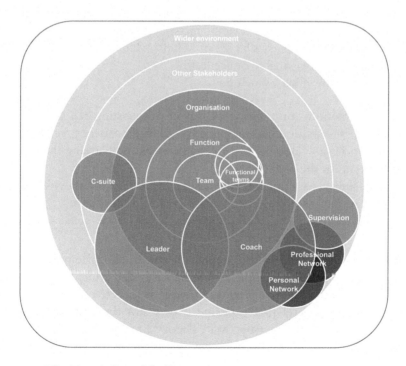

Figure 1.2: The Team's "simplified" system

Turner (2020) STC model (Theory Break 1.2). I use this diagram, and versions of, it throughout this book. Chapter Two describes each element in this simplified system in more depth.

## Cognitive bias and perspective taking

Appreciating that it is impossible for a human brain to see or consider all elements and all connections within a CAS at the same time, the only choice is to simplify observations. The brain uses tricks and familiar thinking patterns to aid understanding, making it impossible for whoever is looking at and describing a system to be completely neutral and objective. This phenomenon is known as cognitive bias (Theory Break 1.3). As an example, to illustrate, someone might look at a set of numbers that sum as expected, making the assumption the numbers that make up the total are correct. However, there might be multiple errors in the data that cancel each other out, which are not seen when focus is on the total, confirmation bias.

---

### THEORY BREAK 1.3: COGNITIVE BIAS

The Cambridge Dictionary defines cognitive bias as "the way a particular person understands events, facts, and other people, which is based on their own particular set of beliefs, (values), and experiences and may not be reasonable or accurate."

Some common biases include:

- Confirmation – only seeing what confirms existing beliefs.
- Hindsight – past events seem more predictable than they really were.
- Self-serving – taking credit for the positive and blaming the environment for the negative.
- Availability – assuming readily available information is evidence.
- Inattention – not seeing things while focus is elsewhere.

---

Another concept central to the premise of this book is the power of perspective taking. In short, people have lenses through which they interpret everything, and those lenses provide a unique perspective of events. Those perspectives are exactly that – perspectives – not the truth and not the correct perspective, just perspectives (Theory Break 1.4). An example is a tall person walking down a street noticing architraves on the buildings they pass by. A shorter person walking down the same street may focus on fences surrounding the same buildings.

---

## THEORY BREAK 1.4: POWER OF PERSPECTIVE TAKING

"Taking a walk in someone else's shoes" is the easiest way to describe the act of perspective taking according to Duffy (2019). It requires both the ability to see another's viewpoint of reality and also understand that viewpoint in the same way that person processes and makes sense of the world. It is more than superficial appreciation; it involves feeling what they feel.

No perspective is correct, or better than another. All are correct and valid, as each is the interpretation of our unique lens through which we make sense of the word.

The power of perspective taking is gaining insight and learning. We do not know what we do not know, and perspective taking is a useful way to expand our own perspective, by learning from other's perspectives. Hopefully resulting in better outcomes for all.

---

The story described in this book could be interpreted by hundreds of different perspectives, built on thousands of different cognitive biases, and all would be valid. However, this book is limited to the five system elements highlighted in Figure 1.2, appreciating that Jane, Michael, Sally, Tammy, John, Rachael and I will each tell a different version of the story based on our own position within the system and our own cognitive bias. By looking at the same events through five different lenses, insight gained is more robust and valuable than considering one perspective in isolation.

## Reflective learning

Useful insight can be gained through reflective learning cycles – an intentional process, where events in the past or present are reviewed and used to inform future events (Dewey, 1910). Another related concept is double loop learning (Gibbs, 1988), where reflective cycles happen in the moment and learning is applied quickly as events play out. Sometimes adapting in the moment is referred to as learning "in action," and reflective learning after an event as learning "on action" (Schon, 1992).

The objective of this book is to share real stories of learning and resilience in the hope that insight gained will be applied in other circumstances. This book is filled with examples of double loop "in action" learning, and single loop "on action" learning. Writing this book has also created an opportunity for a third level of learning – learning occurring now, sometime later, as contributors, including me, have another opportunity to formally reflect on events and gain further insight. Figure 1.3 illustrates my thoughts on the three learning levels included in this book.

Armed with understanding of the premise of this book, the movies *Babel* (González Iñárritu, 2006) and *Sliding Doors* (Howitt, 1998) in mind, and concepts of CAS, STC, cognitive bias, perspective taking, reflective learning at three levels and meta-reflection, I hope this "clapper board" has been useful and the rest of this book will make more sense. Next, we move on to describing "characters," "eras" and "scenes" in the context and approach chapters in Section A.

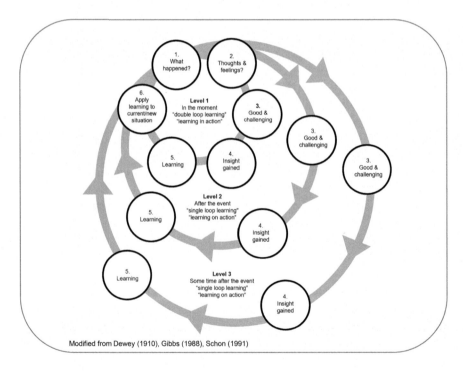

Modified from Dewey (1910), Gibbs (1988), Schon (1991)

Figure 1.3: Three level learning

# References

Cambridge Dictionary. (2022). Retrieved from https://dictionary.cambridge.org/dictionary/english/cognitive-bias.

Cavanagh, M. (2006). Coaching from a systemic perspective: A complex adaptive conversation. In D. Stober & A. M. Grant (Eds.), *Evidence based coaching handbook: Putting best practices to work for your clients*. New York: Wiley.

Clutterbuck, D. (2020). *Coaching the team at work*. London & Boston: Brealey.

Dewey, J. (1910), (1910 edition). *How we think*. New York: Prometheus Books. https://doi.org/10.1037/10903-000.

Gibbs, G. (1988). *Learning by doing: A guide to teaching and learning methods*. Oxford: Oxford Polytechnic.

González Iñárritu, A. (Director). (2006). *Babel* [Film]. Paramount Vantage.

Hawkins, P. (2021). *Leadership team coaching: Developing collective transformational leadership*. London: Kogan Page. https://doi.org/10.1111/peps.12006_5.

Hawkins, P. (2022). *Leadership team coaching in practice: Case studies on creating highly effective teams*. London: Kogan Page.

Hawkins, P. & Turner. E. (2020). *Systemic coaching: Developing value beyond the individual*. London & New York: Routledge. https://doi.org/10.4324/9780429452031.

Howitt, P. (Director). (1998). *Sliding Doors* [Film]. Intermedia Films, Mirage Enterprises, Miramax.

Schon, D. A. (1992). *The reflective practitioner: How professionals think in action*. Farnham, England: Ashgate Publishing. https://doi.org/10.4324/9781315237473.

# Section A – Background

# Context

## Helen Zink

# 2

## Elements of the system

Chapter One introduced the Team's simplified system in Figure 1.1, and this section describes each of the system elements in more depth. Chapter One also explained that it would be impossible to draw all relationships between all system components in play in this case; so instead I use simplified illustrations to help make sense of the system.

DOI: 10.4324/9781003367789-3

## *The Team*

The Team is a senior leadership team comprising five team members, plus the Leader (Michael) and the Coach (me), leading the Consulting Services Function (more on Leader and Coach below), refer to Figure 2.1. The Team was formed at the beginning of Year One as the result of a significant restructure, and all team members, except for Michael and Taylor, were new to the Team and their roles. I describe each team member as neutrally as possible, as their personalities are revealed in greater depth in Chapter Four.

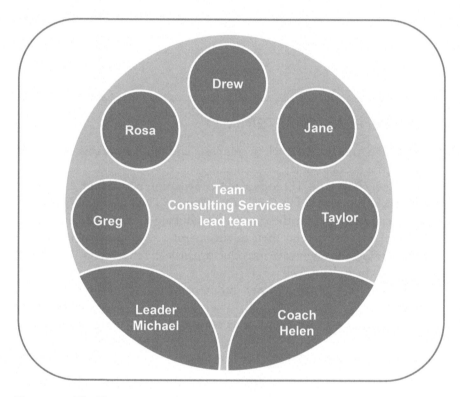

Figure 2.1: The Team

### Greg
At the time the Team was formed, the beginning of Year One, Greg had been working with Consulting Services for around six months as an independent contractor. His new role in the Team was a significant step up, both in responsibility and people leadership. While Greg had good technical

knowledge, he joined the Team with little appetite for development. Four team managers reported to Greg, with teams under them – around 30 staff in total. Team managers were also new to their roles with new responsibilities and expectations.

Rosa

Rosa had been with Green Apple Co for around seven years prior to being appointed to her new role in the Team. She knew the business inside out and had strong relationships with everyone in the Consulting Services Function and across the organisation, with many relying on her for advice and knowledge. Rosa had four direct reports.

Drew

Drew was another independent contractor prior to being appointed to the Team. She had been working within Consulting Services for around a year, and her new role was a significant step up in relation to technical knowledge, responsibility and people leadership. Drew had eight direct reports.

Jane

Jane had been in the organisation for around a year before the Team was formed. She had a small team of three reporting to her. Jane enjoyed the hands-on technical aspects to her role and was apprehensive about leadership expectations in the new structure.

Taylor

Taylor was Michael's EA. She had worked in Green Apple Co for around seven years and with Michael for four years. Her role did not change when the Team was formed on paper, but expectations of her role did. Taylor also had a keen interest in people and wellbeing across Consulting Services.

Team membership changed over the three-year period this case covers. During Year One, Drew left, and Tom joined – only to leave again in Year Two. In Year Two, I also left around the middle of the period, though I continued to work with the Team as an external consultant. Three team members joined temporarily near the end of Year Two and left again as Tom re-joined the Team in Year Three. Rosa also left in Year Three and was replaced by Ethan, and Michael left at the end of Year Three too. Figure 2.2 indicates the movement of team members across three years.

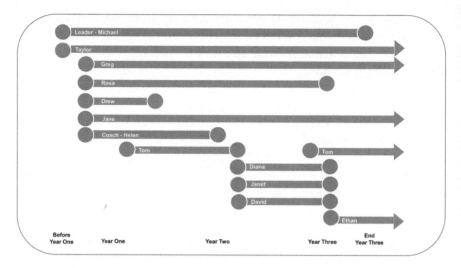

Figure 2.2: Team member movement

## The Leader

Michael had been in his role for four years prior to the beginning of Year One, so he knew Green Apple Co and the area he led well. He reported to the CEO and was a member of the C-suite. Michael also had extensive technical ability, with a history of senior roles in the field of consulting. Figure 2.3 shows Michael as part of the Team and C-suite.

## The Function and Organisation

Green Apple Co was a long-standing organisation of around 3,000 staff, creating apple products sold in the domestic market. Green Apple Co is a well-known brand, with positive customer and public reputation.

At the beginning of Year One, Green Apple Co's internal culture was "top-down" and "siloed." In many ways, these culture characteristics were expected, as standard procedure and regulation dominated the industry. It was not surprising that the same culture permeated through Consulting Services. There was acknowledgement across the organisation that culture needed to change for the benefit of staff and customers, and culture initiatives were in place – discussed more in Chapter Three.

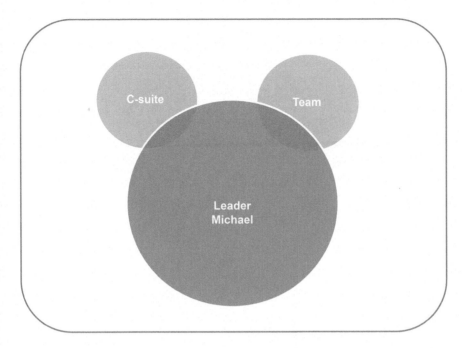

Figure 2.3: The Leader

As this story begins, Green Apple Co was two years into implementing a robust five-year strategic plan, involving fundamental changes to the business model and related processes and systems. Consulting Services' five-year strategic plan supported the Green Apple Co plan. The focus had been process, system and planning of structure changes prior to Year One. Those plans included changes to the Consulting Services structure, which created the Team in this case study. Figure 2.4 illustrates the Consulting Services function within the Green Apple Co organisation, as well as relationships with the Team and Leader.

Consulting Services, comprising around 60 staff, provided internal support services to other functions within Green Apple Co and to some external stakeholders, providing information and support to aid strategic and tactical decision making. Some process and compliance work came under their remit too. Consulting Services' internal reach was wide, with the entire organisation dependent on what they do. A large proportion of staff at the beginning of Year One had been with the organisation for quite some time, and were used to doing things certain ways.

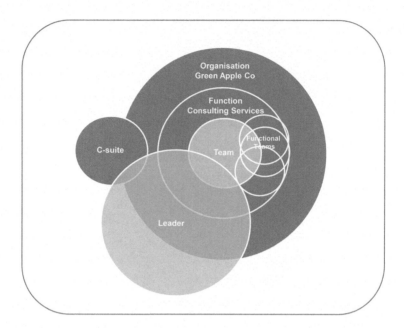

Figure 2.4: The Function and Organisation

The staff of Consulting Services either reported directly to a member of the Team, or a team manager who reported to a member of the Team. Functional Teams varied in size from 5 to 30 staff. Figure 2.5 shows the organisational structure of Consulting Services and Green Apple Co.

## The Coach

My role as Coach was new to the Team and to Green Apple Co at the beginning of Year One. I was the only external appointment to the newly formed Team.

Although there was a position description for my role, there was also an understanding that I would effectively create my role over time. Initial scope at the beginning of Year One included:

- Supporting the Team to develop their leadership skills.
- Supporting Consulting Services more widely with development.
- Working closely with HR and supporting the introduction and application of in-house development tools across Consulting Services.
- Supporting and contributing to organisation-wide culture change initiatives.
- Facilitating strategic planning and implementation across Consulting Services.
- Supporting Taylor in running Michael's office and processes.

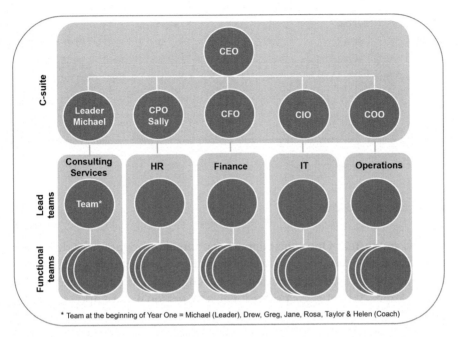

Figure 2.5 Organisation structure Green Apple Co

Note that neither coaching nor team coaching were specifically identified as part of the Coach role at the outset, although, as described more in Chapter Three, the role grew quickly into that. Development and coaching of the Team is the primary focus of this book, and the other aspects of my role listed above are not included in any depth.

My background includes approximately 20 years working in large corporates, including 10 years in senior leadership roles. Since leaving the corporate world I have been working and studying in areas of leadership development, change management, coaching and team coaching. I have a large tool kit to draw from, including positive psychology, change management, and strategic tools and techniques, in addition to coaching and team coaching. All these tools are applied in this case.

The diagram on the left in Figure 2.6 shows my place in the system in Year One. Part way through Year Two, the organisation restructured, and as part of that change, my role was removed. However, I continued to work with the Team as an external service provider as depicted on the right of Figure 2.6.

## Supervision and Other Support

The Supervision and Other Support element of the system relates to my support. I began both professional one-to-one and group team-focused

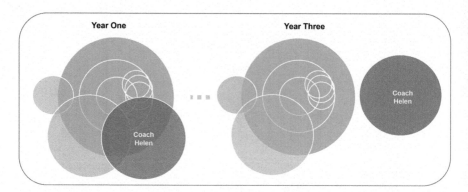

Figure 2.6: The Coach

supervision in Year One. This support continued throughout the three-year time frame this case covers. I was also part of a long-standing peer supervision group focused on one-to-one coaching, which continued in parallel. Other Support relates to professional and personal networks, including people I have come to know through professional coaching bodies, training cohorts, consultants, HR professionals, family and friends. Figure 2.7 indicates where my Supervision and Other Support networks fit into the system.

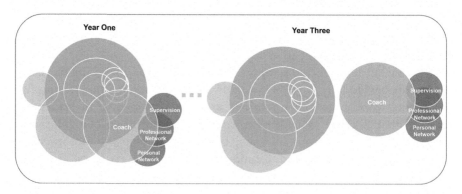

Figure 2.7: Supervision and Other Support

## Other stakeholders and wider environment

Although the majority of the Team's stakeholders were internal to Green Apple Co, there were some important external stakeholders as well, such as the board of directors, funding bodies and regulators. Although there is acknowledgement that these stakeholders impact and are impacted by the system, they are not explicitly referred to in this book – they do not have their own chapter(s) in Section B.

The wider environment has a significant impact on the system in which the Team resides too, described more below and in Section B.

Other stakeholders and the wider environment are added to the system diagram in Figure 2.8. The diagram on the left shows the relationships between elements in Year One. The diagram on the right illustrates the situation in Year Three once I became an external service provider – still part of the system, but no longer part of the organisation.

## Three years

Chapters Four to Eight in Section B are broken down into one-year time periods, where relevant. Partly for convenience and also to highlight significant and distinct environmental impacts during each time period, expanded on next.

### *Year One*

As explained above, the Team was created at the beginning of Year One, and I joined Green Apple Co and the Team at the same time.

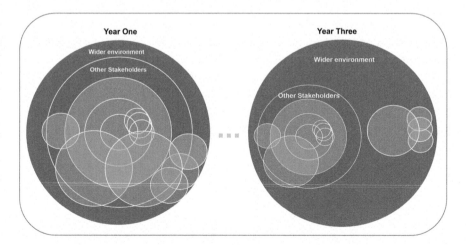

Figure 2.8: Other stakeholders and wider environment

There was a lot of activity within the Team's environment during Year One, including:

- Planning and implementing technology and process changes across Consulting Services and Green Apple Co.
- Recruiting and inducting new staff into the newly formed structure.
- Two unplanned physical location moves requiring immediate and unexpected changes to ways of working.
- Increased focus on development both within the Team and across Consulting Services.
- Challenging team dynamics.
- Team membership changes.
- "Leadership vacuum trap" and "who's the boss" events (more in Section B).

Halfway through Year One all the planned and unplanned changes taking place at the same time severely impacted the Team's ability to deliver services to stakeholders, with wide-reaching implications both across Green Apple Co and externally. The Team refers to this period as a "hailstorm." C-suite pressure at this time was significant, resulting in a review of the Team's strategic and operational priorities, culminating in a "90-day plan" designed to get service delivery back on track. The plan was endorsed by the C-suite, and progress was tracked and communicated well to all stakeholders.

Despite challenges and the extraordinary events impacting the Team, Year One ended on a high. The "90-day plan" was successful, with service delivery back on track well before the end of the 90-day period. Time was spent at the end of the year celebrating successes and acknowledging challenges overcome. Also, at the end of Year One, Michael openly committed to working on his leadership style – a nice lead into Year Two planning.

Figure 2.9 illustrates the main environmental factors in the system during Year One – some planned and some unplanned. Although environmental events are shown in lanes aligning to particular system elements, all events illustrated impact all elements of the system due to the influential nature of a CAS.

## Year Two

Year Two began with great energy. In line with Michael's commitment around his leadership style, the Team invested significant time

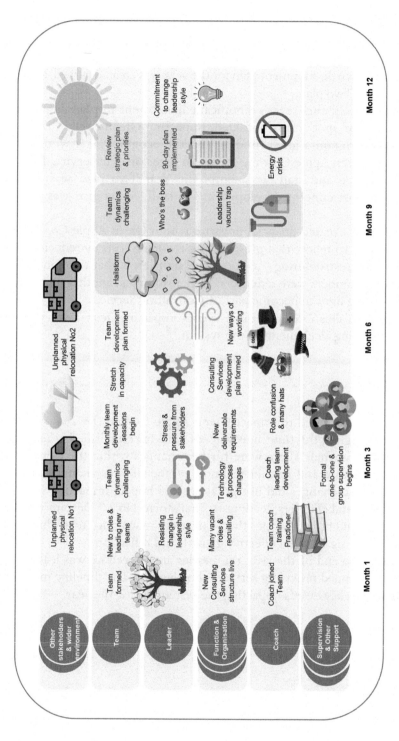

Figure 2.9: Environment Year One

developing the Year Two strategic implementation plan, including clear structure and accountability for deliverables for the year ahead. The Team hosted an all-staff Consulting Services conference, sharing the plan widely. The Team's own development plan for the year was created as well, aligning with the Year Two plan.

Unfortunately, the Team's significant investment in planning was in vain, as a "leaf spot" crisis unfolded, impacting Green Apple Co's ways of working, organisational funding and the economy as a whole. The Team and Green Apple Co were forced to focus on core service delivery, process change and staff wellbeing. The Year Two plan was put on hold, and most content developed in the staff conference was put on hold too.

"Leaf spot" created financial pressure within Green Apple Co. One of the tools used to relieve that pressure was reducing costs by reducing staff numbers and restructuring – again! Some staff left at that time, including me. C-suite numbers were reduced as well, resulting in another team changing reporting lines to become part of Consulting Services.

Figure 2.10 illustrates the main events impacting Year Two, with all events impacting all elements in the system.

## Year Three

"Leaf spot" continued to impact Green Apple Co and the Team in Year Three, although by this time, new ways of working established in Year Two had become normal. There were further changes within the Consulting Services structure and further technology and process changes as well. Some of those changes did not go as well as hoped, impacting internal and external stakeholders, leading to "hailstorm No.2." Despite another "hailstorm" and other changes the Team were managing, Year Three was also a time of significant collective growth and reflection.

Towards the end of the year, the Leader announced he was leaving his role, and I stopped providing services shortly after. The timeline in Figure 2.11 illustrates key events impacting the system during the year.

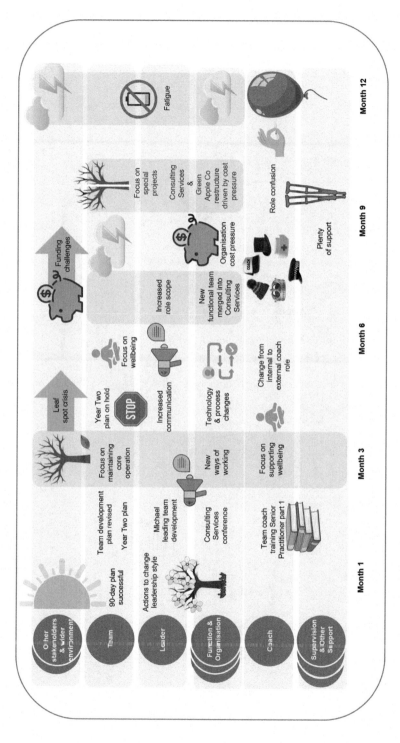

Figure 2.10: Environment Year Two

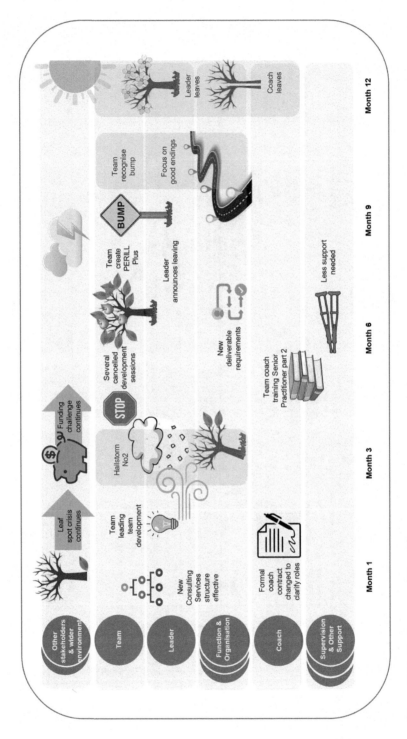

Figure 2.11: Environment Year Three

The interaction of system elements with each other and the environment across all three years is the focus of Section B. However, before moving onto that content, Chapter Three covers more context by describing the development and team coaching approach used in this case.

# Approach

**3**

*Helen Zink*

---

## HOW TO READ CHAPTER THREE

I am Helen, the Team Coach in this case, and this is how this chapter fits into the overall book.

Chapters Two and Three provide information needed for each of the parallel stories told in Section B. Chapter Three, narrated by me, describes the team development and coaching approach applied in this case, including interventions used and outcomes measured. The approach is described as neutrally as possible. Using a movie production analogy, this would be the description of common "scenes" in the movie.

Opinion on whether approaches and interventions used were successful or not is held until Section B, where characters share their respective stories using their own words. Once we hear from all five perspectives in Section B, Section C combines and compares insight from each of those perspectives for further learning.

---

Academics and senior level practitioners would agree there is no right or best practice approach to a team development and coaching engagement. *The team coaching casebook* (Clutterbuck et al., 2022) makes specific mention of this, noting that each situation is unique, incredibly complex and highly influenced by the systems in which the team resides.

Michael described the development approach in this book as an "experiment" from the onset. By describing it this way, he recognised the

DOI: 10.4324/9781003367789-4

uncertainty inherent in the approach and also gave me, and all involved, permission to try, succeed, fail and learn. As the approach in this case is described below, keep the word "experiment" in mind – noting that some parts of the approach were planned and some evolved from and within the system.

## Organisation culture change

As mentioned in Chapter Two, an organisation-wide culture project was already underway as Year One began. The goal for the culture project was to bring to life Green Apple Co's values of collaboration, open-mindedness and valuing the contribution of all, acknowledging that the benefits of this would take time to emerge.

The C-suite were investing in developing themselves as well, with regular monthly development sessions focused on leadership and collaboration. The C-suite team development plan was structured and created well in advance of sessions facilitated primarily by external consultants.

Another stream of development activity involved quarterly senior leader development days, where a combination of internal and external facilitators took senior staff through various leadership and strategic content. The Team was part of the senior leadership group and therefore participated in these sessions.

A fourth area of investment was the creation of in-house resources and tools, designed to support leaders and all staff with their own development. These resources and tools were accessed using a self-service online approach.

## Team development goal and model

As mentioned in Chapter Two, part of my role was to support the Team with their leadership development, acknowledging they were new to their roles, with varying degrees of leadership experience and capability.

Near the beginning of Year One, around the same time I began the role of Coach, I began formal team coaching training at Practitioner level. I had enrolled in the course prior to accepting the Coach position. Although it was not a practice the organisation was familiar with at that time, I was encouraged to continue training in the area and apply the team coaching approach with the Team. The collision of the Team's development journey with a team coaching approach was a complete coincidence facilitated by me being part of the system. The choice of approach was the result of my area of interest at the time – not something pre-planned by the Leader or HR at all!

During that first team coaching training course I became more familiar with Clutterbuck's (2020) HPT PERILL model (Theory Break's 3.1 and 3.2).

## THEORY BREAK 3.1: HIGH PERFORMING TEAM

Katzenbach and Smith (1993) defined an HPT as "A small number of people with complementary skills who are committed to a common purpose, set of performance goals, and approach, for which they hold themselves mutually accountable." Hawkins (2019) added to this definition saying

> A HPT also effectively meets and communicates in a way that raises morale and alignment, engages with all the team's key stakeholder groups in a way that grows performance, and provides constant learning and development for all its members and the collective team.

These definitions were some of the foundations that informed Clutterbuck's (2020) HPT PERILL model used in this case. Refer to Theory Break 3.2.

## THEORY BREAK 3.2: PERILL

**1. Leadership**
Team has type of leadership they need to perform
Typically: coaching, empowering, good communication, development focused, growth mindset, clarifying goals.

**2. Purpose**
Consistent narrative about the future. Collective energy shared vision, goals, priorities.

**3. Relationships**
How the team works together. Respect, trust, collaboration, psychological safety. Accountable for each other's wellbeing, development and performance.

**4. Internal processes, systems and structure**
Clarity of tasks, roles and performance levels. Clear decision making processes. Clear and frequent communication.

**5. Learning**
Ability to respond to and anticipate the environment. Collective continuous improvement and growth.

**6. External processes, systems and structure**
Relationships with stakeholders. Reputation, performance, environmental awareness. Access to resources and support.

All PERILL pillars interact with each other and leadership enables and facilitates interaction between all pillars.

Modified from Clutterbuck (2019)

Green Apple Co's HR team used their own in-house HPT model based on Lencioni's (2002) Five Dysfunctions of a Team (Theory Break 3.3). While I appreciated the in-house model, I thought it lacked recognition of internal and external processes and systems, learning and leadership, which seemed critical to me.

---

## THEORY BREAK 3.3: FIVE DYSFUNCTIONS OF A TEAM

Lencioni (2002) describes dysfunctional teams as having five common characteristics:

- Inattention to results – unclear priorities.
- Absence of trust or mistrusting each other.
- Fear of conflict – prioritising harmony over constructive debate.
- Lack of commitment – focusing on personal rather than team success.
- Avoidance of accountability – not holding each other to account.

The above characteristics are loosely aligned with other HPT models.

---

As I contemplated the in-house model and the approach I was using in team coaching training, I thought the best approach for the Team would be a combination of both. With agreement from HR and Michael, I suggested the Team's development goal of becoming an "HPT that enables others to perform at their best" and framing that goal around a bespoke HPT model combining in-house and PERILL models, refer to Figure 3.1.

HR had also developed their own in-house HPT questionnaire based on their HPT model, and it was already in use with some teams across Green Apple Co. I created a bespoke HPT questionnaire for the Team as well, using in-house questions for the relationships section and PERILL questions for the remaining five elements (PERILL HPT questions were sourced from *Coaching the team at work*, Clutterbuck, 2020). HR and the Leader were comfortable with this, and the Team endorsed the approach as well.

The Team's development goal and model were reviewed regularly throughout the three-year period this case covers, and they remained consistent throughout, with one addition. Around the middle of Year Three, I introduced the Team to an apple tree analogy and image to help embed the

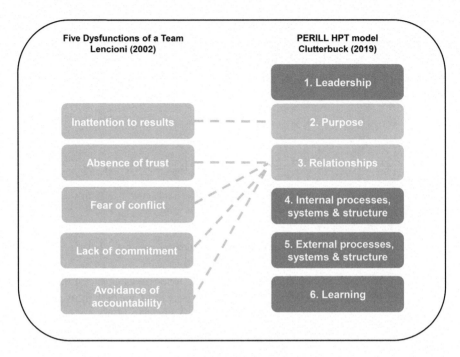

Figure 3.1: In-house versus PERILL HPT models

PERILL model, refer to Figure 3.2. The Team requested a seventh element be added – team resilience and wellbeing. Their new bespoke model is referred to as "PERILL Plus" in this book. I also added questions on team resilience to the Team's HPT questionnaire, reflecting the seventh element.

## Intervention streams

The Team's HPT development goal and model were brought to life primarily through three streams of intervention:

(A) Monthly team development sessions – with me in the team coach role.
(B) One-to-one formal and informal coaching of team members – with me in the coach role.
(C) One-to-one informal coaching of Michael – with me in the coach role.

I would love to say that I thought through the development goal and context, assessed options and planned these three intervention streams based on an assessment of likely effectiveness, but I did not. Michael made the

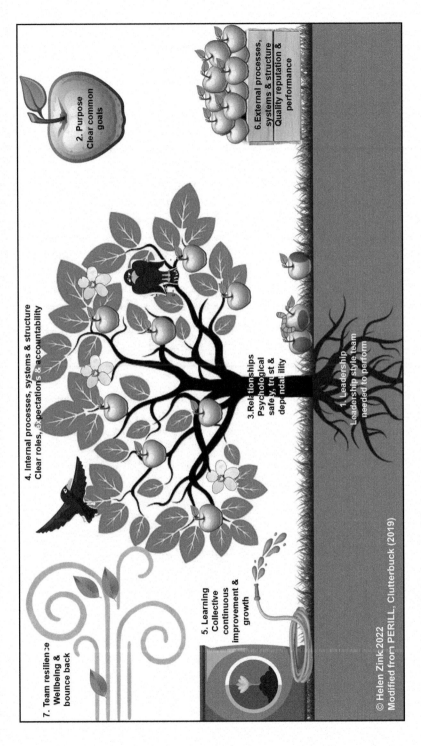

Figure 3.2: "FERILL Plus" HPT model

decision to invest in intervention (A), regular team development sessions, and the other two streams of activity just seemed to emerge. As mentioned in Chapter One, the approach in this case was eclectic and evolving rather than the application of a particular methodology or recommended best practice.

Figure 3.3 shows the parallel nature of interventions taking place across Green Apple Co, the Consulting Services function, and the Team. Despite some interventions being unplanned, all were well aligned across the system.

As mentioned in Chapter Two, the scope of my role included working with the Team on their development. However, I was never formally appointed or described as an internal team or internal one-to-one coach (Theory Break 3.4); it just happened. Given that coaching and a coaching approach was strongly encouraged across Green Apple Co, and I had an interest in coaching and team coaching, it was a natural evolution under the circumstances.

Each intervention stream is discussed in more depth next, including changes in interventions across the three years this case covers where relevant.

## THEORY BREAK 3.4: INTERNAL VERSUS EXTERNAL COACH

St John-Brooks (2013) defines an internal coach as an employee of the same organisation as the coachee, who uses all the tools and techniques of coaching, with the aim of supporting the coachee's professional development. The coach may be a full-time internal coach or may coach for some hours alongside another role within the organisation. The internal coach may be a peer, or more senior or junior than the coachee.

However, St-John Brooks believes the coach and coachee should never be in the same chain of command, and ideally should not even be in the same part of the organisation. The exception is leaders coaching their staff – which is encouraged. Refer to Theory Break 5.2 for more on leader as coach.

In contrast, an external coach is not an employee of the organisation and a formal legal contract for the supply of services between parties exists.

The ICF (2020a) code of ethics recognises that internal coaches experience more challenges managing conflicts of interest, and must be wary of their ability to operate effectively and maintain confidentiality.

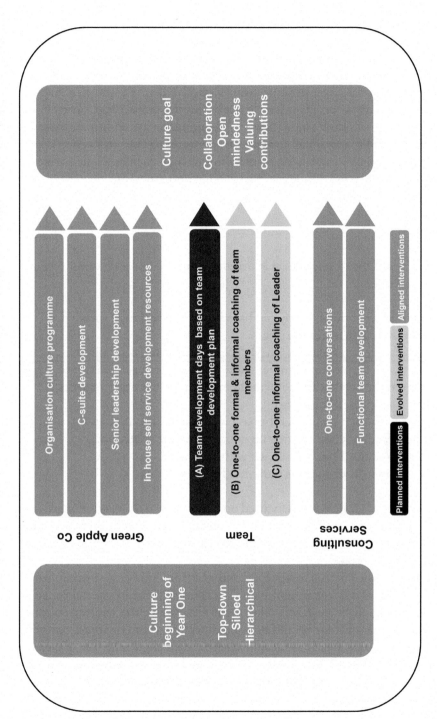

Figure 3.3: Intervention streams across Green Apple Co

*Intervention (A) – Team development sessions*

Monthly team development days became routine throughout the Team's three-year journey. Most sessions took place in person at an off-site location, and some shorter sessions were virtual. Normally, the first half of the day focused on development activity, and the second half on strategy. Development content came from a combination of in-house material designed by HR, my team coaching training resources, and other knowledge and tools in my toolbox, including change management, strategic planning, positive psychology and leadership development.

## Year One

During Year One, a regular cycle around planning and executing sessions was established:

- Agendas were designed by me based on my assessment of what would be most beneficial for the Team.
- Agendas were reviewed with Michael and adjusted if required.
- I met with each team member a few days prior to each session to warm them to the agenda and inform them of any preparation required.
- The session itself took place.
- I met with each team member a few days after each session to debrief, collect feedback and provide an opportunity for reflection.
- I discussed the Team's feedback with Michael.
- The Team's feedback was built into future sessions.

The content of early sessions focused on basics such as team agreements and building trust and psychological safety. I included content on self-awareness and wellbeing as well, as HR encouraged all staff across Green Apple Co to work on these topics.

Figure 3.4 outlines team session content across Year One. I cannot refer to Figure 3.4 as a development plan, as although a plan was established at the beginning of the year, session content was flexible and evolved continually. A better description would be a retrospective record of topics covered.

Figure 3.4 indicates how development topics align with the six elements of the HPT PERILL model with the addition of wellbeing, and also indicates which development modality was used with each activity (Theory Break 3.5). Sometimes the development modality was planned in advance, and sometimes it emerged in the moment. For example, I may have planned

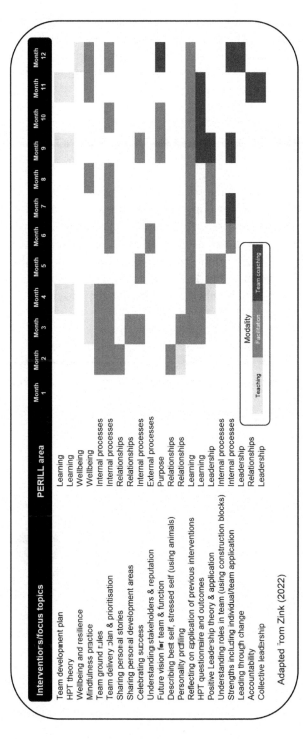

Figure 3.4: Team development activity Year One

for an activity to be heavily facilitated, and as interesting topics came up, I switched to team coaching as a modality to enable further exploration. Conversely, I may have intended to use team coaching, but switched to facilitation or teaching if the Team were not in the right headspace for the intended conversation or we were stuck.

## THEORY BREAK 3.5: TEAM DEVELOPMENT MODALITIES

The *ICF team coaching competencies* (2020b) emphasises the difference between various team development modalities and states that coaches must "Maintain the distinction between team coaching, team building, team training, team consulting, team mentoring, team facilitation, and other team development modalities." Coaches must also ensure they have the capability needed to best suit a client's needs and seek support of others or refer clients to others if they do not.

Training – set syllabus and expected outcomes.
Team building – group activities aimed at improving relationships.
Facilitation – emphasis on process and outcomes often predetermined.
Mentoring – ongoing support and advice from someone more experienced.
Consulting – solicited specific advice based on experience and knowledge.
Coaching – refer to Theory Break 3.6.

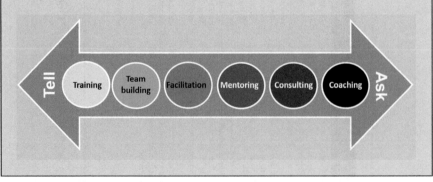

## Year Two

During Year Two, the team development session cycle described above continued, although Michael was more involved with planning content

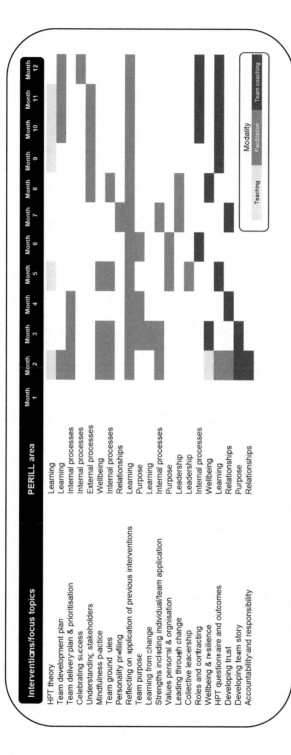

Figure 3.5: Team development activity Year Two

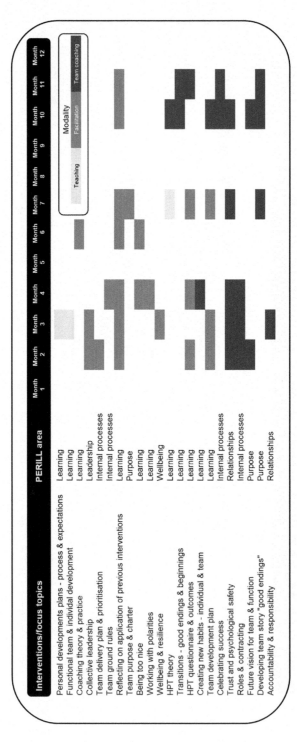

Figure 3.6: Team development activity Year Three

and the delivery of sessions. Figure 3.5 outlines team development activity across Year Two.

## Year Three

During Year Three, the team session cycle changed. Rather than Michael taking a lead role in sessions, team members took turns in the leadership role. Michael was still involved in discussions relating to the agenda, but more in the background. Around the middle of Year Three, I replaced discussions with each team member before and after each session with a simple online feedback form. Figure 3.6 outlines team development activity in Year Three. Some months are left intentionally blank, representing cancelled sessions.

## Intervention (B) – One-to-one formal and informal coaching of team members

In parallel with intervention (A), I initiated one-to-one informal coaching of team members. As illustrated in Figure 3.3, this was not a planned intervention per se, it evolved over time and seemed an obvious opportunity as I spent considerable time with all team members both one-to-one and collectively in fulfilling my day-to-day role.

I also worked with Jane in a formal one-to-one coaching arrangement during Year Two, at Michael's request (Theory Break 3.6). A formal internal coaching contract was put in place, including triad sessions at the beginning, middle and end of the programme with Michael.

### THEORY BREAK 3.6: FORMAL VERSUS INFORMAL COACHING

The ICF (2019), defines coaching as "partnering with clients in a thought-provoking and creative process that inspires them to maximise their personal and professional potential." There are important distinctions between formal and informal coaching.

**Formal coaching** normally involves an agreed series of regular sessions 60 to 90 minutes long, over a period of time, often six months. In most circumstances there should be a formal agreement or contract in place, outlining the roles and responsibilities between parties. The content is often structured, and the coach may use a coaching model or framework to support the session.

The coach will take on the role of asking open ended and powerful questions to help the coachee unlock their thinking. There is often a sponsor involved, who may be the coachee's boss or someone from HR. The coachee, sponsor and coach may meet regularly throughout the process to ensure goals are aligned and progress is acknowledged.

**Informal coaching**, as the name suggests, is more relaxed. There may be no agreement or contract, no set time or frequency, no formally identified roles, in fact there may no mention of a coaching conversation at all. The coachee may not be aware that coaching is taking place and sometimes the coach may not be aware they are taking on the role of coach. The thing that distinguishes this from a normal conversation is the person in the coach role asks open ended and powerful questions that help the coachee unlock their potential and increase their own understanding of a topic.

Whitmore (2009) suggests that coaching should not be limited to a formal scenario, and informal coaching is very powerful. He says, "Coaching is not merely a technique to be wheeled out in certain prescribed circumstances . . . it is a way of thinking, a way of being." He also says, "Superficially the conversation might sound like a normal conversation," but it is not.

## Intervention (C) – One-to-one informal coaching of Leader

Michael and I worked closely together in all aspects of my role, and there were plenty of opportunities for me to provide Michael with advice and informal one-to-one coaching, all of which he was receptive to.

## Outcomes

So far, this chapter has covered the team development goal and model used and described the three main intervention streams applied – although two of the streams were evolutionary rather than planned. The impact of interventions could be seen within trends of two tangible measures.

## Tangible measures

The HPT questionnaire discussed above was completed by the Team every six months throughout the three-year time frame of this case. Figure 3.7 shows trends in the six PERILL areas over three years, with a maximum score of five. A team resilience score was also available at the end of Year Three as resilience questions were added to align with the Team's "PERILL Plus" model.

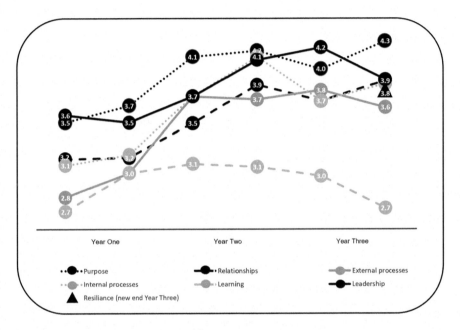

Figure 3.7: HPT assessment scores by PERILL category

Engagement scores were also readily available, and Green Apple Co used a tool that collected and tracked results frequently. Figure 3.8 includes the combined PERILL result and the engagement scores for the Team and the Consulting Services Function, all scores have a maximum score of five.

Opinion on whether approaches and interventions used were successful or not, as well as interpretation of these tangible measures, is held over until Section B, where each system element comments from their own perspective.

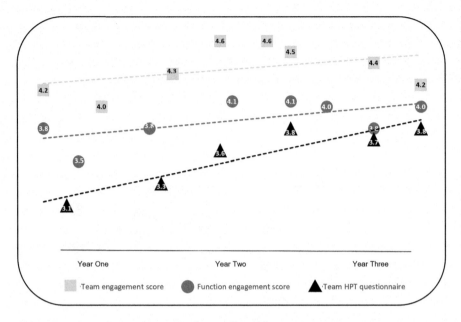

Figure 3.8: Engagement scores and overall HPT scores

## Intangible measures

Intangible measures, such as team member and stakeholder feedback, were not formally collected to ascertain team development progress in this case. However, team members did provide regular feedback after each team session as part of the monthly development cycle. This and other feedback collected from the Team and stakeholders, for the purposes of this book, is included in perspective chapters in Section B.

## Chapter Three summary

Figure 3.9 illustrates the overall content of this chapter, showing the flow in development approach from establishing the team development goal and model, to the three intervention streams used, and the assessment of outcomes. I reiterate that while setting the goal, selecting the HPT model, and establishing monthly development sessions were all planned, other interventions were not. Also note that Figure 3.9 is a retrospective illustration of the approach used in this case, created specifically for this book. It does not represent a predetermined implementation plan.

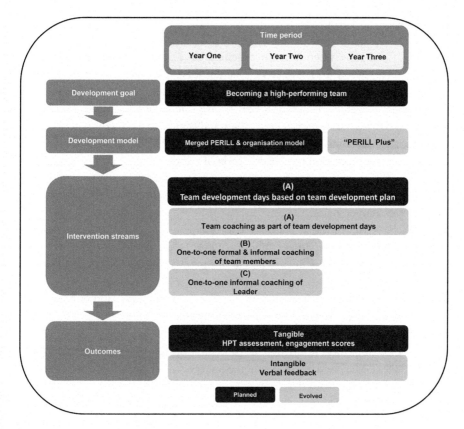

Figure 3.9: Overall approach

With better understanding of system elements and their environment, or "characters" and "eras" described in Chapter Two, and an outline of the development approach or common "scenes" in this chapter, the stage is set for characters to talk through their "parallel plots" in Section B. The first element to describe their perspective of events is the Team, and their story is narrated on their behalf by Jane in Chapter Four.

# References

Clutterbuck, D. (2019). Towards a pragmatic model of team function and dysfunction. In D. Clutterbuck, J. Gannon, S. Hayes, I. Iordanou, K. Lowe & D. McKie (Eds). *The practitioner's handbook of team coaching*. London: Routledge. https://doi.org/10.4324/9781351130554.

Clutterbuck, D. (2020). *Coaching the team at work*. London & Boston: Brealey.

Clutterbuck, D., Turner, T. & Murphy, C. (2022). *The team coaching casebook*. London: Open University Press.

Hawkins, P. (2019). Systemic team coaching. In D. Clutterbuck, J. Gannon, S. Hayes, I. Iordanou, K. Lowe & D. MacKie (Eds), *The practitioner's handbook of team coaching*. Oxon: Routledge. https://doi.org/10.4324/9781351130554-4.

International Coaching Federation (2019). *ICF core competencies*. Retrieved from https://coachfederation.org/credentials-and-standards/core-competencies.

International Coaching Federation (2020a). *ICF code of ethics*. Retrieved from https://coachfederation.org/ethics/code-of-ethics.

International Coaching Federation (2020b). *ICF team coaching competencies: Moving beyond one-to-one coaching*. Retrieved from https://coachfederation.org/team-coaching-competencies.

Katzenbach, R. & Smith, D. (1993). The discipline of teams. *Harvard Business Review*. Retrieved from https://hbr.org/1993/03/the-discipline-of-teams.

Lencioni, P. (2002). *The five dysfunctions of a team: A leadership fable*. San Francisco: Jossey-Bass Wiley.

St John-Brooks, K. (2013). *Internal coaching: The inside story*. London & New York: Routledge. https://doi.org/10.4324/9780429476068.

Whitmore, J. (2009). *Coaching for performance: Growing human potential and purpose*. London & New York: Routledge. https://doi.org/10.1177/0974173920100216.

Zink, H. (2022). The good, the bad, and the unexpected impact of internal coach on a high-performing team development journey. In D. Clutterbuck, T. Turner & C. Murphy (Eds). *The team coaching casebook*. London: Open University Press.

# Section B – Five perspectives

# Team perspective

# 4

*Helen Zink*

---

## HOW TO READ CHAPTER FOUR

I am Jane, a member of the Team, and before beginning this chapter, I will explain how it fits into the overall book.

The five system elements covered in this book describe their own versions of their development story in Section B. This includes thoughts on whether the approach and interventions used in this case, as described in Chapter Three, were useful, what was good, what was challenging, and what was learnt from the experience. Using a movie analogy, Section B involves five "parallel plots," whereby the same story is narrated by different characters, with each character describing themselves and the other main characters in the movie.

Chapter Four is the first parallel plot – the Team's perspective of the story. I narrate the Team's story on our collective behalf, and Figure 4.1 illustrates our view of the system. In this chapter, I cover our thoughts on ourselves as a Team, Michael (Leader), Consulting Services (Function) and Green Apple Co (Organisation), and Helen (Coach).

Content for this chapter comes from our answers to questions Helen asked us for inclusion in this book, voice recordings, notes from team coaching sessions, ad hoc one-to-one coaching conversations, feedback from team development sessions, Helen's memory and our memories.

---

DOI: 10.4324/9781003367789-6

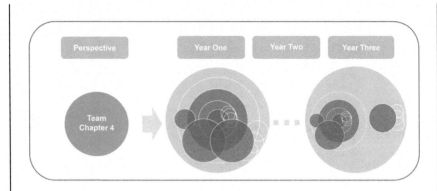

Figure 4.1: Team's perspective of system

I have the pleasure of narrating the first of five parallel plots in this book, the perspective of the Team. I worked at Green Apple Co for about a year before this story began. I also contributed to the design of the Consulting Services structure that went live at the beginning of Year One, including the creation of the Team this book is based on. I feel I am well placed to write this on behalf of the Team, as I was part of the previous lead team, know Michael and team members well, and got to know Helen very well through formal one-to-one coaching with her.

## The Team

I talk about us as a Team first, and our perspective of ourselves within the system is illustrated in Figure 4.2.

### Team development goal – HPT

Helen and Michael talked to us about setting a HPT goal for our team development in one of our team meetings early on. I did not know what it meant to be honest. I also recall that none of us were particularly invested, as we were all focused on our new roles, recruiting staff and teams reporting to us, and managing significant technology and process changes. The HPT goal suggested seemed fine, and we endorsed it without much discussion.

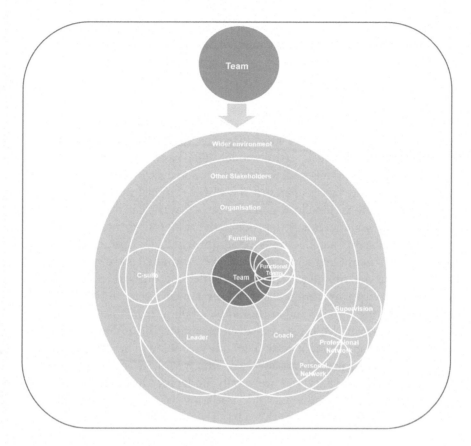

Figure 4.2: Team's perspective of themselves

## *HPT model – PERILL*

### Years One and Two

Around the same time the HPT team development goal was set, Helen suggested we use the PERILL (Clutterbuck, 2020) HPT model as a framework for our development work (Theory Break 3.2). Again, at the time we were completely focused on deliverables and were happy to take Helen's suggestion. I think most of us found discussions around HPT goals and models very theoretical and divorced from reality in many ways an annoyance given our workload at the time. We had other things to focus on that were much more important.

I also recall completing a HPT questionnaire for the first time at the beginning of Year One, and we agreed to repeat the assessment every six months.

We were comfortable enough doing this but did not fully appreciate the significance of the model or the meaning of the questions at the time.

## Year Three

Around the middle of Year Three, just after completing one of our regular HPT questionnaires, Helen introduced us to an apple tree version of the PERILL (Clutterbuck, 2020) model. The basic premise was that the apples we produced needed to meet our apple farmers' (stakeholders') specifications, and various parts of the PERILL model enabled us to meet those specifications. Finally, it made sense – it was clear how all elements of the model were necessary to produce the apples we wanted to produce.

I recall us having a collective eureka moment as we discussed the apple tree. In particular, Greg and Tom were very animated, saying the analogy was fine but was missing components reflecting our struggles, setbacks and challenging environmental conditions. I recall discussing wind, worms and birds eating apples, and rotten apples falling from the tree. As part of that discussion, we insisted a seventh element be added to our HPT model reflecting our team resilience and wellbeing (Theory Break 4.1) – an area crucial to us and our survival, which I talk more about below. It took almost three years, but we finally understood our "PERILL Plus" framework (refer to Figure 3.2). I do not know why Helen did not use the apple tree analogy right from the start; it would have been helpful.

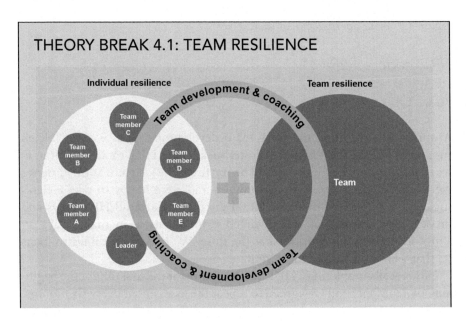

**THEORY BREAK 4.1: TEAM RESILIENCE**

Resilience, defined as the ability to bounce back from adversity, is generally considered on an individual basis, but it applies to the collective nature of a team as well. Hartwig et al. (2020) propose that teams face mutual challenges that may impede their performance or wellbeing, and team resilience relates to the collective response to that adversity, and the ability to overcome it together. Hartwig et al. also share that the level of team resilience comprises many factors, including:

- Characteristics of team members.
- Resilience of individual team members.
- Team processes, such as ground rules, decision making and planning.
- Collective emotional support.
- Psychological safety and trust.
- Team identity and purpose.

The main difference between individual and team resilience is that to be effective, team resilience requires effective communication, collaboration and coordination among team members, which is not necessarily the case for individual resilience.

Therefore, resilience in a team context is the combination of team members' individual resilience and collective team resilience.

## Readiness for team development and coaching

### Year One

We appreciated Helen was with us, she was ready to work with us, and supporting our development was part of her role, but we just did not have time. At the beginning of Year One, I would have preferred support with the process and system changes I was managing rather than what I perceived as another distraction. I know the rest of the Team felt the same. We all tried to excuse ourselves from team development sessions, but Michael was not having a bar of it — he basically forced us to attend, saying it was an expectation of our roles. Greg and Drew were particularly vocal about it, and I overheard some of the heated discussions they had with Michael on the subject.

In contributing to this book, Helen specifically asked us to comment on those early days, and Rosa and I responded with the following.

> Rosa: "We did not understand what a team development journey looked like or what it involved, so initially we were sceptical and pushed back."
>
> Me: "I was not expecting the emphasis on our own development and had reservations about it."

## Years Two and Three

Despite continued environmental and deliverable pressure during Year One, we grew to appreciate regular time spent together, and our appreciation of collective development increased. Over time we felt more connected, understood each other's roles better, and were solving issues together. It became clearer that our development work impacted the way we worked together and ultimately our service delivery. In relation to this, Greg said, "It almost doesn't matter what the content of team days is; the value is in spending time together away from the office."

Rosa and I were also particularly invested in sharing content from our team sessions with staff and teams reporting to us, intentionally spreading our good work and information across Consulting Services.

Tom joined our Team at the end of Year One, and he held different views to the rest of us. He did not see the point in spending time working on topics he was already familiar with and argued that "Our engagement score is high already. Why are we investing more time in this?" I think he missed the point. While he may have been familiar with the topics we covered, not all of us were, and the focus was collective development rather than his individual knowledge. Tom left our Team during Year Two and re-joined again later – returning with the same "anti-development" views.

## Team dynamics

### Year One

Prior to the Team being formed, we all knew each other and had worked together in other roles within Consulting Services – except for Helen. There were existing tensions between some of us at the beginning of Year One, along with some trust and respect issues.

Helen's arrival triggered some interesting and unexpected dynamics within our Team. Most of us were involved in Helen's recruitment process, so we were comfortable with her in the role. However, Taylor was challenged by role boundaries to begin with, saying, "Helen was doing things that had always been my responsibility," and, "She was closer to Michael than I was ever able to get." Rosa was uncomfortable with Helen as well. She had always been Michael's go-to person, and now that seemed to be Helen. She said she was "extremely surprised by the amount of influence Helen had with Michael."

Tom joining the Team disrupted all of us. He wanted to change the way we did things, and his arrival resulted in the formation of a "top-tier" within our Team. Michael, Helen and Tom met regularly and separately from the rest of us, and it was unclear what they were working on. Rosa was particularly annoyed as she considered herself Michael's right-hand, and was not happy to be excluded from the new "top-tier."

As the "top-tier" embedded itself, it became increasingly confusing to identify who made the calls in our Team, as information from Michael, Helen and Tom seemed inconsistent, resulting in rework, increased work-load and frustration. Greg and Taylor were particularly upset and shared their frustrations with Drew and myself. It felt like us ("bottom-tier") against them ("top-tier"). We shared our concerns with Helen, who spoke to Michael about it. It all came to a head in an event we called "who's the boss." Michael called us all to a meeting to discuss our concerns, and although the meeting defused immediate tension, the "who's the boss" dynamic was ever fully resolved.

"The hailstorm" (more below) had good and bad implications. One of the good aspects was collaborating on a "90-day plan" to get delivery back on track. We intentionally micro-managed that plan and ensured priorities were visible across Consulting Services and Green Apple Co.

By the end of Year One, relationships within the team had improved, and I think collective management of the "90-day plan" had a lot to do with it.

## Year Two

In Year Two, relationships between team members improved further, despite significant environmental challenges, including "leaf spot" and changes in team membership. Rosa commented,

There was a lot of disruption around the re-structure, with various people joining and leaving the leadership team, which in effect required forming a new team each time. The people who joined brought valuable contributions, and I missed them when they left, so that wasn't the issue; it was more the chopping and changing. So the dynamic hindered us in some ways and was helpful in others. I don't think it was in our control to do it differently; it was a function of a complex re-structure.

## Year Three

Year Three started hard, and we focused again on managing deliverables and structure changes, as "hailstorm No.2" was brewing (more below). Many of our regular team meetings were cancelled, one-to-ones with Michael were less frequent, and we only really met with each other when urgent delivery matters required input from others. We also cancelled several team development sessions in Year Three, reducing our connection time even further.

During a team session near the middle of Year Three, Helen shared her observations on the way we were operating. I recall her saying something like our reaction to busyness had encouraged us to fall back into old habits. We were focused solely on short-term delivery, resulting in less connection and collaboration with each other, which further increased busyness – a reinforcing cycle of busyness, as depicted in the top loop of Figure 4.3. Helen suggested we needed to maintain some balance and keep connecting, even when we were busy, to enable us to solve issues together – something she, and we, knew we were good at. She was describing the bottom loop of Figure 4.3.

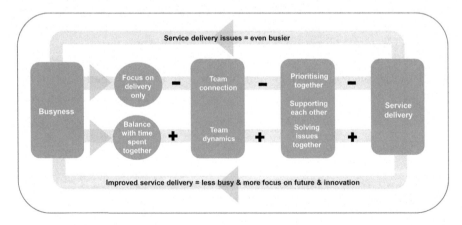

Figure 4.3: Team's busyness cycle

We agreed that Helen's hypothesis made sense. I recall saying at the time, "We had team changes, many challenges, and were managing the ongoing impacts of 'leaf spot'. At the same time, several team development sessions were cancelled, and we lost connectivity. We have lost something, and I want it back." We had a collective aha moment in that session, with the entire Team acknowledging we had "hit a bump" in our development journey and wanted to get ourselves back on track.

Although we agreed on "the bump" and getting back on track, this is an area where individual views within the Team differed. We disagreed on whether cancelling previous sessions was the right call. Taylor and I thought we had made a mistake, and my view was, "When times are difficult and uncertain, connection and collective development is even more important."

In contrast, Greg and Ethan, and, of course Tom, were comfortable we had made the correct decision, and considered delivery more important than development and collaboration at the time.

We agreed to disagree on past decisions, quickly establishing a good collaborative environment for the remainder of Year Three – including getting monthly team development sessions back on track and more time with Michael and each other.

## Impact of the environment

### Year One

Chapter Two describes the extremely challenging environment we experienced in Year One (refer to Figure 2.9). We were all in new roles, embedding a new structure, recruiting vacant positions, managing multiple technology and process changes in flight, managing two unplanned changes in physical location, and managing significant changes in the way we worked and delivered services. We were also short of capacity, and Michael insisted we also increase focus on our development.

All that pressure culminated in a "hailstorm" of issues. It felt like everything that could possibly challenge us and go wrong did. The culmination of environmental impacts and changes we were working through resulted in a drop in service standards. Our stakeholders were extremely upset and vocalised their disappointment. In addition to managing ourselves through the "hailstorm," we were dealing with stakeholder relationship issues as well.

However, there was an unexpected silver lining – our stakeholders loved our "90-day plan." I heard through the organisational grapevine that people were pleased we had owned up to our mistakes, involved stakeholders in priority setting, communicated progress and displayed open camaraderie across our Team for the first time. Our collective reputation improved as a result. In some ways, the "hailstorm" accelerated our HPT journey as it forced us to work together to create and implement the "90-day plan." Once the worst of the storm was over, we reflected on the experience and I recall us talking about post-traumatic growth – similar to when a community bands together during a natural disaster – and we agreed that was what we had experienced (Theory Break 4.2).

---

## THEORY BREAK 4.2: POST-TRAUMATIC GROWTH

A well-known phenomenon, where, despite tragedies and negative events, some good comes from it. Tedeschi (2020) writes specifically about the impact of the COVID-19 pandemic and how many individuals and organisations have experienced some benefit from it, including:

- Recognition of strength and resilience.
- New ways of doing things.
- Improved relationships.

Extraordinary circumstances force people to do things more rapidly, innovatively and collaboratively than they would under normal circumstances.

---

## Year Two

We invested many weeks at the beginning of the year developing a "Year Two plan," and we shared that plan at a very successful Consulting Services conference. However, even before we were able to debrief the conference, our amazing plan was put on hold – "leaf spot" had hit us with a vengeance (refer to Figure 2.10). The implications were significant, requiring immediate redesign of essential processes, the way we delivered our services, and how we worked together. We did what we needed to do quite successfully, I think, by working together in re-prioritising activity, solving challenges collectively, and increasing regular communication amongst ourselves and across Consulting Services.

Again, a crisis had brought silver linings, and this comment from Rosa expresses the situation well. "Our collective leadership in difficult times meant that, ironically, traumatic events brought us closer together. We discovered depths of resilience we didn't know we had. We were much more open with each other and pulled together to solve problems." Again, acknowledgement of our team resilience and post-traumatic growth.

## Year Three

Chapter Two and Figure 2.11 describe further environmental impacts during Year Three, the most notable event being the implementation of another new Consulting Services structure, resulting in changes in staff and responsibilities. Those changes, along with the ongoing implications of "leaf spot," culminated in "hailstorm No.2," and our service delivery dropped again. A wide group of our stakeholders were in pain, and although we quickly put a plan in place to respond, fallout was significant.

The "hailstorm No.2" was disappointing, but some key learning points from the experience were:

- We had not embedded enough learning from the first "hailstorm" to prevent the second.
- Although we had invested heavily in our own team development, the resulting increase in our capability widened the gap between us and team managers reporting to us.
- Busyness caused us to fall back into old familiar habits, and we focused on short-term delivery and working in silos (refer to Figure 4.3).
- Connection and collaboration are important to us and the successful delivery of our services.
- And most significantly, we have strong team resilience.

## Overall reflection

The environment in which we were operating across the three years this book covers was extraordinary. It felt like the universe was throwing everything it could at us. Yet we survived, learnt from our experiences, and became stronger. Back to the theme of team resilience (Theory Break 4.1) – I would not be here writing this on behalf of the Team without it. We all believe the development and coaching work we undertook, discussed next, was central to us building our individual and team resilience.

## Intervention (A) – Team development sessions

### Year One

Monthly team development sessions began soon after Helen arrived. As explained above, we were not supportive to begin with, but we attended. A process around sessions evolved, including some pre-work, a short discussion with Helen prior to each session, the session itself, a debrief with Helen, and feedback incorporated into next sessions. Figure 3.4 outlines topics covered in Year One.

Over time I came to enjoy the time we spent together more and more, and the rest of the Team felt the same – with the exception of Tom, of course.

Helen supplied examples of actual feedback from team sessions during Year One (below). I find our lack of agreement on flexibility of content interesting. Personally, I would have preferred more structure and sticking to agendas in Year One, but it seems others in the Team held different views.

Feedback on areas we appreciated

- "Flexibility of content and adapting to what we need."
- "Short, digestible pieces of useful work that facilitate everyone's participation."
- "Enjoying the opportunity to connect with each other."
- "A good mix of discussion and activity."

Feedback on areas to consider changing in future sessions

- "More structured agenda please."
- "Less content and more time to discuss topics together."
- "Less theory and more focus on collective activity."
- "No time to do pre-work, I just can't commit to doing it."
- "Sometimes topics are not bottomed out – we are not walking away with clear insight or next steps."

## Year Two

By Year Two, we were in a good monthly rhythm, and the benefit of spending time together and working on how we operate, rather than what we deliver, had become apparent. Similar to Year One, we covered many topics – some new and some repeated in more depth (refer to Figure 3.5). We continued to spend time with Helen prior to and after each team session, continuing when she became an external service provider part-way through the year. Examples of actual feedback on team sessions during Year Two follow.

Feedback on areas we appreciated

- "I like the way we step into topics of interest naturally."
- "Weaving together what we have covered before and adding to it and going deeper."
- "Great distraction from everyday work, and connection as a team."
- "Feeling like sessions connect together over the months and build on each other."

Feedback on areas to consider changing in future sessions

- "Maybe fewer topics and go even deeper."
- "Weaving content into more practical application and what is immediately happening for us right now."
- "We have too much on the agenda and we don't get to everything."
- "The high movement of team members is disruptive – although we are managing it well."

## Year Three

At the beginning of Year Three, Michael asked us whether we wanted to continue our team development sessions, and if we did, he wanted to be less involved in the process himself. We decided we would continue and rotate the leadership role in sessions between us, allowing Michael to step out. The idea was that we would take turns working with Helen on the agenda, review content and help arrange logistics for sessions. In some ways, it worked well, and we all learnt from having experience in the leadership role, yet in other ways it was ineffective.

We never seemed to stick to the planned agenda, and while some of us liked that approach, it made it hard for whoever was in the leadership role to keep up with what was going on. As a result, I noticed that Helen often deferred to Michael for guidance in sessions, rather than the nominated lead. It was also challenging having a dual role. I know when it was my turn to be lead, I was so engrossed in topics that I found it hard to help Helen facilitate. Conversely, I was so focused on process at times, I forgot to contribute to content as a team member. I am not sure the rotating leadership concept worked for us, but we continued with it. Some session feedback in Year Three (below) refers to challenges with rotating leadership. Also note more consensus on the benefits of flexible session content in Year Three compared with previous years.

Feedback on areas we appreciated

- "The shared leadership approach meant it wasn't all on Michael and there was more input from the team on content of sessions."
- "Helen supported whoever was in the lead role for sessions."
- "Flexibility of content was good and recognised what was needed in certain circumstances."
- "Focusing on what would help us rather than the pre-arranged plan."

Feedback on areas to consider changing in future sessions

- "Being in the leadership role in sessions is hard."
- "I don't feel comfortable in the leadership role in sessions."
- "On reflection, keep up the connectivity, and don't cancel sessions!"
- "When things are difficult and uncertain, it's even more important to have these sessions."

As mentioned above, there were differing views within the Team on whether we made the right decision to cancel some development sessions in Year Three. However, once we made the collective decision to re-invest and get our development back on track, we did some of our best work – including the creation of "PERILL Plus" (Figure 3.2) and working on "good endings." Helen suggested the "good endings" exercise as a way to acknowledge our development story, celebrate our successes, appreciate our challenges, and identify what we had learnt across our three-year journey together. It was also a great way to say goodbye to Michael, mark his departure, and induct our New Leader, George. I loved it – we all loved it!

## Overall reflection

Now, as I reflect back on the Team's development journey across the period this book covers, I cannot help but smile to myself. We moved from completely resisting development in Year One, to appreciating the benefits in Year Two, to leading our own development in Year Three – with, of course, the exception of Tom, who remained resistant throughout!

It took almost three years to pull together the meaningful team agreement illustrated in Figure 4.4 which captures some of the key outputs from our development work together. While we established initial ground rules in our very first development session in Year One, they continually evolved through the years. We also struggled to reach agreement on whether we needed a written purpose for our team at all, let alone agreeing on the wording of it. Greg was the strongest critic in relation to purpose, suggesting we simply needed to "get s\*\*t done," and spending time on developing anything more substantial was a waste of time. However, we did spend more time on it, and by the middle of Year Three, we had a written team purpose we could all live with.

The simplicity of our team agreement in Figure 4.4 is deceptive – it actually represents many conversations and debates, changes and edits, and hours of collaborative work.

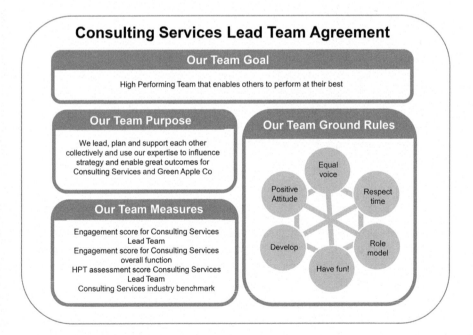

Figure 4.4: Team agreement

## *Intervention (B) – One-to-one formal and informal coaching of team members*

### Year One

It is interesting to reflect on our one-to-one informal coaching experiences with Helen, as we were not really conscious of it happening at the time – I certainly was not. We all regularly spent time with Helen, both as pre-arranged catchups and other meetings focused on mutual deliverables. These conversations often included advice, and, yes, looking back on it now, informal coaching. In my view, these informal conversations, whether they were advisory or coaching in nature, were the most significant benefit of having an internal coach who was part of our Team. I know we all felt the same way.

In contributing to this book, Helen specifically asked us to comment on our experience with informal one-to-one coaching, and we responded with:

> Greg: "I appreciated support for the team and myself when I need to bounce things off someone."
>
> Me: "It was like we had a neutral sounding board and our own HR support within our function."
>
> Rosa: "It allowed for some people to open up to Helen when they may not have felt comfortable doing so with Michael."
>
> Taylor: "Being part of the team meant Helen could get to know us really well, see all sides to us, how we tick, and appreciate our workload and day-to-day issues and how all that affected us."
>
> Greg: "There was no hiding things from Helen, as she knew what was happening. I liked that."

### Years Two and Three

During Year Two, informal coaching and advice continued in much the same way as it did in Year One. Despite Helen moving to an external role part-way through the year, we continued to spend plenty of time with her.

Helen and I also began working together in a formal coaching arrangement in Year Two, which continued as Helen transitioned to an external role. I was feeling quite confused and disillusioned about my role and questioned whether I even wanted it. I enjoyed hands-on technical work, which I had plenty of before Year One. However, the creation of the Team and new Consulting Services structure also created more expectation to lead others rather than do work myself, and I was struggling with it.

My feedback on the formal coaching experience:

> I seem to have actually become a leader! Having gone through a period of not being at all sure that I wanted a leadership role, I've gradually moved through questioning and being overwhelmed, to acceptance and embracing it. This is largely due to the encouragement, support and coaching of Helen, and Michael's belief that I could do it. I'm now seeing the benefits of not always being down in the doing and finding other ways to enjoy my role. This means I now have the headspace to coach my team and support them. I still don't feel that I'm a natural leader, but the effort is working.

By Year Three, my one-to-one formal coaching with Helen was complete, and we did not see much of her outside of team development sessions. I would have preferred to have had more opportunity to connect, but Michael was firm about us needing to stand on our own two feet.

## Outcomes

The only real progress measurements we were tracking were our HPT questionnaire results and our engagement scores. Our HPT score trends upwards over three years, remaining more stable towards the end of Year Three (refer to Figure 3.8). I think this reflects our development journey well – struggling to get traction to begin with, and slow and steady growth later on, plateauing in Year Three. Both our Team and the Consulting Services function engagement scores bounce around in Year One, reflecting the "hailstorm" and other changes taking place (refer to Figure 3.8). This was followed by strong increases in Year Two, and the score dips at the end of Year Three, I think reflecting uncertainty around Michael leaving.

In contributing to this book, Helen specifically asked us to comment on how we thought we had changed as a Team across the three-year timeframe this book covers. Previous comments in this chapter were real-time feedback as the journey unfolded, which Helen refers to as level one and two learning in Figure 1.3. The comments below are our reflections now, after Year Three. Helen refers to this as level three learning in Figure 1.3.

Overall thoughts on how we changed as a Team:

Me: "Michael used to make all the decisions. Now we talk openly, make decisions without the leader, challenge each other, know each other better, have each other's backs, and have a lot of laughs!"

Rosa: "We have learnt the benefits of focusing on development, and we have all invested in this for our direct report teams as well, so the benefits flow across Consulting Services."

Taylor: "We are more open and honest, and we certainly have a more equal voice."

Rosa: "We all have such different personalities, ways of working and getting things done – but in saying that, I do believe that we have become a team that trusts each other and definitely supports each other."

Greg: "I appreciate that we can openly talk about our problems (work, people and personal) and we are there to give advice and carry each other through challenging times."

Me: "We have grown as leaders, having clearer vision on where we are heading and what the end goal is."

Although we were resistant to begin with and our journey was very challenging, we all agree (with the exception of Tom) that the growth in our collective development was well worth the investment we made. I suppose we have transitioned from being active resistors to avid supporters.

## Summary – Team's perspective of themselves

A summary of our collective thoughts on what was good, challenging, and what we learnt from our three-year journey is contained in the Appendix to Chapter Four. Despite early reservations we learnt a huge amount from the experience – much more that we would ever have anticipated. Taylor's thoughts capture our collective thoughts on this: "It is interesting looking back and realising that real change comes from us – starting with ourselves. Aha! The master plan revealed itself!"

The real litmus test of success is whether we would undertake the same journey again. The answer is yes – with a few tweaks. As part of our contribution to this book, Helen asked each of us to identify areas we would change if we had an opportunity to "do over" and themes that came through were:

- We would be more open to the process right up front, and less resistant to investing our time.
- Greg, Taylor and Drew would have taken the opportunity for one-to-one formal coaching with Helen, as I did, as they saw how beneficial it was for me.
- We would have taken more care in understanding the implications of cancelling team development sessions before making the call to do so in Year Three.

## The Leader

I talk about Michael next, our boss, and our perspective of him within the system is illustrated in Figure 4.5.

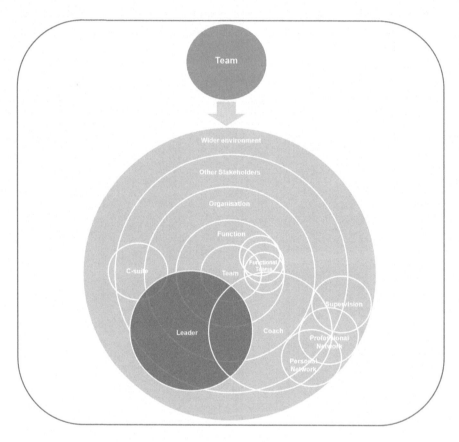

Figure 4.5: Team's perspective of Leader

## *Leadership style*

### Year One

All of us knew Michael before the Team was formed, except for Helen, and we all agreed his leadership style was "top-down" and hands-on at the beginning of Year One. He liked to get into details and have all decisions funnelled through him. I recall saying at the time, "We do not speak up in meetings, we wait for Michael to make all the calls, and nothing happens unless he is there." It was not the leadership style we wanted or needed to be successful in our new roles. Yet, at the same time, we shared deep respect for Michael, valued his technical and organisational knowledge, and knew he cared about and looked after us.

As we moved through Year One, I noticed a gradual change in Michael's style. Team meetings were more structured, had clear purpose, and we all had more opportunity to contribute. Our one-to-one sessions with Michael were also more regular and structured. It felt like Michael was prioritising us more, which we greatly appreciated, given that we were transitioning into new roles and managing significant process and system change at that time. We were getting more of the type of leadership we needed.

It was obvious that Helen was taking on more leadership too, and communication and direction was increasingly coming from her in relation to activity within our Team and across Consulting Services. It was unclear whether the transfer of leadership between Michael and Helen was intentional and planned, or whether Helen just gradually took over. Helen described this as a "vacuum trap" (Theory Break 4.3).

## THEORY BREAK 4.3: LEADERSHIP VACUUM TRAP

A phenomenon that sometimes occurs in coaching/team coaching is where a coach/team coach takes on certain aspects of a leader's role. As coaches tend to be helpful people, they assume filling voids left by the leader is helpful for the leader and team. Leaders, being busy people, may allow it to happen. The result is role confusion. The dynamic often occurs subconsciously, with the leader and coach unaware until someone points it out to them. Clutterbuck (2017) refers to this as the leadership vacuum trap.

As explained above, a "two-tier" leadership team was created when Tom joined us – and it felt like the "vacuum trap" with Helen had become a double trap. While it was great that Michael was sharing leadership with others, he seemed to only be sharing with Helen and Tom. Also, that sharing was not well coordinated or communicated. The resulting "who's the boss" event described above was horrible. We were confused and frustrated, which caused even more angst at a time when we were already overloaded and stressed. Something needed to change!

Near the end of Year One, I recall that Michael made a commitment to work on his leadership style. But we were all so exhausted from the trauma of the past year we did not pay much attention to what he was saying at the time – I know I did not. There was some scepticism within the Team too, and I recall Taylor saying, "He has said things like that before and nothing changed – don't worry about it."

## Years Two and Three

However, the sceptics amongst us were proved wrong! Despite having to put our newly created "Year Two plan" on hold due to the "leaf spot" crisis, we noticed many positive changes in Michael's style. He was focused, more collaborative, and communication with us and across Consulting Services improved considerably. In many ways, the adverse environmental conditions during Year Two reinforced what we needed from Michael, and we saw more of him during that time than ever before.

Towards the end of Year Two, the focus of our team development sessions became Michael's leadership style. In one session, without Michael in the room, Helen helped us create a story board outlining what we appreciated and needed from him. Once comfortable with the content, we shared the story with him, which led to a conversation around how we could support him more to be the leader we needed. The main thread was that, although he was trying, he needed to spend more time mentoring and coaching us so he could delegate more, and this in turn would release more of his time. It was a powerful and emotional session for all of us, and Michael appeared to be receptive to what we had to say.

While we did not notice much change in Michael's style immediately after the conversation described above, we did notice changes as Year Three unfolded.

## Overall reflection

The HPT questionnaire we completed every six months involved a leadership section, including these questions:

- "The leader seeks and makes use of feedback from the team."
- "The leader is a role model for personal development – both their own and coaching others."
- And several others (Clutterbuck, 2020).

Referring to the HPT questionnaire results in Figure 3.7, there was a gradual increase in the leadership score over three years, indicating that we all thought Michael's leadership style was better meeting our needs.

As part of the Team's input to this book, Helen asked each of us to describe the change we observed in Michael's leadership style in a few words. We all agreed that the transformation in his style was significant, and that he shifted from being a "top-down" leader to a more collaborative one. In particular, we noticed:

- Increased delegation.
- Increased communication.
- More mentoring and knowledge sharing.
- Sharing responsibility.
- Stepping back from hands-on work.

## Intervention (C) – One-to-one informal coaching of Leader

We were aware that Helen was supporting Michael with advice on his leadership style in Years One and Two. We assumed the arrangement between them was similar to Helen's approach with us – mostly informal, advisory at times and coaching in nature at other times. We also assume Michael experienced similar benefits to us, in that he had a sounding board and advice on tap.

## Summary – Team's perspective of Leader

A summary of what we found good, challenging, and what we learnt in relation to Michael's leadership style and changes in his style is included in the Appendix to Chapter Four. Our most insightful learning was the impact we collectively had as a Team on Michael's style through open conversation around what we needed. Those conversations were scary, yet useful and rewarding at the same time. It felt good to openly articulate what we needed and I do not think we would have been brave enough to do that without Helen's support.

## The Function and Organisation

The next area I cover is the Consulting Services function we lead, and Green Apple Co as an organisation. Most of our Team's stakeholders were internal to the organisation, so comments in this section relate to most stakeholders. Our perspective is illustrated in Figure 4.6.

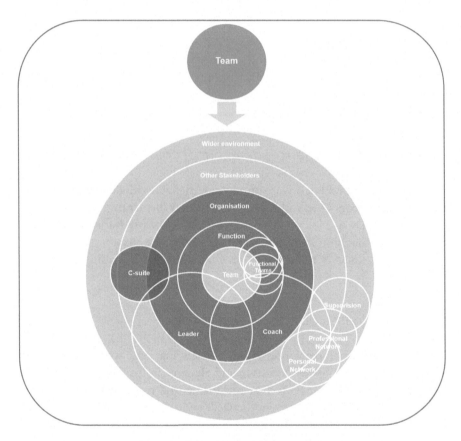

Figure 4.6: Team's perspective of Function and Organisation

### The Function

#### Year One

As mentioned in Chapter Two, Consulting Services comprised 60 or so staff – some reporting directly to us, and others via team managers. As we began working on our own development, I think staff within Consulting Services would have noticed:

- Increased clarity of deliverables.
- More communication from us and Michael.
- More regular one-to-one conversations.

In many ways, we were mirroring changes made in our own Team within the teams we led.

Despite all the work we were putting into increased communication and our staff, tangible measures of change did not reflect our efforts at first. Referring to Figure 3.8, the Function engagement score did not increase at all in Year One; in fact, it dipped in the middle of the year, reflecting the "hailstorm".

## Year Two

As the "leaf spot" crisis hit us in Year Two, we needed to communicate with our staff more frequently to facilitate changes required to processes and ways of working. We focused more on their wellbeing too, and they noticed. Our staff told us they appreciated the increase in attention, and a tangible increase in the Consulting Services engagement score confirmed their views (refer to Figure 3.8).

Another interesting observation in Year Two was the impact, or lack of impact, the merger of another team into Consulting Services had. I recall feedback at the time being positive, and everyone thought we handled the merger well. Again, the Function engagement score was stable during and after the merger period – a good sign.

## Year Three

As Year Three progressed, and we restructured yet again, the Function engagement score dropped (refer Figure 3.8). This was not at all surprising given the wide-reaching impact of that structure change, "hailstorm No.2", uncertainty surrounding Tom returning to the Team, and other environmental impacts described in Chapter Two. It was great to see that by the end of Year Three, scores bounced back, I think for two reasons:

- The new structure began to embed and uncertainty around it decreased.
- Tom invested in a targeted team development programme with staff reporting to him, involving a third of the staff in our Function.

## Overall reflection

As a Team, we talked about the impact we were having across Consulting Services many times. Without investing in our own development as a Team, I do not think we would have been as effective in leading our staff through the multiple environmental crises we experienced – described above and in Chapter Two.

Although the Function engagement scores did not move much to begin with, we take that result as a positive outcome – it could have been much worse given the circumstances! Helen talked to us about the coaching ripple effect (O'Connor & Cavanagh, 2013) many times, and we appreciated the development work we were doing as a Team was positively rippling across the entire Consulting Services function we led (Theory Break 4.4).

---

### THEORY BREAK 4.4: COACHING RIPPLE EFFECT

A study by O'Connor and Cavanagh (2013) confirmed that wellbeing benefits of coaching was not a linear cause and effect equation. Coaching benefited those being coached within an organisation and also positive impacts were felt widely across the organisation. Those most closely aligned to individuals being coached received most positive impact.

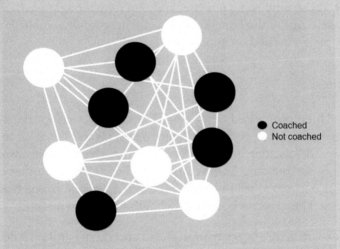

● Coached
○ Not coached

Modified from O'Connor and Cavanagh (2013)

Note this diagram is a simplified version of the results of the study to illustrate the impact of the ripple effect found in the study and does represent the actual results of the study itself.

## The Organisation

Our reputation as a Team and Function at the beginning of Year One was not as strong as we would have liked. Unfortunately, we had inherited the reputation of the previous lead team, and the very visible "hailstorm" involving delivery issues was not helpful.

However, by the end of Year One we were receiving feedback from stakeholders across Green Apple Co that we were working together and communicating better. Our "90-day plan" to address the "hailstorm" was not only effective in bringing delivery back on track; it also improved our reputation.

We managed to maintain delivery during the "leaf spot" challenges in Year Two, which our stakeholders appreciated. However, in Year Three, as "hailstorm No.2" played out, our reputation was hit again. Although factors leading into the storm could have been mitigated, we again managed our way out of that storm with good communication and a recovery plan.

Without our team development work, I think the implications of "hailstorms" and "leaf spot" would have been much greater. Although stakeholders complained at the time, they would have complained a lot more if we had not been able to bounce back and manage our own recovery. The importance of team resilience was discussed above (Theory Break 4.1), and our resilience benefited all of Green Apple Co, whether they fully recognised it or not.

We believe everyone in Green Apple Co experienced the coaching ripple effect too (O'Connor & Cavanagh, 2013) (Theory Break 4.4). Similar to the effect across Consulting Services, our team agreement, effective meeting structure, improved accountability, and better communication skills were new habits applied to every interaction we had across the Organisation.

## Summary – Team's perspective of Function and Organisation

What we found good, challenging, and what we learnt by reflecting on the Consulting Services function and Green Apple Co is summarised in the Appendix to Chapter Four. The most interesting insight is the obvious impact our development had on the wider system, and everyone we worked and interacted with.

## The Coach

The last system element I talk about is Helen, and her dual roles as our Coach and a member of our Team. Our perspective reflecting on Helen within the system is depicted in Figure 4.7.

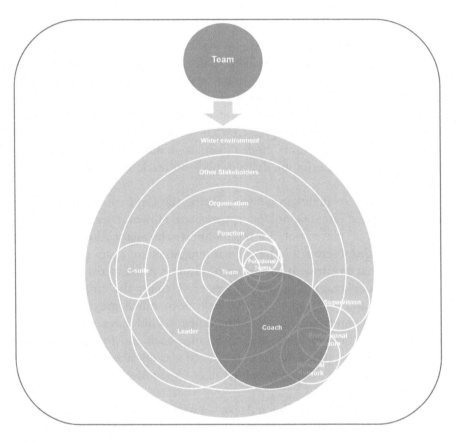

Figure 4.7: Team's perspective of Coach

### Relationship between Team and Coach

We were all involved in Helen's recruitment process and had met her before she joined our Team at the beginning of Year One. She seemed to know her stuff, and the fact her role was not well defined did not seem to bother her.

Despite the team dynamic challenges described above, overall, relationships between us and Helen were positive. We trusted her, she was empathic and supportive, and always found time for us when we needed it. That trust never faltered and continued as she moved to an external service provider in Year Two.

While relationships with us were good, there was an area that bothered some members of the Team – the obvious tension between Michael and Helen. At times, we could feel it and it impacted the environment and effectiveness of our team development sessions in Year Two. In particular, Rosa, who was very sensitive to Michael and Helen's relationship, found it very uncomfortable. Fortunately, by Year Three, the tension seemed to disappear. I assume rotating the lead role in our team development process helped.

## Internal Coach

### Years One and Two

Although Helen knew her role was not well defined when she joined us, it must have been hard for her at the start. In addition to taking on a new role in a new organisation, she had to effectively create that role at the same time. The following comments from Greg and me describe our thoughts on this:

> Me: "I'm not sure any of us had a clear idea of what Helen's role would actually be, including Michael."
>
> Greg: "I think I saw it as an additional HR resource, helping us to deal with bad behaviour, facilitating workshops, and leading cultural change, but I was not sure what that would look like in reality."

As Helen bedded into her role, we found that having an internal coach who was part of our Team worked well for us. She was experiencing the same things that we were experiencing, so it was easy for her to appreciate the context and environment in which we operated. As mentioned above, it also facilitated plenty of opportunity for one-to-one informal coaching and advice, which we all found so valuable.

In contributing to this book, Helen specifically asked us to comment on her role as an internal coach, and we responded with:

> Taylor: "She knew us well, and all our work issues and background. She was able to get us talking to each other much more productively, as she heard both sides of the story."
>
> Greg: "Helen became counsellor to just about everyone in Consulting Services."
>
> Rosa: "It was like we had a neutral sounding board and our own HR support within Consulting Services."

> Drew: "After a short period of time, it felt very natural to see Helen as facilitator and coach in some circumstances and team member in others."
>
> Me: "What could have been an awkward situation was not, thanks to Helen's professionalism, ability to juggle many hats and genuine desire to help people achieve their full potential."

I must also add that having Helen within our Team was not always a bed of roses. To begin with, Helen probably did not feel valued by us. We were pushing back hard on what she suggested we work on, in particular the monthly team development sessions. Furthermore, as explained above, some of the team dynamic challenges we were experiencing were attributable to her role. The "who's the boss" and "leadership vacuum trap" situations are examples of the disadvantage of having a coach involved in day-to-day activity. We also used Helen as an on-tap counsellor, asking her to resolve many people-related issues on our behalf. I know she did not like doing that, and I remember her talking about the "many hats" she wore and the challenges she faced around role clarity.

More comments from us:

> Taylor: "It must have been difficult for Helen to be one of the team."
>
> Me: "We were all guilty of leaning on Helen as a coach and forgetting that she also needed support as a team member. The relationship was too one-sided – we were happy to take support, but we did not give."

## External Coach

### Years Two and Three

About halfway through Year Two, Helen left our Team and Green Apple Co. In many ways things did not change. We still had the same person supporting us with regular monthly team development sessions, we still communicated frequently and we could still call on her for advice.

In contributing to this book, Helen specifically asked us to comment on the transition of her role to an external coach, and we responded with:

> Me: "It was hard to begin with, as the implication of the change was uncertain. It was also sad to see Helen leave, but I think that the transition went remarkably smoothly, considering the circumstances."

Taylor: "A positive from the situation was that Helen was no longer involved in internal politics or work deliverables, so she could step back from it and bring new and more independent perspectives."

Greg: "As she was still close to the Team, it was clear there was sometimes difficulty separating being an external consultant from her previous role as one of the Team."

Rosa: "The transition from being a team member to a purely external coach changed her approach – she was coaching us to decide on the development goals and roadmap without contributing input as she had done in the past as a member of the Team."

As we moved into Year Three, the scope and support Helen provided reduced significantly. We had very little communication with her outside team development sessions. It must have been hard for her, as she had to work with a different member of the Team each month, and many sessions were cancelled or de-scoped at the last minute. Despite the frustration, her awareness and flexibility around our changing needs was a true testament to her professionalism.

More comments from us:

Greg: "It must have been hard figuring out what the Team had the mental capacity to deal with and to manage all the last-minute changes to agendas and content to accommodate this."

Me: "Helen often reminded us that her role was different now and she was reliant on us to tell her what was going on in our Team; she did not have inside knowledge anymore."

It was sad to see Helen leave us completely at the end of Year Three. We were not expecting that to happen, but we also appreciated being able to work on "good endings" with her before she left.

## Summary – Team's perspective of Coach

It has been interesting to reflect on the journey by focusing attention on Helen – not something we had done prior to contributing to this book. The experience must have been hard for her, and as a Team we all agree that we should have looked after her better. What we found good, challenging and what we learnt by reflecting on Helen as Coach is summarised in the Appendix to Chapter Four.

## Chapter Four summary

It has been a privilege to pull this chapter together on behalf of the Team, and I am confident I have expressed our collective voice fairly. I have also made a point to highlight areas where individual team members' views differ.

Helen asked us to identify the best thing about this journey, the most challenging part and the most significant thing we learnt. There was good consensus amongst us that:

- The best part was spending time together as a Team, reflecting and learning together.
- The most challenging aspects were, without doubt, the impacts of "hailstorms," "leaf spot" and other unexpected environmental impacts.
- The most significant thing we learnt was the value of team and individual resilience. Without investing in our collective development as we did, we would not be here now.

Before signing off, I feel it is important to emphasise the rocky ride we experienced over the three-year period this book covers. The circumstances and environment we found ourselves in was extraordinary, and the universe literally threw everything it could at us. When we reminisce on these three years, Greg often pipes up with comments like, "It was unbelievable – we could not have made this stuff up!" And yet we survived. I do not think it was a coincidence that we moved from actively resisting development, to appreciating the benefits, to leading our own development in Year Three! We grew and matured together.

I look forward to telling you about our Team's plans for Year Four and our future in Chapter Eleven. Until then this book moves through other perspectives of the story, with Michael up next, talking about his experience as Team Leader.

## References

Clutterbuck, D. (2017). *The leadership vacuum trap and how coaches and mentors can avoid it*. Retrieved from https://www.coachingandmentoringinternational.org.

Clutterbuck, D. (2020). *Coaching the team at work*. London & Boston: Brealey.

Hartwig, A., Clarke, S., Johnson, S. & Willis, S. (2020). *Workplace team resilience: A systematic review and conceptual development*. Organisational Psychology Review. 2020, Vol. 10(3–4) 169–200. https://doi.org/10.1177/2041386620919476.

O'Connor, S. & Cavanagh, M. (2013). The coaching ripple effect: the effects of developmental coaching on wellbeing across organisational networks. *Psychology of Well-Being: Theory, Research and Practice.* 3:2. https://doi.org/10.1186/2211-1522-3-2.

Tedeschi, R. G. (2020). Crisis management: Growth after trauma. *Harvard Business Review.* Retrieved from https://hbr.org/2020/07/growth-after-trauma.

Appendix to Chapter Four: Good, challenging and learnt – Team's perspective

| Good | Challenging | Learnt |
|---|---|---|
| | Team development and coaching | |
| Eventually we valued our investment in monthly team development days, with flexible content. | Initial resistance to invest in development (Y1). | Regular team development sessions are a good investment. |
| Our feedback on team sessions was incorporated into future sessions. | Team dynamics were complex. Our poor reputation (early Y1). | A team's appreciation of the value of team development can grow. |
| "Hailstorms", 90-day plan & leaf spot forced us to work together & collaborate. | Team development sessions: <br> • Flexible content. <br> • Topics not bottomed out. <br> • Cancelled sessions (Y3). | There is a relationship between investment in connection & development & delivery. |
| We shared leadership of our development (Y3). | "Hailstorms" & other events forced us to focus on navigating storms & BAU. | Invest time in learning from challenges/mistakes so they are mitigated/not repeated. |
| We added resilience to the HPT model (Y3). | We did not learn enough from the "hailstorm" to prevent "hailstorm No.2" (Y3). | Team development sessions: <br> • Balance structure & flexibility. <br> • Bottom out topics. <br> • Align to where team is at. <br> • If sharing leadership, spend time on role clarity & expectations. |
| We cancelled some team sessions to concentrate on BAU (Y3). | Rotating team development leadership role (Y3). | As a team develops & steps up, it may expose capability gaps. |
| We recognised the "bump" in our development journey (Y3). | As we stepped up, the gap between us & team managers reporting to us widened. | The team development path is bumpy; expect ups and downs; it takes time to see results. |
| Investment in "good endings" was useful (Y3). | | |
| We have strong team resilience. | | |

| Good | Challenging | Learnt |
|---|---|---|
| We changed – tangible measures & verbal feedback improved (Y2 & Y3). | Implications of cancelling team sessions was not thought through (Y3). Changes took time to become visible in engagement scores. | *Team development builds team & individual resilience, which facilitates more team development – a cycle. And team resilience is important. (Most valuable learning for the Team).* "Good endings" are a good investment. Good management of adversity can create silver linings. Team development has a ripple effect across an organisation. |

**Leadership development**

| Good | Challenging | Learnt |
|---|---|---|
| Helen worked closely with Michael supporting one-to-one informational coaching & direct advice (Y1 & Y2). Michael made a commitment to change his leadership style (end of Y2). Michael's leadership style did change. | Michael's "top-down" leadership style (Y1). "Leadership vacuum trap" & "Who's the boss" events (Y1). Helen moving from internal to external coach role reduced Michael's on-tap support (Y2). | If sharing leadership responsibilities, communicate well with team & all stakeholders. Support from an on-tap coach is helpful. Explicitly talk about the leadership style the team needs. A team can provide valuable support for a leader to change their style. Leadership style can change – it just takes time. |

(continue)

(continue)

| Good | Challenging | Learnt |
| --- | --- | --- |
| | Coaching in general | |
| Helen had the skills, knowledge & attitude we needed for the role. | Experimental & green fields nature of Helen's role created uncertainty. | There are advantages & disadvantages of an internal coach versus an external coach – it is not clear cut. |
| Being an internal coach & part of our Team meant Helen understood us & provided on-tap support (Y1 & Y2). | Helen's many roles/"hats" seemed to bother her. | Employ a coach with suitable experience, & also look for attitude, flexible mindset & tenacity. |
| Helen provided formal & informal one-to-one coaching of team members (Y1 & Y2). | Tension between Michael & Helen impacted all of us. | On-tap advice & one-to-one coaching of team members is very helpful. |
| We all built strong trust with Helen. | Helen changing from internal to external coach role meant less on-tap support for us (Y2). | Trust between the team & the coach is important. |
| Helen became our counsellor across Consulting Services & resolved our people issues (Y1). | | Coach needs awareness of what the team can handle. |
| Helen's approach was flexible & appreciated our needs. | | If there is any tension in any relationship with the coach, address it, as it impacts everyone. |

# Leader perspective     **5**

*Michael the Team Leader and Helen Zink*

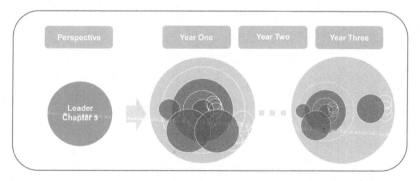
DOI: 10.4324/9781003367789-7

the system. In this chapter I talk about the Team, myself (Leader), Consulting Services (Function) and Green Apple Co (Organisation), and Helen (Coach).

Content for this chapter is sourced from specific points of self-reflection, video recordings, voice recordings, notes from team coaching sessions and ad-hoc, one-to-one coaching conversations, feedback from team development sessions, Helen's memory and my memory.

Long before this story began, my vision for Consulting Services was to be "world class consultants." Though the achievement of this was in our gift, the reality was we had a lot of work to do to get anywhere close to that goal. As we set off on the development journey in Year One, I knew the road ahead would be bumpy. However, I did not anticipate the number of potholes, gravel ruts and collapsed bridges we would encounter, nor did I anticipate that one of the most significant things to change along the journey would be me.

## Strategic context

### Strategic alignment

I embellish on the strategic context outlined in Chapter Three as it is important context for this story. We had a robust five-year plan in place across Green Apple Co, and within Consulting Services the first two years of implementation focused on technology, system and process changes to enable key organisational-wide five-year objectives.

As we began planning the third year of implementation, I was acutely aware that technology, processes **and people** needed to align for our strategy to be successful. My thinking was reinforced by the outcome of strategic reviews with my leadership team at the time, together with key stakeholders across Green Apple Co. Based on feedback gathered, there was consensus that the next area that required focus was **people**, including changing the structure and style of Consulting Services.

When Helen joined the Team, at the beginning of the third year of strategy implementation, she confirmed my thinking again, with reference to McKinsey's Seven S's model (Peters & Waterman, 2006) (Theory Break 5.1). The "hard S" elements of change were already in progress, but the "soft" elements needed significant work. I will touch on my thinking and approach around each of the "soft" S's and structure.

The new structure for the Function, which also created the Team this book is based on and Helen's role, became effective at the beginning of Year One. I had actually designed the new structure three years prior, but the timing was not right, nor did I have the capacity or mandate to implement it until Year One and the new structure needed to be in place before we could tackle the "soft S's."

### Staff and skills

While thinking through the new structure, a key consideration was the type of people required in my leadership team to enable it. Previous team members did not have the philosophy or key skills required to make the change envisaged. I needed the right leaders, which ultimately led to a whole-sale change in team membership, and the creation of the Team in this case.

## Shared values and style

I knew a critical part of strategy enablement was changing the entire culture of Consulting Services. To enable that, I needed a Team with a modern leadership philosophy based on trust and collaboration, rather than traditional managerial effectiveness. Although I believed I now had the right structure and staff in the Team, I knew they needed support to change their skills sets, the way they worked with each other, and the way they led their teams – their style.

## THEORY BREAK 5.1: MCKINSEY 7 S'S MODEL OF CHANGE

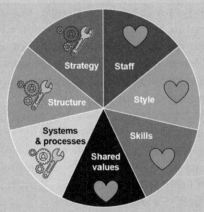

Modified from Peters & Waterman (2006)

Seven interrelated factors that influence an organisation's ability to change. Lack of hierarchy among these factors implies significant progress in one part of the organisation will be difficult without working on the others. Strategy, systems and processes, and structure are referred to as "hard S's". Shared values, style (culture), staff (the right staff), and skills (the right skills) are considered the "soft S's."

*Coach and team coaching*

## Coach concept

The concept for the Coach role came about as a result of a conversation I had with a consultant supporting us with the design of our strategy. We talked about the need for people-focused strategic enablement and gaps in my own capacity and capability to lead that type of change myself.

As thinking progressed, I was concerned the Team would not achieve the level of development and commitment of time required if we used external support to help us – support which we would only see from time to time. I felt we needed more continuity. One of the biggest calls in the design of the Team was the creation of a full-time support role, who was also part of the Team, the Coach role.

## Coach recruitment

The original scope of the Coach role was wide. We were looking for someone who could lead process improvement and delivery management, as well as design and lead our people strategy enablement. It was a challenging recruitment process, as candidates tend to be good at one or the other – not both. We selected Helen as she had the skills and capability we were looking for in relation to people and also had a good appreciation of the functional aspects of the consulting services we provided. Her mandate was to focus on people first, beginning with the Team, as we, the Team, believed we were capable of managing technology and process changes ourselves.

## Team coaching

Helen talked about team coaching when she joined. Although I was not familiar with the term, or how it differed from other types of team development, or what it would mean for us, I was happy to support this approach for the Team's development path (Theory Breaks 1.1 & 3.5). I also supported the team coaching training Helen was undertaking at the time. My view was the investment would be beneficial for the Team, Helen and all of Green Apple Co.

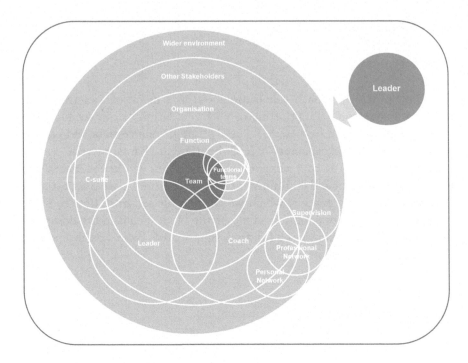

Figure 5.2: Leader's perspective of Team

## The Team

With more appreciation of strategic context, I begin looking at elements within the system. I focus on the Team first, and my view of the Team within the system, is illustrated in Figure 5.2. As indicated, I was also part of the Team.

### Team development goal – HPT

As Helen settled in, spent time understanding the strategy of Consulting Services and Green Apple Co, and met with the Team, staff within Consulting Services, C-suite, HR and other key stakeholders, she suggested the goal of "becoming a HPT" (Theory Break 3.1). I was aware of the HPT concept from a previous organisation, and the concept was completely in line with my vision of world-class performance and our overall strategy. It worked for me. Interestingly, I tried establishing a HPT team-development goal with previous incumbents of my lead team some years before, and it crashed and burned.

Once the HPT development goal had been socialised with me and HR, Helen took it to the Team for their thoughts. From memory, the Team accepted it; however, I suspect they did not fully understand what it would mean for them in practice. I knew I would be asking the Team to let go of the familiar ways of operating they had relied on for many years and embrace new styles and ways of thinking.

The HPT goal endured into Years Two and Three. I think it served us well, and there was no need for change.

## HPT Model – PERILL

### Year One

Around the same time our HPT development goal was set, Helen suggested we use the PERILL (Clutterbuck, 2020) HPT model to frame up our work (Theory Break 3.2). I had not heard of this particular model before, but it seemed logical and consistent with our direction of travel, and I endorsed it. I was also pleased Helen adapted the model to incorporate Green Apple Co's own in-house HPT model. It was critical that Helen used in-house development material, where possible, to maintain a consistency of approach across the organisation. The use of in-house concepts was also essential to maintain good relationships with HR. We needed ongoing buy-in from HR to support our dedicated internal coach model. The rest of the organisation relied on part-time internal HR resources for their development needs, and we needed to prove our model would work.

Helen discussed the PERILL HPT model with the team, and again, they appeared to accept it, but I am not sure any of us fully appreciated what it meant at the time.

### Years Two and Three

We referred to the PERILL HPT model frequently over the three years. The Team, including myself, also completed a HPT assessment every six months as a tangible way to track progress and highlight development priorities. In Year Three, we even added an additional component to the model – team resilience and wellbeing – a critical areas for us as a team. Helen refers to our bespoke model as "PERILL Plus" (Figure 3.2) in this book.

*Readiness for team development and coaching*

Year One

Did I think the Team was ready for focused team development and/or coaching process at the beginning of Year One? If I am honest, no! They had a new structure to implement, new roles, new challenges, new technology and processes to implement, new teams to recruit and build, and I was asking them to work on their leadership and how we operated as a team at the same time. Unsurprisingly, the Team were hesitant about the process to begin with, partly because it was new to them, and partly because there was trade-off between getting work done now and investing in longer-term development. Figure 2.9 illustrates the complexity of the environment the Team were experiencing in Year One. Despite this, my view was that we had a clear strategy in place that included focus on people as an enabler, and we had Helen lined up and ready to go. We were doing it!

Looking back now, I made the right decision. As hard as it was for all of us to carve out the time during Year One, if we had not, the impact of environmental changes in Years Two and Three, such as "hailstorms" and "leaf spot," would have destroyed us. I am convinced there is never a good time or a right time to begin focusing on team development – just start!

Years Two and Three

Years Two and Three proved to be just as challenging as Year One, and the team continued to experience an extraordinary amount of pressure. Figures 2.10 and 2.11 illustrate the complexity of the Team's environment in Years Two and Three.

Despite continued environmental and operational challenges, conversations with me about team members needing to attend development sessions were not required in Year Two. By then, the team were looking forward to development days, as they gave us a chance to refocus, take a different mindset and connect – buy-in from the team had turned 180 degrees. By the end of Year Two, understanding of what was expected of the Team as leaders was solid, although there was still work required to translate leadership expectations into outcomes that stakeholders would appreciate, and to develop the next level of team managers reporting to the Team.

*Team dynamics*

Year One

I knew all the team members when I pulled the Team together, and they all knew each other, except for Helen. Some I had worked with for many years, and some I knew less well. I considered all had the capability to step up into their new roles with support from myself and Helen. I was also aware there were existing tensions between some individuals in the Team, and the arrival of Helen complicated things further. Some thought she was encroaching on their turf (more later).

*Two tier team*

When Tom joined the Team late in Year One, everyone seemed to have concerns, which I found curious as all were involved in his recruitment process. I think the main challenge related to his high level of experience. He had his own way of doing things, which often differed from the Team's way, and he did not communicate clearly the rationale for changes he made. In addition, Tom's role was designed to work closely with Helen and myself, with the three of us collectively leading the team, freeing up more capacity for me. Effectively, by adding Tom to the Team, I had created a two-tier leadership team.

*Who's the boss*

Initially this backfired. The two-tier approach bothered some team members who found themselves in the bottom tier, resulting in frustration which impacted our culture. Furthermore, the creation of the top-team resulted in confusion around who and where instructions and guidance were coming from. The Team said it felt like they had three bosses, all with slightly different opinions on things, and conveying different messages. Team confusion culminated in the "who's the boss" event. As the Team Leader, it was a truly challenging position to be in. The team I had personally selected and employed, and wanted to develop and empower, was on the edge of implosion and rebelling against me.

Surprisingly, "who's the boss" also came with a silver lining. It was the first time the Team spoke openly and honestly about concerns they had with me, and each other, collectively, and in front of each other. If we had not been working on our own development, I am not sure we would have communicated so openly and the opportunity to reset.

By the end of Year One, some Team dynamics had improved, some remained the same, and some were works in progress. However, the monthly team development sessions were providing regular opportunities to connect and learn together, and trust and psychological safety, although fluctuating, were improving overall.

## Years Two and Three

Improved dynamics and trust continued into Year Two, although there was some disruption as team members changed frequently during this period.

As Year Three unfolded, it become increasingly challenging for the Team to connect. Due to environmental impacts, we were again completely focused on managing deliverables and structure changes. There were fewer team meetings, one-to-one conversations with me, conversations between team members, and we also cancelled several team development sessions. During a team session near the end of Year Three, we openly acknowledged we had "hit a bump" in our development journey and needed to focus more on relationships and reconnecting. Which we did.

## Intervention (A) – Team development sessions

### Year One

The idea of monthly team development days to support the Team's development progress was mine. The C-suite were doing the same; I was part of those C-suite sessions; I had experienced similar in other organisations; and it seemed a logical approach here too. Monthly team off-sites were scheduled in for the year, with half of the day focused on development and the other half on strategy work. I was keen for the Team to spend some informal time together as well, so we also built in a social component.

### Team development session process

Helen and I worked together on agendas for the development part of sessions. I wanted the Team to come to each session prepared, so often

Helen would share an article to read in advance or a topic to reflect on. Having said that, I often did not have the time for preparation myself and did not always set a good example. Although I was aware of, contributed to and approved the content of the development component of the team days, I left it mainly to Helen.

The content of development sessions was extremely fluid and flexible. Often agenda items were changed several times leading up to a session, the morning of a session, and sometimes in the moment during a session. Helen discussed and agreed all changes with me.

## Team development session challenges

The flexibility of sessions did not suit everyone. The Team was caught in the conundrum of appreciating the benefit of fluidity and spending more time on relevant topics as they arose, normally at their own request, versus content dropped from the agenda. We had good days, and yet sometimes we felt defeated by only covering part of what we intended to cover. The dynamic around this made it hard for some team members to engage.

Sometimes it felt like we did not fully bottom out topics and were not walking away with clear insights or next steps. Sometimes topics "left hanging" like this were picked up in subsequent sessions, a month later. A break to reset and re-evaluate topics was beneficial at times, but at other times we were unable to recreate "the moment" or flow, and potential benefit was lost. I do not believe this situation could have been avoided completely, but I know some of the Team were bothered by it.

Sometimes topics and conversations that took place triggered emotional responses from team members and from me. I was not concerned, as in my view, emotion shows vulnerability and helps build trust. However, as the leader of the Team, I could have been more aware and supportive of those who were not comfortable with challenging conversations and visible emotion. At times I did not pick up on emotional cues from team members and Helen needed to step in with support.

## Team feedback

Feedback from the Team members on session content was mostly favourable. Again, some would have preferred more structure, some were happy as things were, and some would have preferred not to be there at all. Greg and Taylor, in particular, believed the real value of sessions was spending time together as a team, and content was almost a side benefit.

Tom made it abundantly clear he found little value in our team sessions and thought we should focus on delivery instead. Although he participated, because I told him how important it was to me, there were times his disengagement was obvious, and it impacted the vibe in the room.

## Year Two

We continued with monthly team development sessions in Year Two for several reasons:

- The Team had reached a point where they better understood the benefits of the work we had done together in Year One.
- We thought revisiting some topics in more depth would be helpful.
- It was a great opportunity to onboard new team members and continue the development journey as our composition changed.

At the beginning of Year Two, in line with an increased focus in my own leadership development (more below), I took a more active role in team development sessions. Helen continued to make recommendations, and I involved myself more in planning and preparation. This extended into the later part of Year Two, where Helen's role became external to the organisation.

### Focus on the Leader

Across the second half of Year Two the focus of development content was on my leadership style. While I consented to this, and I am comfortable being challenged, I felt increasingly uncomfortable as sessions progressed. It seemed to become our sole focus and felt out of line with the original intent of us developing together as a team. I also felt like the Team were aiming for perfection and creating unrealistic expectations of me that I knew I would struggle to fulfil.

## Year Three

At the beginning of Year Three, the Team and I discussed the team development programme for the year without Helen in the room. We all acknowledged there was value in sessions, but there were other factors involved in our decision-making process:

- I was not comfortable with the focus on my leadership style at the end of Year Two, and felt focus needed to turn back to the collective team.
- The Team raised concern that I was not spending enough time with them one-to-one. On reflection, time I was spending preparing for team sessions in Year Two could have been spent with them instead.
- The Team felt the ratio of team development versus strategic planning was increasingly weighted towards strategic planning and we needed to reset with a development focus.
- My ability to prepare strategic planning content for team days was limited due to other issues demanding my time. The lack of preparation seemed to increase tension between Helen and me (more below) which impacted the Team.

We did consider not proceeding at this point. However, rather than me making the decision for the Team, as I had in Years One and Two, I specifically gave the Team the choice of whether to proceeded or not in Year Three. After some debate, the Team agreed they wanted to continue.

## Rotating leadership

To mitigate the factors bulleted above, we talked through the concept of rotating leadership for the purposes of team development sessions. I would still be there, keeping an eye on content, however, the leadership baton would be passed from me to the Team and to each team member, respectively. Helen seemed comfortable and happy with the new arrangement and focus; however, she acknowledged working with a different person in the lead role each session would pose some challenges around continuity. We all agreed to try it.

The first development session in Year Three was different from our previous pattern of sessions for a few reasons:

- Time was spent discussing how the rotating roles concept would work and individual expectations and responsibilities around this.
- It was the first session with a team member in the leadership role.
- Content was structured in a way that allowed the Team to create their own team development plan for the year ahead.

After the first session it felt like we were all set for the year with a firm development plan in place – or so we thought!

## Impact of environment

As wider environmental factors arose again, we were once more completely focused on managing deliverables and structure changes. Although we saw less of Helen in Year Three, she had some insight into what we were going through and wanted to tackle the pending "hailstorm No.2" head-on as part of our development sessions. I pushed back on it for two reasons:

- I did not think the Team were in the right headspace to be challenged directly on this when they were in the thick of managing the impacts.
- I did not have the leadership capacity to face it, given organisational strategic projects I was involved in at the time.

Tension and pressure within the Team around this time was high, and something had to give. One of the casualties was team development. Many sessions were cancelled, some at very short notice, and others were descoped on the day with content shifted to lighter topics. While I did not personally support the decision to cancel sessions, I intentionally left the decision to the Team to make for themselves. I wanted them to take full responsibility for their own development, and they were.

Looking back now, a better approach would have been to formally reduce the frequency of sessions – perhaps one session every two months. This would have provided more certainty and ability to plan. In hindsight, I should have made this suggestion to the Team for our collective consideration.

## Good endings

Around two thirds of the way through Year Three, I announced I would be leaving my role at the end of the year. I let Helen know my plans, and soon after, she came back to the Team and me with a proposal to park the development plan, which by this time was being shuffled constantly due to session cancellations, and focus the rest of the year on "good endings" work which the Team described in Chapter Four. The Team and I agreed. It certainly seemed there would be value in collectively reflecting on shared successes and acknowledging our challenges. The Team also asked Helen to build enough time into the agenda to focus on future development as well – in effect, allowing time for the Team to create their own team development plan for Year Four.

The "good endings" sessions were amongst the most valuable times we spent together as a Team. It felt like everyone contributed to the collective story with an equal voice. With hindsight, we saw the significant impact our journey had on us. I really appreciated the "good endings" sessions from a personal perspective as well. It was a cathartic experience in many ways and helped me process my departure as leader of Consulting Services and the Team – a Team I had been part of for a good proportion of my career, and one I had designed and created from scratch.

## Overall reflection

In summary, over the three-year period, the style of team development sessions, the content and the approach Helen used, adapted to meet my needs and those of the Team. Overall, I was very comfortable with the effectiveness of this intervention across all three years.

## Co-coaching

I had not heard the term co-coach or acknowledged the fact that I was taking on such a role until I began working on my contribution to this book. Terminology aside, I was supporting Helen with content and agreeing how we would work together within team development sessions, and I believe this meets the definition of co-coach (Theory Break 7.13).

I talked to Helen several times about using an independent external coach from time to time. I hoped this would allow Helen to be a more equal member of the team and contribute more content. In team sessions, I sensed she was holding back to avoid disturbing flow, and focused on process – meaning she was unable to contribute content as a team member at the same time. We put her in a tough position with her dual role in these sessions, and I was keen to experiment with having someone else in the coach seat.

Helen arranged for an external coach to join us for one session, late in Year One. It was an interesting dynamic, and I sensed Helen had not fully vacated the coach seat and was continuing to hold back.

Helen resisted my suggestion of ongoing use of an independent external coach after that – I am not sure why, as we never fully explored it. There were so many distractions for me, the Team and Helen during Years Two and Three that I did not raise the co-coach conversation again. On reflection, I should have insisted that we continue to experiment, whether that role was framed up as a co-coach or a sole coach role. I was, and still am, curious about the impact this opportunity might have had – an opportunity missed.

### Intervention (B) – One-to-one formal and informal coaching of team members

#### Year One

One-to-one informal coaching was one of the greatest benefits of having an internal coach who was part of the Team. As Helen worked alongside the Team on a day-to-day basis, there was plenty of opportunity for her to reinforce behaviour and remind us of agreed actions. I know the Team were aware of this and valued it too.

#### Year Two

During Year Two, the informal coaching dynamic described above continued.

I also asked Helen to work formally with Jane, who was struggling to assimilate into her new role. I knew there was some risk with this arrangement as Helen had expressed having challenges with Jane personally, and I wondered whether she was able to remain independent enough to be effective. However, Jane trusted Helen, and she was readily available, so we all agreed to try it.

The outcome was a huge success. The transformation of Jane's attitude, behaviour and willingness to take on the challenge of her new role was one of the most significant changes in leadership I have ever witnessed. Cheers to the power of coaching! Note formal one-to-one coaching with Jane continued as Helen moved to being an external service provider around the middle of Year Two.

## Year Three

During Year Three, Helen had little opportunity to support one-to-one informal coaching, apart from time spent working with whoever was in the nominated leader role. Jane's formal coaching was complete by this stage as well.

## Leader as coach

This period also saw some of the strongest changes in my own leadership style, including increased commitment to one-to-one time with team members. As mentioned above, the Team had identified this as a problem in Year Two. Although I understood the concept of leader as coach well, having been a recipient of it, historically I had failed to apply it successfully within teams I had led, leaning on mentorship and direction instead. In Year Three, I fully embraced the role of leader as coach (Theory Break 5.2), and I suppose the baton of one-to-one coaching had been passed from Helen to me (more below).

---

### THEORY BREAK 5.2: LEADER AS COACH

Ellinger, Beattie and Hamlin (2010) describe the characteristics of leaders with a coaching mindset as:

- Open to personal learning and feedback.
- Empathy with others.
- Empowering others.
- Developing and supporting others.
- A belief that others want to learn.
- High standards.

Learning is most effective when it is integrated with work, along with feedback and support. A strong case for an ask rather than tell, or coaching mindset. In contrast, traditional management is about directing and coordinating and telling others what to do.

Importantly, Ellinger, Beattie and Hamlin (2010) also emphasise that leaders may need to take on both roles, depending on the circumstances. Effective leadership includes the ability to identify which role is required at that time and having the ability to switch between roles.

---

*Internal Coach – and change to external*

Year One

The decision to have an internal coach, and someone permanently embedded within the Team, had significant advantages:

- Development was prioritised, rather than being relegated behind BAU.
- Continuous connection between work done in development sessions and real-world execution.
- Immediate intervention when habits the Team or individual team members were working on required additional support or modification in the moment.

I do not think I would change anything in relation to the internal coach model during Year One. It gave us sharp focus to enable the people aspect of our strategy, and created a lot of strength in our Team.

Having said that, there was a strange power dynamic inherent within the role. Formally, the role reported to me, with accountability to me, but in many ways, Helen was directing my development and holding me accountable to it. On reflection, we did not invest enough time working through the reality of how our roles, expectations and relationship would work. As a consequence, Helen, the Team and I suffered from the implications of lack of role clarity (more below).

Year Two

The Coach role was removed from the Team to meet organisation-wide cost-saving targets in Year Two. It was hard to justify retaining the role given the extensive cost pressure we were under. My thinking was we could continue to work with Helen as an external part-time service provider, retaining some continuity for the Team, for me, and for Helen. I was also curious how we would perform as a leadership team once the "safety-wheels" that our internal coach provided were removed – how wobbly would we be?

When Helen was with us, my internal dialogue was that "It did not really matter if we bought into something we were working on, as Helen was there to pull us back on track." The impact of losing Helen as an internal resource I expected was twofold:

- The Team would receive less in-the-moment development support.
- Responsibility for development would shift from Helen to me and the Team.

In reality, the transition of development responsibility was not handled well. We did not identify and make new expectations of parties explicit enough. Helen was trying her best to operate as an external service provider, albeit with an unusually high level of inside knowledge. At the same time, the Team, including me, were behaving as we were prior to the change. I believe this contributed to Helen's frustration, and ultimately to the need for formal contract changes at the beginning of Year Three.

Looking back now, I think part of my motivation to move the Coach role to an external position was the hope it would help clarify the complex role dynamic between us (more below).

## Year Three

As we moved into Year Three, opportunities for communication between Helen, the Team and me were limited to team development sessions themselves. Helen had little visibility of the environment in which we were operating, which was one of the major positives of her internal role in Year One, and she also had no awareness of progress we were making. To Helen, lack of visibility, combined with the frequent cancellation of development sessions, may have seemed like nothing had changed, or worse, the Team was going backwards. I think this impacted Helen's engagement in the programme towards the end. We failed to recognise the need to brief Helen on how the Team were operating day-to-day when she could no longer see it for herself. This highlights again the pros and cons of working with an internal coach versus working with an external supplier. There are benefits and challenges with both models – it is not clear cut.

## Outcomes

Measuring the outcomes of our team development journey was not managed as well as it should have been. Apart from the HPT assessment Helen was running for us every six months, and engagement scores we were already tracking across Green Apple Co, we did not discuss, agree or create other tangible measures. Ironically, we were creating a measurement framework for other deliverables and strategic change we were working on during Year One. We should have included development measures in the framework as well – another opportunity missed.

## Tangible measures

However, I believe the two tangible measures available told an accurate story. Figure 3.8 shows the HPT assessment score trending upwards over the three-year time frame, remaining more stable towards the end of Year Three. I think this reflects both the trajectory of the Team's development and also the Team's increased understanding of the HPT model we were using. The Team engagement score bounces around in Year One, clearly reflecting the "hailstorm" that occurred in the middle of the year. This is followed by a reasonably steady increase through Year Two, before dipping towards the end of Year Three. I suspect the final dip related to new uncertainty surrounding news I was leaving.

## Intangible measures

Although intangible measures were not collected formally, we did receive regular verbal and written feedback from the Team as part of the monthly team development process. The Team share examples of their feedback in Chapter Four. I also received feedback as Leader, in one-to-one sessions with each team member. Again, an opportunity was missed to collect and share intangible feedback in a more formal way.

## Change in Team

From my perspective, I saw significant changes in the Team during Year One, including improved:

- Understanding of interrelationship of their roles and connections between them.
- Self-awareness and self-improvement.
- Confidence.
- Accountability.
- Support and trust of each other.
- Open challenging of each other and me.

The growth I observed in Year One continued into Years Two and Three. The changes I observed in the Team were positively impacting others as well, and I saw the benefits of the work we were doing across Consulting Services and Green Apple Co.

While working on this book, Helen asked me to consider a team maturity model (Theory Break 5.3). At the beginning of Year One, the Team were operating in the survival zone, and by the end of Year Three, had grown into the internal cohesion zone. However, progress from zone one to five was in no way linear. While the overall maturity trend was increasing, we slipped back into survival mode several times, most notably when working through the "hailstorms" – resulting from challenging change management events.

## THEORY BREAK 5.3: TEAM MATURITY

The hierarchy of team maturity illustrated here was created by Barrett (2010) and extended by Hawkins (2022). The rationale is that teams sit in a particular stage and, depending on that stage, they may be limited in their ability to focus on higher stages.

The ability of a team to move between stages depends on many factors including:

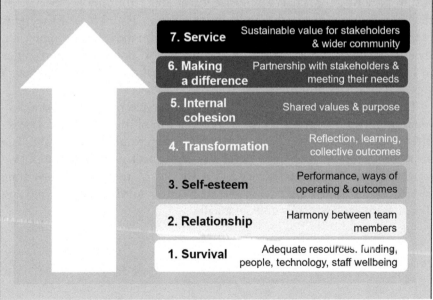

| | |
|---|---|
| **7. Service** | Sustainable value for stakeholders & wider community |
| **6. Making a difference** | Partnership with stakeholders & meeting their needs |
| **5. Internal cohesion** | Shared values & purpose |
| **4. Transformation** | Reflection, learning, collective outcomes |
| **3. Self-esteem** | Performance, ways of operating & outcomes |
| **2. Relationship** | Harmony between team members |
| **1. Survival** | Adequate resources. funding, people, technology, staff wellbeing |

- Historical position – newly formed or an established team.
- Organisation context – clear mandate and access to resources needed.
- Business context – market conditions and pressure.
- Team leader – maturity and leadership style.
- Development – attention and investment in team learning.

Hawkins (2022) recommends that team coaching style and focus is matched to where the team is at on the team maturity scale.

In summary, we could have, and should have, created a formal tangible and intangible measurement framework for our development journey. However, having said this, it would only ever have told part of the story. I noticed changes in how the Team were talking to each other, how they were getting along, and how they were interacting with stakeholders. Being able to sense the increased level of trust within the Team was the most significant benefit, and I am not sure how we would ever have been able to measure a sense of that. I could feel it!

## Summary – Leader's perspective of the Team

A summary of good, challenging and learnt areas from my perspective of the Team is contained in the Appendix to Chapter Five. Most of the items in the learnt column are not new to me, although I did not fully appreciate their importance until events played out in this case. Some are opportunities missed, like experimenting more with an external co-coach and creating a robust measurement framework.

The most important way to measure the success of the team development approach described above is whether I think the Team and I benefitted. The answer is yes. Given the opportunity, would I do it again? The answer is again yes, with some tweaks. Looking back now, I am grateful we started the development journey when we did, as the groundwork done in Year One played a big part in the Team and I surviving years Two and Three, both professionally and personally.

## The Leader

I now get to talk about myself, the most fun part of this chapter and the ultimate opportunity for self-reflection. My view of myself as Leader in the system is illustrated in Figure 5.3.

### Leadership style

Year One

I care about people and get a lot of energy from supporting others' development, so I was genuinely passionate and excited about the opportunity we were embarking on with my new Team. As mentioned above, I had effectively been waiting three years for my plan to come to fruition.

### Top-down style

Coming into Year One, I knew I relied on what others describe as a "top-down" leadership style. I made most decisions myself and did not delegate

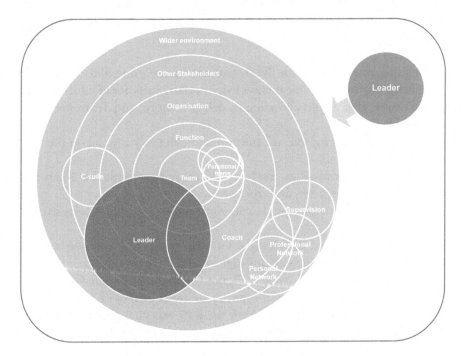

Figure 5.3: Leader's perspective of himself

enough. There were many reasons why I had not focused on changing my style previously:

- I felt my style was necessary to deliver organisational needs at the time.
- The urgency around deliverables did not support consultative delegation.
- Prior to Year One, the overall capability of the lead team reporting to me was not where I needed it to be.
- I gain energy from hands-on, detailed work and solving problems, so I sometimes took on detailed work that I found interesting for fun.

I was also under a huge amount of stress with demands from both internal and external stakeholders, and, as such, I focused on wider organisation pressures rather than the Function I led. I was working long hours and dealing with challenging experiences in my personal life as well. In parallel, my manager, the CEO, and other senior and influential stakeholders told me I held too much organisational knowledge, and this was a significant risk to Green Apple Co's continuity.

I know I am not describing a high-performance leadership style here, and when Helen joined, she quickly picked up on my style and personality characteristics. Within a few days, she was challenging me, recognising my style needed to change if I wanted the Team to work towards our HPT goal. Helen's suggestions included:

- Spending more time with the Team, both one-to-one and collectively, and sharing more technical knowledge and organisational information.
- Over time, this would allow me to delegate more, and Team members would learn more.
- Reduce involving myself in hands-on work and rely instead on the new Team I had created.
- This in turn would allow me to spend more time with the Team and reinforce the delegation and trust cycle.
- As a result, in theory, I would experience more capacity and less stress.

Figure 5.4 was created specifically for this book and summarises the suggestions above and conversations Helen and I had on this topic.

Intellectually, I knew the cycle in Figure 5.4 would be beneficial, but as is often the case, finding the initial capacity to invest time with the Team up front to kickstart the cycle (arrow on the left) was challenging. My focus in Year One was on significant technology and processes changes in flight,

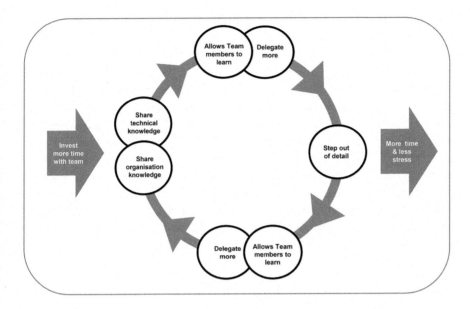

Figure 5.4: Leadership delegation and trust cycle

the success or failure of which would impact Green Apple Co's ability to operate. Besides, one of the reasons I created Helen's role was for her to lead some work on my behalf, not add to my list of things to work on. I admit my resistance to Helen's suggestions were strong during most of Year One.

Looking back now, I did not emphasise the importance of timing when Helen and I spoke about the cycle in Figure 5.4. If I had made it clear to Helen, the Team, my boss and other key stakeholders that I agreed I needed to change, and was willing to invest time in it later, some of the tension in the system may have been mitigated. The lesson I learnt here is communication! I see now that my pushback might have felt like complete resistance to Helen which contributed to the pressure she was experiencing and the tension in our relationship.

## Leadership vacuum trap

As we moved through Year One, it was obvious Helen had high leadership capability, not just in relation to supporting leadership development in others, but hands-on leadership as well. So over time, more and more leadership activity moved from me to her. She stepped in for me some-times, spoke on my behalf at staff meetings, covered my role while I was on leave, and led significant projects like the "90-day plan." I was also aware she was covering for me in informal ways as well. Filling gaps she saw seemed natural for her, and I think most of her actions were subconscious. Helen referred to the unfolding phenomena as the "leadership vacuum trap" (Clutterbuck, 2017) (Theory Break 4.3). I knew it was happening, and I let it, as I prioritised wider organisational deliverables and pressures.

Later in Year One, I made the decision to increase capacity in the Team by bringing in Tom. Effectively this created another "leadership vacuum trap" resulting in the "who's the boss" episode mentioned above. While I think there were pros and cons in how these events played out, I should have proactively and more explicitly communicated why some leadership activity was coming from Helen and Tom rather than me.

## Commitment to change

I received consistent and persistent messages around changing my leader-ship style. My boss, my colleagues, the Team and Helen all said the same thing – change!

Towards the end of Year One, organisation-wide pressures had eased a little, the "who's the boss" situation required us to work more on role clarity, and we had successfully navigated through the "hailstorm." Things were looking up.

Around the same time, in one of our team development sessions, I asked each member of the team what they needed from me as their leader. Weighing up the situation, I made an active and open commitment right there and then to focus on changing my style. I also made it clear that I expected the Team to commit to work on their individual leadership styles as well, and we would continue to work collectively on our HPT goal – Figure 5.5 summarises key messages from that session and our dis-cussion. The time was right! Although I was very enthusiastic about what the shift would mean for me, the Team and for Consulting Services, I also knew it would not be easy.

As I think back now, my personal commitment to work on my leadership style should have come earlier in the journey. My understanding around the critical role that a team leader plays in high performance and team change is one of the most significant things I learnt from this experience (Theory Break 5.4).

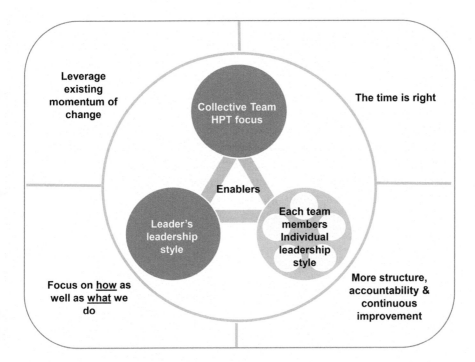

Figure 5.5: Leader's commitment to change

## THEORY BREAK 5.4: CRITICAL ROLE OF TEAM LEADER

The team leader has significant influence on the team. In an extensive study by Gallup (Clifton & Harter, 2019), they found that 70 per cent of the variance in team engagement is determined by the leader of the team.

This supports the role of the leader in Clutterbuck's PERILL model (2020). In PERILL it is emphasised that the team leader strongly influences the other five elements of the model. The team leader normally hires and fires team members, approves spend on development, systems and other critical team resources, decides how much team time to dedicate to particular activities, holds key relationships with senior stakeholders, often has sole authority to make certain decisions, and decides how much investment to make in team development. So, the team leadership role, buy nature, is disproportionate in influence within a team.

Yet, Clutterbuck (2020) also says that high team performance is related to the ability of the team to lead collectively, which may seem a contradiction.

The critical message here is that the team leader role is crucial in team development, and a team, including the team leader, need to explicitly work through how roles are divided, when collective leadership works best for them, and when the leader takes the lead. And ironically, it is the team leader that creates the environment, and encourages enough trust and psychological safety for this type of discussion to happen in the first place.

## Year Two

In the beginning of Year Two I was focused on enabling the new leadership approach I committed to at the end of Year One. I put several things in place to initiate and support my new focus.

I was more conscious and actively working on changing the way I was working, including more active involvement in leadership matters – closing the "leadership vacuum traps."

We created a "Year Two plan," including formalised initiatives to enable our strategic objectives, clear accountability for those initiatives, and a process to track and regularly report progress to all stakeholders across Consulting Services and Green Apple Co. I ensured that all initiatives were assigned to members of the Team, ringfencing myself into a sponsorship role. Accountability and responsibility were crystal clear.

We also held a Consulting Services staff conference for the first time in years. The purpose was to share the collective strategic path we were on, provide an opportunity for the Team to shine and openly display their leadership, solicit input from staff across Consulting Services into initiatives within our plan, get to know each other better and have some fun. The energy in the room was great and we achieved all that we set out to do and more.

### Best laid plans on hold

The same week, just as we had great momentum and plans in place, my world, and all of our worlds, changed. An unexpected personal situation needed my full attention requiring immediate time off work. At the same time a "leaf spot" infestation impacted our environment, requiring complete and rapid reengineering of how we worked.

A few weeks later, once I had returned to work, it felt completely unfamiliar, like I had been in a time warp. During my absence, the Team had led Consulting Services through significant process change, established regular wellbeing checks for all staff and were actively working together and supporting each other. It was the best example of collaborative problem solving I had seen from the Team – and they had done it without me. Although the benefit of the development work we had done in Year One did not appear obvious at the time, I am convinced it was a significant contributor to the Team's ability to successfully manage the transition described above.

A casualty of the "leaf spot" infestation and the unfolding of related circumstances was that our "hot off the press" Year Two plan needed to be descoped and some content was put on hold.

My operating environment continued to be very challenging during the remainder of Year Two. Much of my attention was focused on managing organisation-wide implications of the infestation. I also no longer had the luxury of Helen providing informal coaching, advice and capacity, as the role moved to an external resource. In addition, the responsibilities of my role increased following a restructure, and a new team was merged into Consulting Services and under my remit.

## Change in Style

Despite all the challenges, I believe changes in my leadership style were coming through by the middle of Year Two. Also, although descoped, the essence of our Year Two plan was back in play, and the strategy I had owned in the past was now shared across team members, and they were fully responsible for executing that strategy.

These shifts enabled me to focus more on communicating long-term vision and sponsoring strategic enablement. Effectively, the leadership delegation and trust cycle Helen and I were talking about early in Year One, Figure 5.4, had come to fruition. I also received confirmation from the Team, my boss, colleagues and Helen that they saw some change in my style too.

## Timing of change in Style

On reflection, my shift in style came about for several reasons:

- My conscious decision to focus on change – I meant what I said.
- The groundwork we had done as a team in Year One and the first part of Year Two was coming together for me.

- The team development days, one-to-one informal coaching, direct leadership advice from Helen and others, as well as C-suite development activity taking place, were consistent, and, combined, gave me the platform I needed.

I am sure Helen would describe these factors coming together in a systemic way, perhaps something like "reinforcing system forces" – I say, "the universe aligned."

I think there were two learning points here for me:

- Most of the messaging I received around needing to change the way I led was subtle and gradual; I may not have realised the compounding impact.
- While I heard and intellectually understood the rationale for change and may have subconsciously used lack of capacity as an excuse, the shift did not come until I genuinely bought into it and made a conscious and explicit decision to change.

While writing this chapter, Helen drew my attention to a change formula (Theory Break 5.5) and asked whether it was valid in my situation. In short,

## THEORY BREAK 5.5: CHANGE FORMULA

This change formula represents that change will only happen if the pain of staying the same is greater than the pain of changing. And changing is made up of dissatisfaction with the status quo, desirability of the alternative, and practicality of implementing the change.

Cost of changing

Dissatisfaction with status quo

Desirability of alternative

Practicality of change

Modified from Beckhard & Harris (1987)

it was. I believe I changed because the balance of the equation shifted – dissatisfaction with the way I was leading, desirability of leading a new way, and good timing and the practicality of change, all outweighed my perception of how hard it would be – "the universe aligned."

## Year Three

As mentioned above, one of the most impactful changes in my style in Year Three was focusing on leader as coach (Theory Break 5.2).

I was also feeling confident that changes I had made were embedding, and having built a stronger team, I began considering my own longer-term priorities both professionally and personally. This ultimately led to the decision to leave my role at the end of Year Three. The uncertain impact of my pending departure undoubtedly influenced aspects of my leadership style and the team development programme at that time as well.

## Overall reflection

At the beginning of Year One, as we set off on this journey, I did not appreciate how much my leadership style would change, how much I would learn, and how significant the personal impact would be. It has genuinely been a transformational experience for me, with most growth in areas of:

- EQ-centred leadership.
- Leader as coach.
- Sharing leadership.
- Sharing knowledge and delegating.
- Improved communication.

Helen asked me to consider my leadership style with reference to the leader maturity model (Theory Break 5.6). I think I was operating in the team manager and team leader zones in Year One. As explained above, I had long-term vision, but the opportunity to fully focus on the team or myself was not available. In Year Two, I was beginning to move into the higher zones of team orchestrator and coach, and by Year Three I was much more comfortable in those areas. It seems it is possible to teach an old dog new tricks – it just takes time.

The Team supported the view that I changed as well, with evidence coming through in our regular HPT assessment results. Figure 3.7 shows a positive trend in the leadership component of PERILL across three years, with the decease at the end of Year Three reflecting my decision to leave.

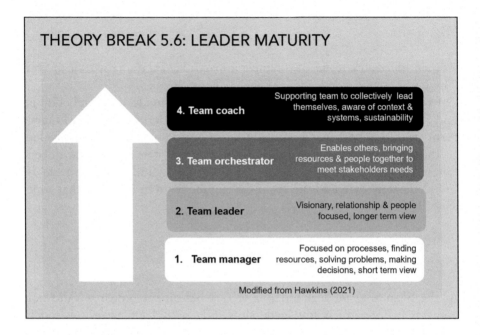

**THEORY BREAK 5.6: LEADER MATURITY**

**4. Team coach** — Supporting team to collectively lead themselves, aware of context & systems, sustainability

**3. Team orchestrator** — Enables others, bringing resources & people together to meet stakeholders needs

**2. Team leader** — Visionary, relationship & people focused, longer term view

**1. Team manager** — Focused on processes, finding resources, solving problems, making decisions, short term view

Modified from Hawkins (2021)

With the benefit of hindsight, I wonder what the leadership graph in Figure 3.7 would have looked like if I had made the decision to work my own leadership earlier in the journey. I could have enabled this by adding more capacity to the Team at the beginning of Year One to work on change and delivery improvements, rather than waiting until the end of Year One to employ Tom. We might have avoided or at least mitigated the "hailstorm," "leadership vacuum traps" and the "who's the boss" events, and perhaps the Year Two plan would have been the Year One plan.

## EQ-centred leadership

I would like to share one last piece of self-reflection in this section. While contributing to this book, and reflecting on my personal growth and leadership style, I have increased my passion for EQ-centred leadership (Theory

Break 5.7). Traditionally, my profession and functional discipline is technology and process led, hence the original leadership style I began this journey with. Shifting to an EQ focus has helped me, and I believe will help other leaders, navigate a rapidly changing environment and better support service delivery to customers and stakeholders.

---

## THEORY BREAK 5.7: EMOTIONAL INTELLIGENCE (EQ)

Goleman (1995) describes emotional intelligence as encompasses the following five skills:

- Self-awareness – recognising our own emotions as they play out.
- Regulation – managing our own emotions and reactions.
- Motivation – ability to complete tasks we take on and delay gratification.
- Empathy – recognising the emotions and needs of others.
- Social skills – building relationships with others.

It is also argued that EQ is more important than traditional intelligence (IQ) for successful leadership.

---

### Intervention (C) – One-to-one informal coaching of leader

### Year One

As mentioned above, within days, if not hours, of her arrival, Helen was giving me leadership advice and coaching me informally. Sometimes it was solicited and sometimes offered, often in-the-moment. The scenario that played out here was one of the significant benefits of having an internal coach as part of the team. Helen was right there with me experiencing a lot of what I was experiencing, and she was literally on the spot offering advice and coaching as events played out.

On reflection, there were pros and cons to this approach. A positive aspect was rapid response as events unfolded. A negative was I sometimes felt overwhelmed by the volume of suggestions I was receiving in parallel with other pressures I was experiencing. Helen's feedback may have been even more beneficial with stronger agreements between us on how support would be provided. I think a more structured, less frequent approach might have been easier for me to digest.

## Bespoke leadership model

In the past, I was proud of my ability to apply a consistent, authentic leadership style in all situations. One of the most powerful areas Helen and I worked through together was the realisation that I actually had five leadership styles. The key was building self-awareness to enable me to select the style that most appropriately matched circumstances. Figure 5.6 illustrates my styles; arrows indicate areas I was trying to use more, and areas I was trying to play down. Note the downward arrow next to compassion is not a misprint. Sometimes I was too compassionate and did not hold others to account enough. It is also extremely important that I remain authentic and natural through everything I do, also depicted in the diagram.

This model we created worked and still works well for me – it was custom-built, completely genuine and authentic. My model will not be

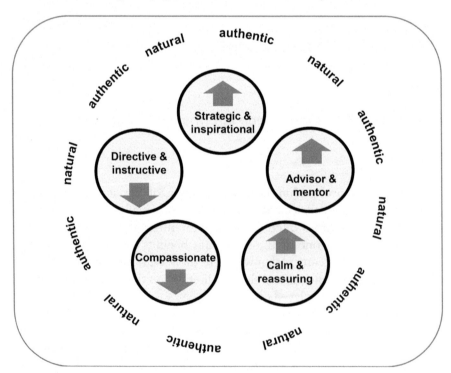

Figure 5.6: Leader's leadership model

found in any leadership textbook and is a great example of the power of one-to-one coaching – albeit informal coaching in this case.

## Formal one-to-one coaching

As we worked together, Helen asked me to consider formal one-to-one coaching several times. I was hesitant, as, although Helen was extremely keen to support me, I was not comfortable with the role-reversal scenario this reflected, given that Helen reported to me. The power dynamics between us were already complex, and I felt adding this additional dynamic would complicate things further. Also, I was working on other areas of development in my personal life at the time and did not feel I had the capacity to take on more.

## Year Two and Year Three

There was little change in the one-to-one informal coaching and advice pattern between the Helen and I during the first part of Year Two. During the second part of the year, when Helen moved to an external service provider role, I continued to work with her to some extent, although I focused more on implementing leadership changes identified in Year One.

As the Team were rotating the lead role in relation to team development sessions during Year Three, I did not spend much time with Helen at all and received minimal coaching support.

## Relationship between Leader and Coach

### Year One

The investment in change I was making with the Team and across Consulting Services meant Helen and I spent a lot of time together. Our mutual trust built very quickly, we supported each other with personal challenges as well as professional ones, and became friends.

The time I spent with Helen also meant I had less time for other members of the Team, given capacity pressures described above. A dichotomy existed here where Helen required my time to help me plan and develop the change she thought was necessary in my leadership style, while at the same time she was concerned I was not spending enough time with the Team to kickstart the leadership delegation and trust cycle illustrated in Figure 5.4.

In parallel, Helen's perception that I was not willing to work on my leadership style would have been hard for her to digest. She was also working with a Team that were resisting investment in the programme she was running. As a result, Helen was frustrated with the organisational context, the Team and me – fair, given the circumstances.

At the same time, the power dynamics between Helen and I were complex. As explained above, as part of her role, she was supporting my development, mentoring, advising and coaching me, while in the structure she reported to me. It felt very unnatural – the role of mentoring, advisor and coach should have been mine. As explained above, one of the reasons I created Helen's role was to support the Team's development, yet I felt she was overly focused on me, so I was frustrated too.

Adding to an already complex scenario, I was experiencing significant challenge and change outside of the work environment. Given how authentic both Helen and I are, it was difficult to blend all aspects of my life easily – and we did share personal conversations as friends.

The combined impact of everything above was clear frustration and tension resulting in many emotional conversations which further increased the frustration we both felt. As Year One progressed, I also received feedback that the tension between us was increasingly obvious to the Team and other stakeholders, with some questioning whether we had any form of boss–employee relationship at all.

Looking back now, I think there were some things we should have done differently:

- We did not talk enough about the unusual situation we were in, our challenging role dynamics, and the impact it had on us, the Team and other stakeholders.
- We spent too much time talking about the "tension" and not enough time talking about the root causes of what we were experiencing – the causes of our "frustration." This was an opportunity missed, and we could have established more robust initial agreements that might have mitigated some challenges and tension.
- Boundaries around personal versus professional conversations were not tight enough. This interplay added an additional colleagues–friends layer of complexity to an already difficult situation with dichotomies of boss/employee and coachee/coach relationships.

## Year Two

The tension in our relationship continued throughout Year Two, with one change. We experimented with explicitly identifying whether conversations would be professional or personal in nature in advance, including physically separating these conversations. I found this approach much easier to manage, although I do not think it benefited Helen much, and she continued to feel frustrated.

As mentioned above, I hoped that one of the consequences of moving Helen from an internal to an external role would be improved role clarity, and less tension. In reality, I think the new dynamic was helpful for the relationship between Helen and the Team, but less successful for the relationship between Helen and me, as the tension between us remained.

## Year Three

As already mentioned above, we re-assessed all services provided by Helen at the beginning of Year Three. We also amended our formal written contract to include clear responsibilities and expectations of the Team, Helen and me. In conjunction with this, Helen and I agreed to cease all personal communication. It was a harsh way to set boundaries, but effective. The change made my role simpler and clearer, which I think improved engagement and ultimately benefitted the Team.

## *Summary – Leader's perspective of himself*

A summary of good, challenging and learnt areas of my own development journey is included in the Appendix to Chapter Five.

I am a genuine and authentic leader and I have shown considerable vulnerability in sharing my leadership development story in this book. Being part of, and instigating this "experiment," has allowed me to discover, practice and apply:

- EQ-centred leadership.
- Leader as coach techniques.
- Matching my leadership style with circumstances.
- Visible sharing of leadership.
- Sharing knowledge and delegating.
- Better communication.

Contributing to this part of the book has been a great self-reflection exercise, and I have learnt a lot from reflecting on my growth again now, sometime after the change journey itself. Helen refers to this as level three learning in Figure 1.3. It has been both a valuable and cathartic experience. I can now say with confidence I have higher EQ in both my professional and personal life than I did at the beginning of Year One. The leadership road I travelled, although rocky at times, was well worth it.

## The Function and Organisation

It makes sense that the organisation in which a team resides has a significant influence on everything to do with that team, including strategy, resources, priorities, technology, processes, ways of working, culture, relationships and, of course, their development. In this section, I discuss the wider Consulting Services function and Green Apple Co from my perspective as Leader of the Team, and also as a senior leader within the organisation and a member of the C-suite, as illustrated in Figure 5.7.

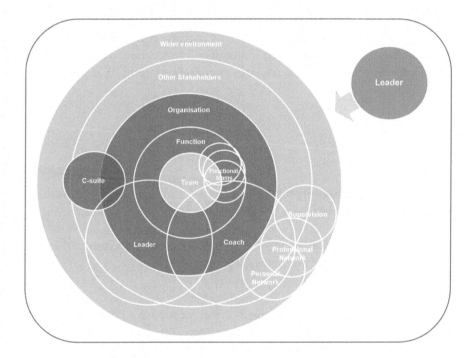

Figure 5.7: Leader's perspective of Function and Organisation

### Organisation culture

Year One

As described in Chapter Two, the Organisation's culture was "top-down" and "siloed" at the beginning of Year One, with that culture permeating within Consulting Services. There were plans in place to change that. Throughout Green Apple Co there were streams of activity taking place (refer to Figure 3.3 and Chapter Three). The work we were doing with our Team and Consulting Services was all completely in line and mutually reinforcing. I am also sure the interventions we undertook would have been less impactful without the culture activity taking place across the organisation as support.

## Years Two and Three

As described in Chapter Two our environment was severely impacted by "leaf spot" and other global events in early Year Two, and some organisation-wide culture change activity was delayed and put on hold. This meant the work we were doing locally with our own team development was even more important – as a means to maintain some traction while still being anchored in foundations set across the organisation during Year One.

## *The Function*

### Year One

As the Team began focusing on development, I think staff across Consulting Services would have noticed a few things in relation to the Team:

- More investment in manager–staff one-to-one conversations.
- Clearer accountability for deliverables.
- More support of their own development.

I think staff throughout Consulting Services would have observed changes in my leadership style as well, including increased communication (both written and face-to-face), more visibility and more delegation.

In addition to development work within the Team, all functional teams across Consulting Services participated in some level of team development work, although it was less intense.

As changes in the Team were taking place, the impact was not immediately visible in the Consulting Services engagement scores. Figure 3.8 shows a flat score throughout Year One, and I think this reflected the long tenures of many staff in the function at the time who were sceptical of change.

It was also becoming clear that team managers within Consulting Services, the layer of management below the Team, exhibited both technical and leadership capability gaps. This constrained the ability of the Team to step up to the level I expected of them as they developed. I noticed team members compensating for team managers reporting to them, even stepping in with hands-on work at times, to ensure deliverables were met. The challenges I had stepping up as a leader in the past were now exhibiting themselves in the next layer down.

## Year Two

Wider environmental events in Year Two (refer Figure 2.10) required the Team to increase focus on staff wellbeing and regular communication across their respective teams. I think the work we did as a team in Year One established a good platform for this, and staff took notice. Referring to Figure 3.8, the Function engagement score began to increase in Year Two.

As mentioned above, another team merged into Consulting Services late in Year Two. Although the merged team were part of Green Apple Co, they of course brought their own team subculture with them, which could have had positive or negative implications. I think the transition went reasonably smoothly, and Figure 3.8 shows a stable engagement score throughout that merger period.

## Year Three

Two significant events impacted staff within Consulting Services during Year Three. A large number of staff were subject to another restructure, including the appointment of new team managers to address gaps at that layer, as highlighted above. And Tom, who left at the beginning of Year Two, returned to lead a new team formed by merging two teams.

There was a lot of uncertainty during this time, evidenced by the dip in Function engagement score in the first part of Year Three (refer to Figure 2.10). It bounced back quickly once structure changes were clarified, and I think changes across Consulting Services were managed well by the Team, influenced significantly by the development groundwork undertaken in Year One.

## Overall reflection

It was clear the development work we had and were doing as a Team positively impacted staff reporting to Team members and the entire Consulting

Services function. Helen refers to this positive influence as the coaching ripple effect (O'Connor & Cavanagh, 2013) (Theory Break 4.4).

## The C-suite

At the beginning of Year One, the C-suite, my colleagues, had little direct contact with the Team or Function, apart from interacting with dedicated relationship managers we had assigned to each of them.

However, over time, I believe the C-suite observed more shared leadership, and the gap between myself and members of the Team closing. For example, early in Year One, I presented all Consulting Services content at C-suite meetings. Gradually, members of the Team presented their own work to the C-suite and other stakeholders. I think by Year Three the gap closed even more, with reliance moving to the Team rather than resting solely with me. My colleagues told me general respect for the Team's leadership capabilities had improved as well.

## The wider Organisation

It would be fair to say that the reputation of the Team and myself coming into Year One was variable at best. Some stakeholders thought we performed well, while others voiced their concerns very negatively and loudly across Green Apple Co. The "hailstorm" in Year One only exaggerated the negative perceptions of some. Due to the storm, we were unable to deliver services to the expected standard. Unfortunately, the "hailstorm" hit before the Team had a chance to benefit from, or embed much, if any, of the development work we had begun. As a result, I doubt the benefits of our early work would have been evident to staff across wider Green Apple Co at all.

Despite the impact of the "hailstorm," I think our well-communicated "90-day plan," created to address the storm, was well received. I felt our reputation across Green Apple Co began to shift towards the end of Year One. It was obvious to all that members of the Team were working together, communicating with each other and the wider organisation, and taking open responsibility for our collective setbacks.

Similar to the C-suite comments above, the wider Organisation would have noticed me stepping back and Team members stepping up by fronting meetings, conversations and deliverables themselves in Year Two. By Year Three, shared leadership across the Team would have been evident across the entire organisation.

*Summary – Leader's perspective of the Function
and Organisation*

A summary of good, challenging and learnt areas arising as I reflect on the
Function and Organisation is included in the Appendix to Chapter Five.

The most significant learning was the huge impact early investment in
team development in Year One had on the way the Team led Consulting
Services through the environmental impacts experienced in Years Two and
Three. This reinforces my view that I made the right decision to start this
development journey when we did.

## The Coach

Now turning my attention to Helen and her dual roles as team coach and a member of the Team, and later an external service provider. The journey described throughout this book must have been very challenging for her. I know she considered leaving us several times. She does not seem the type to give up easily, indicating the difficulty of the role.

I have already covered many of my thoughts on Helen and her role in previous sections of this chapter and will use this section to fill any gaps. My view of Helen within the system is depicted in Figure 5.8.

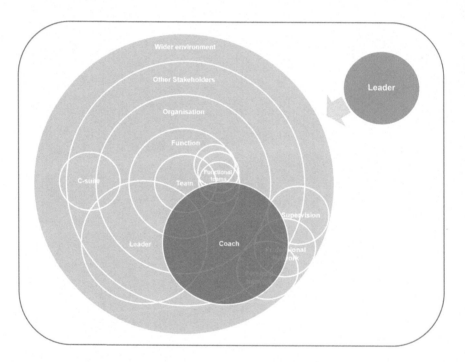

Figure 5.8: Leader's perspective of Coach

### First impressions

When I interviewed Helen during the recruitment process, she came across as smart, passionate about the opportunity we were offering and had the experience and background we were looking for. Most importantly of all, she did not seem concerned with the experimental nature of the role – in fact, it motivated her. It was clear in interviewing her that her focus was on the people development side.

As expressed previously, I should have considered the capacity we needed to focus on changes in service delivery at that time as well – avoiding the need to drag Helen into the overall change space as much as we did.

I expect Helen's first few weeks were tough, as they are for anyone starting a new role. This situation was even harder than most, as although we had a draft position description, she effectively needed to create her own role, her own goals and her own priorities. In hindsight, it may have been beneficial to provide more context and depth of understanding of our strategy and objectives. As it was, we left a void, and Helen developed her own green field approach and programme.

I am also aware that once Helen began to know Green Apple Co and people, there were some early disappointments. I know the capability of the HR team was an area that concerned her. This created a challenge for me as I needed HR buy-in to support and maintain her dedicated role in the Team. I needed to be supportive of the HR function, and I wanted to respect the perspectives Helen brought with her as well. As a result, I sometimes felt as though my allegiances where split.

## Relationship between Coach and Team

### Year One

I have touched on this already above. There were some challenges when Helen joined our Team and some tension in relationships with individual members. Taylor felt Helen was encroaching on her turf both in relation to deliverables and as my confidant – a role often unique in an executive/ EA relationship. While I think the relationship between Taylor and Helen improved somewhat over time, I continued to feel like I needed to pick sides.

In relation to other members of the Team, Greg was a delivery-focused person and could not relate to "fluffy stuff". To begin with, he was not convinced Helen was adding value but was comfortable to go with the flow. Interestingly, over time, Greg became one of the strongest supporters of Helen's approach and the Team sessions.

Drew, Jane and Rosa were a little unsure of Helen's approach at first but understood the strategic context and were happy to go with the flow – once I convinced them to attend sessions.

Tom, who joined near the end of Year One, was not at all happy to go with the flow. He thought the team development process focused too much on "soft" EQ aspects of leadership he already knew, and he wanted to focus on process improvement and deliverables. I am not aware there were any personal issues between Tom and Helen, just a lack of buy-in with the process we were in.

## Years Two and Three

The main relationship change in Year Two occurred between Jane and Helen. One-to-one formal coaching was taking place, and, as mentioned above, the benefit Jane experienced was substantial. The respect Jane had for the Helen and her craft understandably increased as a result, and Jane become a strong advocate for both one-to-one coaching and team coaching.

There were a lot of team membership changes during this period, including Helen leaving the Team herself. From a relationship perspective, I do not think changes in team membership impacted the Team and Helen much; however, it did mean many aspects of the development programme needed to be repeated as new members were inducted and brought up to speed.

## Overall reflection

In summary, team dynamics were complicated, and constantly moving, and Helen was part of that. I do not think that anything that played out here was unusual within a team and, on the whole, relationships between Helen and team members was good. She handled the fluidity of dynamics well, gained trust quickly and maintained trust as team membership changed.

### Relationship between Coach and Leader

### Year One

Helen never considered or accepted me as her boss, nor did I treat her as a staff member – in my eyes we were equals. This contributed to the complex power dynamic between us, described above, with inherent positive and negative implications I expand on next.

Positives included mutual on-tap advice, support, friendship and professional sounding boards in each other. Another positive was the open way we discussed, debated and challenged each other in relation to our respective work areas.

While challenging each other helped us create more robust outcomes, we often blatantly disagreed as well. While I am comfortable having my opinions challenged, officially Helen reported to me, and, ultimately, accountability and therefore final decisions rested with me. While Helen knew that, sometimes my decisions did not sit well with her, resulting in more tension between us. I know members of the Team saw this play out.

Another negative area was one-to-one conversations. I had one-to-one conversations with all members of the Team, focusing on their development. Sometimes I used a coaching style in these conversations, and, of course, I took the same approach with Helen. I recall having one or two successful sessions, but overall, the dynamic between us was not working. Helen openly admitted she was challenged by the situation and resisted me in the coach role. The implication was that she was not getting the development support she needed from me, which was one of the main drivers for arranging external professional supervision. While I think the use of an external support for Helen was essential for her development, it weakened the boss–employee perspective of our relationship even further, as she was not looking to me to support her needs.

The most significant negative was the constant tension in our relationship, already described above.

## Years Two and Three

As mentioned above, Helen moving from an internal coach to an external supplier of services had less impact on our relationship than I had hoped.

It all came to a head at the end of Year Two, and Helen required changes to our formal contract to continue to provide services in Year Three. On reflection, we should have established firm formal boundaries earlier in the piece, as soon as we recognised the negative impact role clarity was having on Helen, the Team and me.

As Year Three played out, some team development sessions were cancelled, and others were descoped, as explained above. The inconsistency of sessions gave Helen the impression we were no longer committed to the development journey. We talked about the Team's commitment around the middle of the year, and I tried to reassure her that we were committed; we simply needed to prioritise other activity. I think her perception of lack of commitment impacted her sense of professional achievement and ultimately her engagement with us and the programme that year.

## Coach development journey

### Year One

As Helen's manager during Year One, I was naturally invested in her development journey, as I was with all members of the Team. When Helen joined, I was aware she had general coaching experience, team development and culture change experience, and considerable hands-on leadership experience. However, I was also aware she was at the very beginning of her team coaching career. The decision to use team coaching as one of our development modalities was a risk but I was comfortable we had a good starting point and Helen's team coaching experience would grow over time while she worked with us. It was all part of the "experiment."

I was aware of how challenging Helen's position was, and as explained above I was also aware that I was unable to provide the development support Helen would normally have expected from her boss. When Helen requested sponsorship by way of professional supervision, I was very happy to support it. Occasionally Helen talked to me about her supervision sessions, sometimes sharing insights she had gained, or asking my opinion on subjects that had been discussed. One of the topics I recall her bringing to me was the "many hats" she wore, and the confusion she and all of us were experiencing around role clarity. I think the work she was doing in supervision helped her make sense of what was happening. I also appreciated that independent input was not only valuable for Helen, but it was also good for all of us, as ultimately the support she received was benefiting the Team and myself.

The coach role, team development sessions, and one-to-one informal coaching provided plenty of opportunity for Helen to experiment with team coaching models and theories, many of which I understand she was trying for the first time. In effect she was using our "experiment" as a self-development platform.

Overall, I think the biggest development shifts for Helen during Year One were a greater appreciation of system dynamics and improved self-awareness.

### Year Two

The first part of Year Two played out in a very similar way to Year One. During the second part of Year Two, as Helen transitioned to an external service provider, her main development area was navigating that transition.

## Year Three

From my viewpoint Helen's standout development shift in Year Three related to role clarity and activating the formal agreement we had established around that. Another area of improvement I noticed was increased patience and agility. While we had always taken a flexible approach to development session content, Year Three required Helen to navigate carefully through fluctuations in approach, modality, logistics, timing, team attention and commitment – including her own commitment.

## Overall reflection

In summary, while it was a very challenging experience, I am confident Helen learnt a significant amount about team coaching, the complexity of systems and herself over the three years this case covers. I have no doubt the unique and challenging circumstances of this case provided an opportunity for her to "experience it all," and I am pleased she is now able use what she has learnt to benefit her ongoing career. I also know she is passionate about sharing what she has learnt with others – hence this book.

## *Summary – Leader's perspective of the Coach*

The Appendix to Chapter Five summarises good, challenging and learnt areas as I reflect on Helen's experience as her manager in Year One and part of Year Two, and as the recipient of services for part of Year Two and Year Three.

It has been interesting reflecting on the journey from this angle, as it provided me with an opportunity to put myself in Helen's shoes – shoes that perhaps I had not fully appreciated before this exercise. As a result, I have gained insight about Helen and the system I would not otherwise have been conscious of.

## Chapter Five summary

Given the high volume of content in this chapter, Helen asked what my one best and one most challenging experiences were. With the benefit of hindsight, I am pleased our journey achieved our goal of stronger leadership within our Team, and leadership styles based on EQ, rather than technical excellence alone.

The most challenging thing was the recognition that in addition to focusing on people development at the beginning of Year One, we should have added more capacity to the Team to ensure change was managed well and service delivery was maintained. Our delivery issues throughout the journey, in particular the "hailstorms," slowed down and masked the benefits being achieved in our individual and team development.

Helen also asked what my greatest learning was. A hard question to answer, as there were many learning areas and layers of insight. Some learning occurred during the journey itself and was applied in-the-moment, and some learning is more obvious now as I reflect on the experience from different angles while writing this chapter. Helen refers to these as level one and level three learning, respectively, in Figure 1.3.

It is too hard to select one great learning, so I settled on two:

- The importance of leader as coach based on EQ-centred leadership. The one-to-one conversations I was having with each individual team member in parallel with our collective team development supported the work we were doing. It was a chance to work with each individual member of the team on their own unique leadership journey, focus on their positions and personalities, reflect on how they were impacted and changing, and help them customise key elements of the Team's collective journey in a way that worked for them.
- I also learned I was capable of personal change in a manner and to a degree I had not even thought possible. The "old dog" learnt some new "tricks"!

### *Advice for leaders*

Before signing off from this chapter, I will take the opportunity to share parting comments and advice for other leaders embarking on, or part way through, a journey such as this.

Systems are complex, so, while on the journey, do not fixate on the outcome you visualised at the beginning. Instead, focus on and trust the process. Over time you will find that outcomes have emerged from the system, developed organically, and differ from your original vision. Those outcomes may in fact be greater than what you anticipated at the start. Also, recognise that a journey like this is not a stand-alone team development exercise. It is a complete reengineering of how you operate as a team, as leaders, as a system and as people, and it takes time and consistent, continual, investment.

At the very beginning of a journey such as this, the team may not seem ready; it may not feel like the right time to start. However, my advice is do it anyway. I am proud and relieved that we invested when we did, as the groundwork done in Year One was the main reason we were able function and succeed during the challenging environmental circumstances in Years Two and Three.

The Team, Helen and I learnt a huge amount through our three-year journey together. For me personally, this period was a time of significant development in both my professional and personal EQ.

Obviously, the learning in this chapter is drawn from my experience with this team on this journey. However, all are equally valid considerations that apply to any leader in any situation, team coaches, external or internal coaches, team members, HR professionals, consultants and academics. My hope is that you find some nuggets in this chapter you can apply to your own practice and with your own teams in your own situation. I encourage all leaders to invest in team development and coaching like we did, and remember it relies on a lot of faith and trust in the power of the coaching process.

I talk about the application of what I learnt from this "experiment" to my future in Chapter Eleven. However, next we hear from Sally my former C-suite colleague, who talks through the journey from the perspective of the Function and Organisation.

# References

Barrett, R. (2010). *The new leadership paradigm*. Lulu.com.

Beckhard, R. & Harris, R. (1987). *Organizational transitions: Managing complex change*. Wokingham: Addison Wesley. https://doi.org/10.5465/ame.1987.4275847.

Clifton, J. & Harter, J. (2019). *It's the manager*. New York: Gallup Press. https://doi.org/10.1002/joe.21971.

Clutterbuck, D. (2017). *The leadership vacuum trap and how coaches and mentors can avoid it*. Retrieved from https://www.coachingandmentoringinternational.org.

Clutterbuck, D. (2020). *Coaching the team at work*. London & Boston: Brealey.

Ellinger, A., Beattie, R. & Hamlin, R. (2010). The manager as coach. In E. Cox, T Bachkirova & D. Clutterbuck (Eds), *The complete handbook of coaching*. London: Sage.

Goleman, D. P. (1995). *Emotional intelligence: Why it can matter more than IQ for character, health and lifelong achievement.* New York: Bantam Books. https://doi.org/10.1037/e576082010-001.

Hawkins, P. (2021). *Leadership team coaching: Developing collective transformational leadership.* London: Kogan Page. https://doi.org/10.1111/peps.12006_5.

Hawkins, P. (2022). *Leadership team coaching in practice: Case studies on creating highly effective teams.* London: Kogan Page.

O'Connor, S. & Cavanagh, M. (2013). The coaching ripple effect: the effects of developmental coaching on wellbeing across organisational networks. *Psychology of Well-Being: Theory, Research and Practice.* 3:2. https://doi.org/10.1186/2211-1522-3-2.

Peters, T. & Waterman, R. (2006). *In search of excellence: Lessons from America's best-run companies.* New York: Harper Business.

Appendix to Chapter Five: Good, challenging and learnt – Leader's perspective

| Good | Challenging | Learnt |
|---|---|---|
| | Strategy enablement and change management | |
| My passion & excitement that the strategy I designed was finally coming to life. | "Top-down" & "siloed" culture within Green Apple Co (early Y1). | Development of people is a critical part of strategy enablement – focus on "soft S's." |
| Clear alignment of our work with Green Apple Co strategy. | Organisation-wide people interventions slowed due to impacts of "leaf spot" (Y2). | Alignment of interventions streams across Organisation & Team & Function, supports & helps embed change. |
| Green Apple Co organisation-wide people initiatives. | No formal framework for measuring progress & success. | |
| "Hard S's" of strategy enablement were in place. | | Have a structured progress & outcomes measurement framework. |
| Tangible outcomes improved & so did positive feedback. | | Tangible evidence of growth & improvement may take time. |
| | | Sense of change might be more insightful than formal measures. |
| | | Do NOT lose sight of delivery standards when embarking on change, including development change. |

(continue)

(continue)

| Good | Challenging | Learnt |
|---|---|---|
| | **Team development and coaching** | |
| We started the journey at the beginning of Y1, despite resistance from the Team (Y1). | Poor reputation of Team (early Y1). Initial resistance of Team to invest in development (Y1). | Even if the team is not "ready" to start team coaching – just start! Regular team development sessions are a good investment. |
| Investment in monthly team development days, with flexible content. | Team dynamics were complex & trust & psychological safety fluctuated. | Team coaching is a fluid & holistic form of development, with high rewards. |
| Team eventually recognising long-term benefits of development (Y2). | "Hailstorm(s)" slowed down & masked the benefits of development (Y1 & Y3). | Appreciation of the value of team development can grow. |
| Growing trust & psychological safety evident – I could "feel" the change. | Some aspects of team development sessions, including flexibility of agendas. | Team development sessions:<br>• Commit to pre-work.<br>• Balance structure & flexibility.<br>• Bottom out topics. |
| Team recognised the "bump" in development journey & appreciated it was temporary (Y3). | Overall lack of clarity around roles & responsibilities between Team, Helen & me. | • Align frequency & timing with other commitments. |
| Team understood the importance of resilience. | As the Team stepped up, the gap between them & team managers below them widened. | • Moderate topics depending on where team is at. |
| Investment in "good endings" was useful for the Team & cathartic for me (Y3). | Change took time to become visible in tangible measures. | Invest in clarifying roles & responsibilities of team, leader & team coach. |
| Stakeholders noticed improvements & increase in Team's maturity evident over time. | Team maturity zig-zagged, it slumped sometimes. | Team dynamics & hence trust & psychological safety is fluid. |

| Good | Challenging | Learnt |
|---|---|---|
| | Leadership development | |
| I understood I needed to invest time upfront to be able to delegate & share leadership. | My "top-down" leadership style (early Y1). | The "people" part of strategy enablement begins with leaders being in line with the goal. |
| One-to-one informational coaching & direct advice from Helen was helpful (Y1 & Y2). | Consistent messages that my leadership style needed to change. | A shift from delivery focus to an EQ-based leadership approach is the best way to deal with volatility |
| Strong trust & friendship between me & Helen. | I was under pressure, stressed & a knowledge risk to Green Apple Co. | & change, & meet stakeholders needs. |
| My open commitment to change my leadership style (end Y1). | Initially I resisted working on changing my leadership style (Y1). | *Leader as coach & one-to-one support of team members in parallel to collective team* |
| I came to understand I had several leadership styles. | "Leadership vacuum trap" & "Who's the boss" (Y1). | *development helps embed change.* (Most valuable learning for Leader). |

The team development path is bumpy, Team maturity is not linear; expect ups & downs.

As a team steps up, new gaps between them & other parts of the system may be exposed.

Team development has a ripple effect across an organisation.

"Good endings" are a good investment.

(continue)

(continue)

| Good | Challenging | Learnt |
|------|-------------|--------|
| | Leadership development | |
| Active implementation of leadership change enablers (early Y2). | Challenging power dynamics between Helen & me. | If sharing leadership responsibilities, communicate well with stakeholders. |
| My focus on one-to-one coaching of team members (Y3). | Time spent with Helen meant less time spent with my Team (Y1 & Y2). | One-to-one coaching & advice for leader is helpful to embed change – agree how to give & receive it between parties. |
| My leadership style did change. | The volume & frequency of leadership advice from Helen felt overwhelming at times. | Shift in leadership style comes from an active decision to do so & timing of that decision is important. |
| My transformation was personal as well as professional. | Helen moving from internal to external role reduced on-tap support & had less impact on role clarity than I expected (Y2). | There is no correct leadership style. Create your own bespoke model. |
| | | Shared leadership & increased communication improves reputation & reduces perception of knowledge risk. |
| | | Leadership style can change – it just takes time. |
| | | *Working on leadership style can fundamentally & positively change you as a person. (Most valuable learning for Leader).* |

| Good | Challenging | Learnt |
|---|---|---|
| | Coaching in general | |
| Helen had the skills, knowledge & attitude we needed for the role. | Experimental & green field nature of Helen's role. | There are advantages & disadvantages of an internal coach versus an external coach – it is not clear cut. |
| Having Helen as an internal coach who was part of the Team provided focus (Y1). | Having an internal coach & her being part of the team created role clarity issues (Y1). | Invest time inducting the internal or external coach & keep them up to date with changes in environment. |
| Helen had good relationships with members of the Team. | Team dynamics included dynamics with Helen as well. | On-tap advice & one-to-one coaching of team members in parallel to collective team development helps embed change. |
| One-to-one informational coaching & direct advice from Helen was helpful (Y1 & Y2). | Tension & unusual power dynamics between Helen & me. | The coach is part of the team dynamic & system, may disrupt team dynamic. |
| Helen changing from internal to external role provided some role clarity & shifted onus of development to Team & me (Y2). | Opportunity to experiment with formal co-coaching not taken. | Agree with the coach how role dynamics & any tension will be resolved. And be careful with personal boundaries. |
| | Helen moving from internal to external role had less impact on role clarity than I expected (Y2). | Experiment with co-coaching. |
| Formal contract with Helen amended to clarify roles & responsibilities (Y3). | Helen's visibility of our context reduced (Y3). | If changing a coach or responsibilities of their role, invest time in clarifying roles. |
| Complexity of the role & environment provided great learning for Helen. She "experienced it all" & I saw her develop. | | If there is tension & lack of clarity of roles & responsibilities, consider formal contracts with the coach. |

(continue)

(continue)

| Good | Challenging | Learnt |
| --- | --- | --- |
| | Coaching in general | |
| | | Employ a coach who has suitable experience, but also look for attitude, willingness to experiment & learn, & an agile & flexible mindset. |
| | | The coach learns just as much from the experience as the team & leader. |
| Good | Challenging | Learnt |
| | Coach support | |
| I supported Helen's development in team coaching & professional supervision (Y1 & Y2). | I was unable to provide Helen with normal boss–employee development support (Y2 & Y3). | Check the coach (whether internal or external) has all the support they need. |

# Function and Organisation perspective 6

*Helen Zink*

---

## HOW TO READ CHAPTER SIX

I am Sally, a member of the C-suite. Before beginning this chapter, I will explain how it fits into the overall book.

The five system elements covered in this book describe their own versions of their development story in Section B. This includes thoughts on whether the approach and interventions used in this case, as described in Chapter Three, were useful, what was good, what was challenging, and what was learnt from the experience. Using a movie analogy, Section B involves five "parallel plots," where the same story is narrated by different characters, with each character describing themselves and the other main characters in the movie.

Chapter Six is one of the parallel plots – the Function and Organisation's perspective of the story. I narrate the story in this chapter on behalf of everyone across Consulting Services and Green Apple Co. Figure 6.1 illustrates our view of the system. In this chapter, I cover our thoughts on the Team, Michael (Leader), ourselves as key stakeholders (Function and Organisation), and Helen (Coach).

Content for this chapter comes from answers to questions Helen asked us for inclusion in this book. Although information gathered was not an extensive 360 review, this chapter is a good indication of key stakeholders' perspectives. Figure 6.2 indicates stakeholder areas across Green Apple Co that have contributed content and as you can see there is good coverage across all areas.

DOI: 10.4324/9781003367789-8

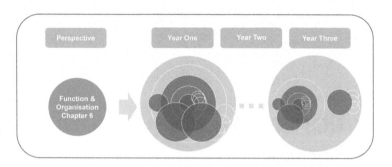

Figure 6.1: Function and Organisation's perspective of system

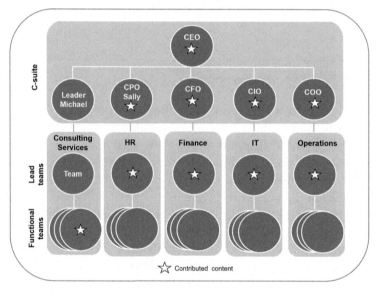

Figure 6.2: Source of content Chapter Six

I was the CPO in Green Apple Co and a member of the C-suite during the period of this case. I contributed to the design of the Consulting Services structure that went live at the beginning of Year One, including the creation of the Team this book is based on. I was involved in designing the overall strategy for Green Apple Co, knew Michael well and understood his vision for the function he led, and had awareness of the culture within Consulting Services by way of my role as head of HR. I feel I am well placed to write this on behalf of key stakeholders across Green Apple Co.

## Strategic context

### Year One

By our own admission, and as mentioned in Chapter Two, the culture in Green Apple Co was "siloed" at the beginning of Year One. We were fully aware of the issues, hence our focus on culture change activity depicted in Figure 3.3. My C-suite colleagues and I also knew that it takes time to change culture and our programme had a five-year time horizon – we were in it for the long haul.

In addition to culture change initiatives, we actively supported one-to-one coaching as a development enabler. We taught and encouraged leader as coach skills as part of our senior leadership development programme (Theory Break 5.2). We also used professional external one-to-one coaches when required for senior members of staff and coordinated an internal peer coaching programme for other staff as well. We also encouraged collective team development, including the creation of our own in-house HPT model and HPT questionnaire as described in Chapter Three.

At the same time, our internal HR resources were extremely limited, and most development enablers were designed as self-help options, where managers and staff accessed online learning and development resources.

The creation of the Team and Consulting Services structure at the beginning of Year One was completely in line with our strategic trajectory as an organisation. The creation of the Coach role within the Team, while unique to that particular Team, was also in line with strategy. There was discussion at the time as to whether the coach role should report to Michael or fall within my HR team. In the end, we agreed the role would report to Michael with a dotted line to HR.

We wanted Michael to have full autonomy in how the resource was utilised – if he had control, he might be more receptive to change himself. Other areas of Green Apple Co had not prioritised development as much as Michael had, relying on internal self-help tools, stretched internal support within my HR team and ad hoc external consultancy as required.

### Years Two and Three

We were aware the Team continued with their own development work in Year Two, despite descoping the overall culture change programme due to "leaf spot" implications. There was no issue with the Team continuing on their path, as long as their work remained in line with our overall people strategy, and they had the budget for it.

At the beginning of Year Three, some of our internal HR staff undertook basic team coaching training to upskill internal capability in areas of team development. We wanted to reduce reliance on expensive external consultants.

## The Team

With the context of being comfortable with and supportive of the Team's development approach, I will talk about our perspective of the Team within the system, as illustrated in Figure 6.3.

### Team development goal and HPT model

The Team's HPT development goal in Year One was completely in line with our internal HPT philosophy. However, Helen preferred the PERILL

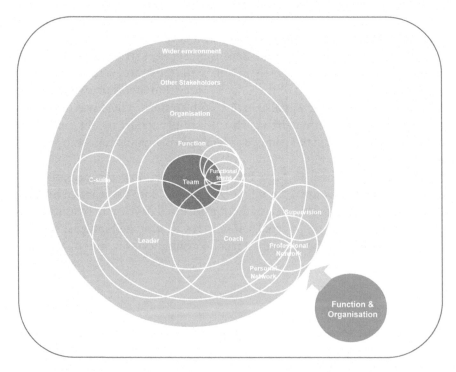

Figure 6.3: Function and Organisation's perspective of Team

(Clutterbuck, 2022) HPT model over our in-house approach. To "meet in the middle," my HR team endorsed Helen's idea of combining our in-house model with the PERILL (refer to Figure 3.1). I am also aware that Helen combined our in-house HPT questionnaire with PERILL questions.

## Intervention (A) – Team development sessions

### Year One

We were aware the Team were participating in monthly team development sessions, similar to the C-suite. Initially Helen shared the Team's development plan and content of monthly sessions with us, trying to keep us updated as content changed. But to be honest, our resources were stretched and we were not able to keep close tabs on everything – after all, Consulting Services comprised only three per cent of our total workforce of 3,000 staff, they already had Helen as a dedicated resource, and we had other issues to deal with.

Our main interest was ensuring the work Helen was doing aligned with activity across other parts of the organisation – and we were comfortable this was the case. Michael was also a hard man to please, and as long as Michael and the Team were happy, we were happy too.

### Years Two and Three

As Helen moved to an external supplier role in Year Two, we essentially lost connection with her and the Team's development programme. Michael managed the relationship with Helen himself and we left him to it.

By Year Three, in-house HR capacity had increased, and so had our team development capability. I felt the use of Helen as an external provider was no longer in-line with our strategic intent, and although I did not mandate it, I would have preferred the use of in-house support.

On reflection, our involvement in the Team's monthly development sessions and our relationship with Helen should have been managed differently in Years Two and Three. Once an external resource, the primary relationship between Helen and the organisation should have been with the HR team reporting to me, rather than Michael. However, due to lack of capacity within HR early on, the close relationship between Michael and Helen, and Michael holding the development budget for his own Team, we chose not to interfere.

## Intervention (B) – One-to-one formal and informal coaching of team members

As Helen was a member of the Team in Year One, we were very aware she was supporting the Team in an advisory capacity – after all, availability of on-tap support was one of the main reasons her role was placed within the Team. I cannot comment on whether Helen was advising or coaching – I suspect a bit of both.

The team also participated in a senior leader peer coaching programme coordinated by our HR function.

I cannot comment on one-to-one coaching arrangements once Helen moved out of the organisation in Year Two, as I had no visibility.

### Tangible outcomes

I keep a close eye on all engagement scores across Green Apple Co as part of my role. Although many factors influence engagement scores, they do provide a good indication of the vibe and culture within an area. Leading into Year One, both the Team and Consulting Services functional engagement scores were higher than the average across Green Apple Co.

Figure 3.8 shows stable results across Year One – surprising given the turbulent environment we were all operating in and the inherent cynicism of longer-serving staff. By the way, scores in other parts of the organisation dropped dramatically during that time.

Despite the "leaf spot" crisis in Year Two, Consulting Services engagement scores increased that year, which I see as a testament to good communication and increased focus on wellbeing across the entire organisation.

There were multiple structure changes across the organisation and within Consulting Services in Year Three, so I was not at all surprised by the drop in scores during that time. All in all, very pleasing results for Consulting Services and much better results and less volatility compared with most other parts of the organisation.

As mentioned above, I was aware a HPT questionnaire was being used with the Team, and I saw the results of the first assessment taken at the beginning of Year One. I did not see results after that, so I cannot comment on trends in that area.

## *Intangible outcomes*

In contributing to this book, Helen specifically asked some staff within the Consulting Services function, members of the C-suite, including me, and staff across Green Apple Co, (refer to Figure 6.2 for sources of content) what they noticed about the Team across the three-year period this case covers. I have reviewed that feedback which informs the following comments. In many ways I find this type of verbal information more insightful than hard numerical engagement scores.

## Function

In their feedback, Consulting Services staff said it was strange they were not asked what they wanted and needed from the Team over the period of this case. However, despite a lack of direct input, most of their feedback was positive. Themes related to changes in the Team's willingness to collaborate and communicate, and increased positivity and energy. They felt there was a more positive working environment as a result, making it easier for them to access the Team and get support they needed to deliver their work.

Some direct comments relating to changes in the Team:

- "Previously, the Team always gave me the impression they were stressed and unapproachable. Now I feel like they have time for me."
- "I got the feeling they were pleased to be on a journey of change."
- "The Team appeared to be happy, working well together and supportive of each other and us."
- "Strategy is clearer and well communicated."
- "The Team seem happier and less stressed despite all the challenges they have faced."
- "The Team was finally addressing long-term staff issues that their predecessors had not. It was great to see rotten apples removed from our basket."

As I reviewed feedback from Consulting Services staff, it seemed they got what they needed in the end, but it took some time to get there. Some staff specifically mentioned that if asked, they would have suggested the Team prioritise approachability and communication in their development plan and questioned the process which omitted them.

Some comments relating to the process:

- "We should have been engaged more throughout the process."
- "A customer engagement group would have been useful."
- "Seeking input from other parts of the organisation would have added value."
- "A 360 view would have identified what people want."

## C-suite

As a C-suite, we did not see much, if anything, of the previous Consulting Services leadership team prior to Year One, and not much changed as the new Team formed at the beginning of Year One. Michael continued to front almost all interaction and communication with us.

Ironically, the "hailstorm" seemed to change that. Although service delivery was an issue, and we were all adversely impacted by the storm, it was the first time we saw the Team work together collectively, communicate with us and plan well. It was great to see them come out of hiding – although a shame it took a "hailstorm" for the change to happen.

Over time, the Team became more and more visible and communicated better. By Year Three, members of the Team attended C-suite meetings, presenting their work and papers for our information, feedback and approval. It was great to see them at our table more often.

Some comments from C-suite members relating to changes in the Team:

- "I saw camaraderie in the Team; they collaborate much more and have some fun at the same time."
- "Team members were more visible, and we were getting to know them better."
- "Better planning and communication, which is really important to us."
- "Leadership was being shared more, and we saw more support from team members in C-suite meetings, which was very fresh and constructive."
- "It was great to see improving and consistently high engagement scores compared with the rest of organisation."

There was consensus amongst my colleagues and myself that the Team's overall management of change was lacking in some areas.

Some comments from C-suite members relating to change management:

- "I know the Team was going through development and change, but they lost sight of delivery."
- "There was just too much change and too much expected of Team all at the same time."
- "The first hailstorm was not great, but the second was extremely hard for us to manage."
- "We were not involved in the Team's development process at all – the first time we were asked to provide input was contributing to this book."

As I reflect now, given the magnitude of the change being undertaken and the importance of the Team to the overall operation of Green Apple Co, we should have insisted on a formal and documented change programme with C-suite sponsorship. That change programme would have integrated, prioritised and managed risks associated with all changes the Team were managing at the time, including systems and processes, structure and people, and their own development.

## Wider organisation

Similar to other stakeholder groups, staff across the wider organisation were not asked to contribute to the Team's development process. However, Helen did ask them for input to this book. In summary, their feedback was consistent, and they noticed positive changes in the way the Team were working together and leading others.

Some comments from staff across Green Apple Co relating to the Team:

- "It was clear that there had been a shift in recognising the need for change, and also that this change was positive rather than something that implied failure or criticism."
- "I think the rest of the organisation were grateful for improved communication and the Team was on the right path."

There were themes coming through around a lack of involvement in the process and slow progress as well. Some comments:

- "While we appreciate the Team were under a lot of pressure which led to the 'hailstorm' in Year One, the 'hailstorm No.2' should never have happened."

- "If asked, we would have requested the Team focus on providing services in an EQ-centric way – we need services tailored to our needs and a collaborative relationship-based delivery model."
- "While we saw great improvements in Year Three, improvements should have happened earlier in the Team's journey."

## Summary – Function and Organisation's perspective of Team

The Appendix to Chapter Six summarises collective thoughts on the good, challenging and learnt aspects of the Team's journey from the Function and Organisation perspective.

Overall, stakeholders, including myself, observed positive change and found the Team easier to work with. The quality and reliability of their services improved as well. However, reflecting on areas learnt, there are two clear messages from the stakeholders I represent:

- Do not forgo delivery standards when embarking on change.
- Involve stakeholders throughout the team development and coaching process.

Without acknowledging the importance of stakeholders and involving them throughout (Theory Break 6.1) there is danger that team development becomes self-absorbing and insular. I think this happened in this case to some extent.

---

### THEORY BREAK 6.1: IMPORTANCE OF STAKEHOLDERS

Stakeholders determine a team's success or failure, or "legitimacy" as Clutterbuck (2022) would phrase it. The external processes and systems element of his PERILL model (Theory Break 3.2) reflects this, citing stakeholder relationships, reputation and performance as critical.

Why involve them?

- Understanding what stakeholders need and value helps a team prioritise their development efforts to those that are most impactful.

- Some stakeholders have strong voices, influence others, and ultimately determine a team's reputation – and a team's reputation impacts their ability to secure resources they need to deliver.
- Involving staff and understanding their needs improves staff engagement, which helps attract and retain good staff.
- Stakeholders involved may become a team's strongest advocates; communicate for them and build reputation on their behalf (Theory Break 6.2).

There are many tools available to support stakeholder identification and analysis. The diagram below is based on the Hawkins and Turner (2020) model and includes: staff; internal and external customers; suppliers and partners; regulators; funders; physical environment; future and past generations; and, most importantly, careful consideration of stakeholders you might have missed, as they may interfere when least expected and cause issues.

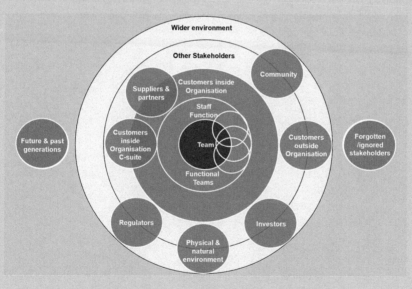

Modified from Hawkins & Turner (2020)

## The Leader

In this section, I focus specifically on Michael my C-suite colleague. Again, I represent everyone in the Function and Organisation, and our view of Michael in the system is illustrated in Figure 6.4.

### *Leadership style*

Michael's leadership at the beginning of Year One was "top-down," which, to be fair, was consistent with the style of several other senior leaders in Green Apple Co at that time – a style we were trying to change. All members of the C-suite, including myself, were telling Michael to delegate more, keep out of detailed work, share leadership, and share technical and organisational knowledge. We also had grave concerns about Michael holding too much organisational knowledge himself – we identified he was as a significant risk to Green Apple Co business continuity. His style was also impacting his own stress levels and health, which concerned all of us too.

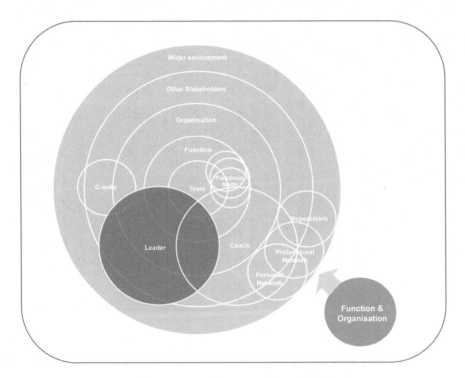

Figure 6.4: Function and Organisation's perspective of Leader

Michael did take our comments on board, and we observed a gradual change in his style over the period of this case. I think the development work we were doing as C-suite was a significant contributor to that change.

Helen specifically asked a sample of staff within the Consulting Services function, members of the C-suite – including me – and staff across Green Apple Co (refer to Figure 6.2 for source of content) what they noticed about Michael's leadership style across the three-year period this case covers.

Some comments on changes in his style:

- "Michael become more visible by holding all department team meetings in open areas and sharing all kinds of information, including new HR approaches to managing people. I had not seen Michael do that before."
- "Michael was stepping back more and allowing his Team the freedom to make their own decisions. There was good flow-on impact for me, as I could go directly to members of the Team for information and not have to wait to find some time with Michael."
- "He increased focus on communication, delegation, collaboration and empowerment of others in his overall approach. This helped me learn a lot more about my role too as work was delegated to me."

Overall feedback themes related to better communication, more trust in others to lead, more visibility and approachability, more delegation, more inclusivity and collaboration, coaching others, embracing feedback, and less defensiveness. Michael should be very pleased with these observations!

Although the change in Michael's style was positive, there were some bumps along the way. It is unrealistic to expect behavioural changes to stick one hundred per cent all of the time, and we did notice him slipping back into old habits at times. A staff member contributed: "At times, I observed Michael falling back into a more controlling style when under pressure. I never doubted that his intentions were to include others, but sometimes the priorities of delivery got in his way."

Some stakeholders reported they saw very little or no change in Michael at all. Perhaps the change was so gradual it was hard for some to notice. Perhaps some had known Michael for such a long time that they were locked into old perceptions that could not be budged. Perhaps C-suite colleagues saw a side of Michael others did not. Or, perhaps for some, their experience of Michael genuinely did not change. All valid explanations – but I observed positive change myself.

## Intervention (C) – One-to-one informal coaching of Leader

Michael and Helen worked closely together, and we in the C-suite referred to Helen as his confidant – we knew she had his ear. At times we took advantage of that relationship, speaking to Helen about things we wanted to see in Michael, knowing her influence was strong.

We cannot comment on the nature of communication between Michael and Helen, whether she gave him advice, or whether a coaching approach was used. However, whatever the nature of their interaction, it was clear that the one-to-one support Helen provided contributed to the change we saw in Michael. I know that some of us in the C-suite, including the CEO, saw Helen's role as a way to directly influence Michael in the direction we wanted and needed. The close interaction between them was one of the main reasons we endorsed the creation of the role within the Team. In a way, we used Helen as our influencer and spy.

## Summary – Function and Organisation's perspective of Leader

The Appendix to Chapter Six summarises thoughts on the good, challenging and learnt aspects in relation to Michael and changes in his style from our collective perspective as key stakeholders.

The most prominent learning is acknowledging that leadership style can change, even with the most stubborn leaders, but it takes time. It follows that if a leader is working on changing their style, all stakeholders and the leader themselves require patience and persistence to embed the change they want to see. My advice to anyone working alongside a change effort such as this – be realistic and be supportive!

## The Function and Organisation

In this section, I talk about the role that staff within the Consulting Services function, C-suite, including myself, and the wider Green Apple Co had in the journey. Our view of ourselves as stakeholders within the system is depicted in Figure 6.5.

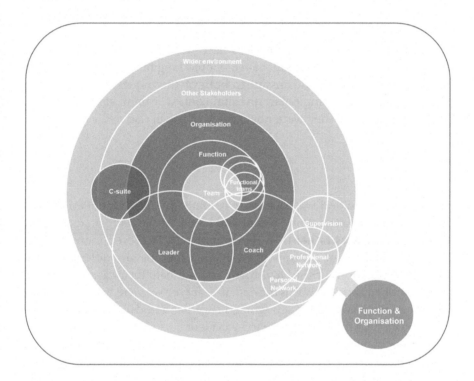

Figure 6.5: Function and Organisation's perspective of themselves

## Role of Function and Organisation

### Function

Of what I knew of staff in Consulting Services and reviewing their contributions to this book, I believe the Function was suffering from change fatigue. The impact of the new structure at the start of Year One was substantial, with all staff either reporting to brand-new managers or adjusting to changes in reporting lines. In addition to a new configuration, staff were grieving the loss of staff who were asked to leave at that time.

Then, Soon after the new structure was live, all staff had to physically move buildings twice in quick succession. Due to changes in location, equipment and processes needed to be adapted. Then, as illustrated in Figure 2.9, the "hailstorm" hit, along with other environmental challenges. In addition to working through the implications of the "hailstorm", they received a lot of criticism from other staff across the organisation, including me, if I am honest. And that was all in Year One. Figures 2.10 and 2.11 indicate many more challenges in Years Two and Three, including more restructures, "leaf spot" and another "hailstorm."

Could staff in Consulting Services have been more supportive of the Team as they worked through change? Could tangible engagement scores have improved earlier? The answer to both of those questions is maybe – but given the challenging environmental context, I think staff did well to hold on and survive; they were not capable of much else.

## C-suite

The Team's reputation was lacklustre coming into Year One. Perhaps our opinions were unfair to some extent and based on the performance of the Team's predecessors rather than the incumbents. However, there were no early signs that the newly appointed Team would be any different to the last, and implications of the "hailstorm" did not help their case.

As described above, towards the end of Year One we were beginning to see improvement in how the Team worked together and delivered outcomes – but it took a long time for change to be evident.

Looking back now, I can see that we were not as supportive as we could have been. Given the importance of the Team's services and the magnitude of the change they were working through, we should have directed our energy into supporting them rather than complaining. Using our energy more positively by insisting on being involved, offering change management resource, guidance and sponsorship, would have been much more effective. I think increased support from us would have accelerated the Teams improvement substantially.

## Wider organisation

Similar to my own experience and that of others in the C-suite, staff across the wider organisation did not know the Team well in Year One. It was not until the "hailstorm" and "90-day" plan that team members became visible.

Similar to the C-suite comments above, staff in the wider organisation did see positive change in the Team, but it took time.

Could staff across the wider organisation been more supportive and helped the Team through their change programme? The answer is maybe – however, most of the environmental impacts illustrated in Figures 2.9, 2.10 and 2.11 impacted everyone in Green Apple Co, and staff were focused on managing their own local challenges – so in reality I do not think there was capacity for much support.

## Summary – Function and Organisation's perspective of themselves

The Appendix to Chapter Six summarises the good and challenging aspects in relation to us, the Function and Organisation, and our impact on the Team. The key message from this section is that while support from us was not as evident as it could or should have been, particularly from the C-suite, it was difficult to contribute in a proactive way when all of Green Apple Co was subject to complex and challenging environmental impacts at the same time.

We missed an opportunity to find ways to support the Team in this case. And taking a wider lens, we missed an opportunity for all parts of the organisation to support each other through significant change. We had spent a lot of time and money creating the five-year strategic plan for Green Apple Co but as an organisation we did not invest as much as we should have in enabling that plan well. Food for thought!

## The Coach

The final system element I will talk about is Helen, the Coach. I and others in the C-suite and across Green Apple Co can only comment on Year One, as once Helen left and became an external service provider, we had no visibility of her or what she was working on with the Team. Our view of the Coach in the system is illustrated in Figure 6.6.

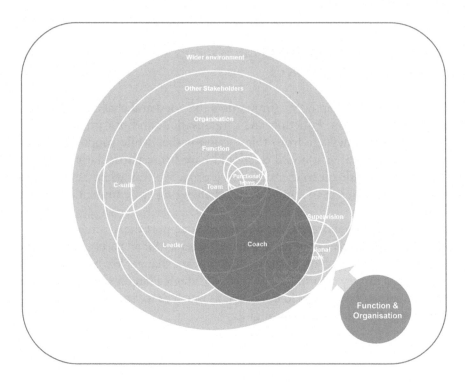

Figure 6.6: Function and Organisation's perspective of Coach

*Relationship between Function and Organisation and Coach*

Function

Staff across Consulting Services loved Helen. Their feedback included comments around energy and positivity, and they said she was approachable and always there to help at any time. They seemed to like having her around, and her impact on culture within the Function was immediately evident. In Year One, I observed more talking across teams within the Function, more staff meetings, increased focus on staff development and more communication.

## C-suite

At the very beginning of Year One, Helen met with me and all C-suite members as part of her induction. She seemed experienced, confident, and gave us all the impression she would get what we needed done.

However, I am also aware there was lack of consistency amongst us as to what exactly it was "we needed done." Some of us thought Helen was there to support issues with operational delivery. Michael's boss, the CEO, believed a significant part of her role was to support Michael in changing his leadership style. And some of us thought she was there to change wider culture within the Function.

Reflecting back now, I can see how lack of clarity at our senior level would have added to the challenges the Team, Michael and Helen faced in relation to their overall change programme. In addition to sponsoring the Team's change programme, alignment in understanding of Helen's role and priorities within the C-suite would have been helpful.

Helen became visible across Green Apple Co as soon as she joined, and during Year One she attended C-suite meetings from time to time, discussing projects she was involved in, such as the "90-day plan." However, as I reflect back now, I realise she never spoke about the development work she was doing with the Team – strange!

## HR

The HR team reporting to me had a good relationship with Helen in Year One. In particular, one of my team managers, Erica, was involved in designing her role, her recruitment and her induction. Erica worked very closely with Helen, and she told me they shared knowledge and worked on projects together. Helen was there for input and as a sounding board, and my HR team created in-house development material she used and applied. Helen also worked with my HR team in relation to our organisation-wide culture change project – there was a lot of cross-pollination.

However, in Year Two, around the same time Helen moved to an external service provider role, Erica also left us. Following that, the connection between my team and Helen was sporadic at best. The Team, who seemed happy with their development support, were not an HR priority for us at that time anyway.

## Wider organisation

All members of the Team were members of the Green Apple Co senior leadership group, including Helen. Outside of regular senior leadership development sessions, staff across the wider organisation had little visibility of her or what she was working on, and once she was no longer an employee, they had no visibility at all.

## Summary – Function and Organisation's perspective of Coach

The Appendix to Chapter Six summarises the good, challenging and learnt areas identified above, reflecting on Helen from the collective perspective of the Function and Organisation. The standout learning area here relates to better understanding and shared agreement of Helen's scope and priorities in Year One and maintaining connection with her once she left the organisation.

## Chapter Six summary

It has been enlightening working on this chapter on behalf of staff across Consulting Services and Green Apple Co. The opportunity to reflect on events some time afterwards has highlighted areas that could have been managed better by the C-suite and the HR team in particular. Helen refers to this post-event reflection as level three learning, refer Figure 1.3.

However, I am not going to beat myself up too much, as it is important to recognise the extreme environmental circumstances faced by the Team and the entire organisation over the three years this case covers. Just as one set of obstacles was managed, another set arrived – the onslaught was relentless. As a whole organisation, we were pushed into focusing on short-term delivery and local challenges within our own direct areas of responsibility and did not have capacity to support the Team in their development endeavours.

Helen asked us to identify the best thing about the journey, the most challenging part and the most significant thing we learnt. There was consensus amongst feedback I reviewed that:

- The best part was we saw positive changes in the Team and Michael.
- The most challenging aspects were not being directly involved in the process until contributing to this book.
- The most significant thing we learnt was that we missed an opportunity to find a way to support the Team and each other through change across the whole organisation.

Contributing to, or insisting we contribute to, the Team's development journey may have resulted in more rapid change. There would have been other benefits too. If representatives from various parts of Green Apple Co had worked with the Team, perhaps as a cross-organisation working group or steering committee, more staff would have understood the Team better.

Better understanding of the Team's successes and struggles might have turned some critics into advocates – ultimately improving the Team's perceived performance and reputation across Green Apple Co highlighting the importance of psychological contacts between teams and their stakeholders (Theory Break 6.2).

I wonder how different outcomes would have been if we had been directly involved right at the beginning and throughout. We will never know the answer to that question but going forward I am much more conscious of the need for stakeholder involvement, which I emphasise in Chapter Eleven as future intensions.

The next perspective we hear from is Helen, and her version of the story as Coach and also as an employee of Green Apple Co in Year One.

## THEORY BREAK 6.2: PSYCHOLOGICAL CONTRACTS WITH STAKEHOLDERS

Clutterbuck (2022) describes psychological contracts between teams and their stakeholders as extremely beneficial. Including stakeholders in a team's development programme not only ensures good prioritisation of development areas, but it also improves relationships. There is evidence that strong relationships, involving mutual trust and cooperation, impact perceptions of performance. To put it simply, if stakeholders are involved in the development work of a team, they will feel valued and trusted. This in turn may result in a perception of performance that is better than it actually is, and more forgiveness of performance issues. Also, stakeholders who were critics may become advocates, and new advocates are likely to favourably influence the opinions of other critics.

## References

Clutterbuck, D. (2022). *The challenge of the incoming team leader.* Retrieved from https://www.coachingandmentoringinternational.org

Hawkins, P. & Turner, E. (2020). *Systemic coaching: Developing value beyond the individual.* London & New York: Routledge. https://doi.org/10.4324/9780429452031

Appendix to Chapter Six: Good, challenging and learnt – Function and Organisation's perspective

| Good | Challenging | Learnt |
|---|---|---|
| Strategy enablement and change | | |
| Clear alignment of approach with strategy & Green Apple Co's culture intervent ons.<br><br>Leader as coach & coaching culture encouraced across Green Apple Co. | Organisation culture "top-down" & "siloed" (early Y1).<br><br>HR resources limited.<br><br>Culture change interventions across Green Apple Co slowed down due to "leaf spot" crisis (Y2 & Y3).<br><br>Environmental challenges impacted all Green Apple Co staff & processes.<br><br>Staff across Consulting Services (& Green Apple Co) suffered from change fatigue.<br><br>Change across Green Apple Co was not well coordinated or supported internally. | Development of people is a critical part of strategy enablement.<br><br>Ensure the team's development approach & models are aligned with the organisation's approach.<br><br>EQ & relationship focused service delivery is important to stakeholders – data is not enough.<br><br>Do NOT lose sight of delivery standards when embarking on change.<br><br>It may take time for stakeholders to notice change.<br><br>If there is a lot of change, consider investing in coordinated organisation-wide change management. |

(continue)

(continue)

| Good | Challenging | Learnt |
|---|---|---|
| | **Team development and coaching** | |
| Long-term issues with some staff addressed. | The Team's reputation was poor (Y1). | On-tap advice & one-to-one coaching of team members is very helpful. |
| More attention on staff communication & wellbeing (Y2 & Y3). | Some staff in Consulting Services, C-suite & other senior staff were cynical & unsupportive. | Team development has a ripple effect across the organisation. |
| Tangible outcomes & verbal feedback on Team showed improvement (Y2 & Y3). | "Hailstorms" & "leaf spot" impacted service delivery (Y2 & Y3). | Include stakeholders when setting development goal & use their support throughout the development process. (Most valuable learning for Function and Organisation). |
| Increased visibility & involvement of Team in senior level meetings (Y3). | Felt like it took a crisis to see any change in the Team (Y1). | If the change anticipated is significant, manage it formally: |
| | Stakeholders were not explicitly asked to contribute to any part of the Team's development. | • Change programme.<br>• C-suite sponsorship.<br>• Formal measurement of tangible & intangible outcomes. |
| | | Support & empathy from stakeholders is helpful. |

| Good | Challenging | Learnt |
|---|---|---|
| **Leadership development** | | |
| Consistent messages that Michael's leadership style needed to change. | Michael's "top-down", hands-on leadership style (early Y1). | One-to-one support & advice for leader is helpful to identify & embed change. |
| Michael benefitted from one-to-one support & advice Helen provided (Y1 & Y2). | Michael was stressed & a risk to organisation – held too much knowledge personally (Y1). | Expect bumps if a leader is working on changing their style. |
| Michael's leadership style did change. | Michael slipped back into old habits when under stress. | Leadership style can change – although it might take time. |
| | Some stakeholders observed no change at all. | |
| **Coaching in general** | | |
| Having an internal coach & Helen being part of the team provided significant focus (Y1). | C-suite & senior leaders were unclear on purpose & mandate of Helen's role (Y1). | There are advantages of an internal coach versus an external coach. |
| Good relationship between HR & Helen – sharing insight & support (Y1). | Connection between Helen & HR lost (Y2 & Y3). | Relationship between organisation & coach should not rest solely with the leader – keep connected. |
| Helen provided on-tap advice to team members & others across Consulting Services (Y1 & Y2). | By Year Three use of external coach was out of line with Green Apple Co's strategic approach (Y3). | Ensure there is clarity of coach role, priorities & mandate. |
| Staff in Consulting Services liked & trusted Helen & appreciated her support (Y1 & Y2). | | |

# Coach perspective

# 7

*Helen Zink*

---

## HOW TO READ CHAPTER SEVEN

I am Helen, the Coach in this story, and this is how this chapter fits into the overall book.

The five system elements covered in this book each describe their own versions of their development story in Section B. This includes thoughts on whether the approach and interventions used in this case, described in Chapter Three, were useful, what was good, what was challenging and what was learnt from the experience. Using a movie analogy, Section B involves five "parallel plots," whereby the same story is narrated by different characters, with each character describing themselves and the other main characters in the movie.

Chapter Seven is one of the parallel plots – the Coach's perspective of the story. I narrate my own version of the journey, and Figure 7.1 illustrates my view of the system. In this chapter, I discuss the Team, Michael (Leader), Consulting Services (Function) and Green Apple Co (Organisation), myself (Coach) and the role of my Supervision and Other Support networks in this case.

Content for this chapter comes from: Notes from team coaching and supervision sessions, ad hoc one-to-one coaching and other conversations, feedback from team development sessions, and my memory.

---

DOI: 10.4324/9781003367789-9

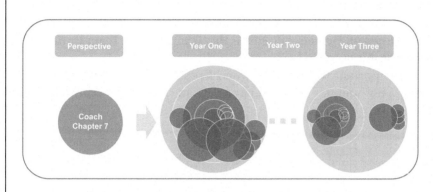

Figure 7.1: Coach's perspective of system

I am the Coach in this case, and I was also a member of the Team I was coaching in Year One. When I started my role with Green Apple Co, I was very excited and optimistic about being part of the "experiment." Although new to team coaching, I was confident I could contribute a great set of tools, techniques, experiences and knowledge (more in Chapter Two). I walked into the system knowing that my role was not well defined, and the Team were green. However, there were many surprises and disappointments along the way, and it felt like I was riding a "stay or leave see-saw" throughout the engagement.

## The Team

The first system element I discuss is the Team, and the Team from my perspective is illustrated in Figure 7.2.

It is important to note that when I refer to the Team, I mean a collective and unique entity separate from individual team members (Theory Break 7.1).

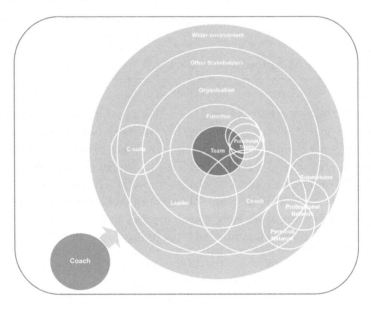

Figure 7.2: Coach's perspective of Team

## THEORY BREAK 7.1: CLIENT IS THE TEAM

The ICF Team Coaching Core Competencies (2020b) state that a critical difference between one-to-one coaching and team coaching "is the nature of the client . . . The client in a team coaching context is a team as a single entity, comprising multiple individuals." The standards go on to say that team coaches need to remain objective, not favour any particular team member or members, and any and all content of discussions with individual team members must remain confidential and not shared with others in the team or with the team collectively.

## *Team development goal – HPT*

### Year One

The first month in my role was spent meeting stakeholders and understanding strategic drivers of change within Consulting Services and Green Apple Co. Once I felt I had digested enough, and themes began to emerge, I suggested the Team's development goal of "becoming a HPT" (Theory Break 3.1). I was confident the goal suggested was in line with Green Apple Co's overall people strategy and HPT approach, as discussed in Chapter Three. Although technically my suggestion was endorsed by Michael, the Team and HR, I got the sense they would have accepted anything I suggested at that point. I recall Rosa and Greg saying at the time, "We are not a team anyway, so it's not clear why this goal discussion is relevant."

"Not a team" rang alarm bells. Did the Team not see the reliance they had with each other to deliver services? Did they not see that in the eyes of stakeholders they were mutually accountable for all they delivered? I could see it, and Michael knew it, but the Team, or at least some team members, thought there was no commonality at all (Theory Break 7.2). It was clear I had a lot of work to do, and the Team were at a very early stage of maturity as Michael discussed in Chapter Five. (Theory Break 5.3).

---

### THEORY BREAK 7.2: GROUP VERSUS TEAM

Katzenbach and Smith (1993) explain that being a team is much more than calling yourself one, and the following characteristics distinguish a team from a group:

| Group | Team |
|---|---|
| Strong leader | Shared leadership |
| Individual accountability | Both individual and mutual accountability |
| Generic purpose | Purpose created themselves |
| Outputs are individual | Collective reliance |
| Effectiveness measured individually | Effectiveness measured collectively |

## Years Two and Three

At a higher level of maturity in Year Two, we reviewed whether the HPT goal was still appropriate, and the Team chose to retain the goal as originally worded.

During Year Three, I floated the idea that a HVT goal might be more appropriate (Theory Break 7.3). I was conscious that stakeholders were not considered enough in the Team's development programme. We had done some work on stakeholder mapping and creating personas, but there had been no direct input from stakeholders themselves. I hoped a change in wording might increase the Team's appetite to engage stakeholders directly in their development, but there was no traction, and the goal was not changed.

---

### THEORY BREAK 7.3: HIGH VALUE TEAM

Hawkins (2022) argues that "we need to understand that a team's performance can only be truly understood through its capacity to co-create value with most and / or all of its stakeholders . . . Its ability to create added value for an organisation." A focus on HPTs may result in performance measures based on bettering previous performance or outdoing other teams around them, rather than focusing on what stakeholders need and value.

---

## HPT Model – PERILL

### Years One and Two

As described in Chapter Three, the PERILL HPT model and questionnaire (Clutterbuck, 2020) (Theory Break 3.2) were used with the Team and adjusted to incorporate Green Apple Co's own HPT approach.

The selection of this model was riddled with confirmation bias (Theory Break 1.3). I was studying Clutterbuck's work at the time and made no attempt to consider the merits of other models or approaches that might suit the Team better. On my advice, the Team accepted the PERILL model. Again, I felt they would have accepted anything I suggested at that point.

### Year Three

Despite referring to the PERILL (Clutterbuck, 2020) framework frequently over the years, I sensed the Team were still struggling with relevance partly due to workload pressure and other environmental impacts (more later). Around the middle of the year, I made the call (with Michael's endorsement) to simplify everything we were working on, including the PERILL framework.

That simplification was the main motivation behind the apple tree metaphor (Theory Break 7.4), described in Chapter Three. I hoped a visual apple tree concept might help clarify how each element of the model was important and how elements interrelated.

---

### THEORY BREAK 7.4: METAPHORS

Metaphors are common in change management, therapy, coaching and coach supervision. The use of a metaphor we are familiar with allows our brains to understand a new and potentially complex situation by substituting complex mental processing with something we are familiar with, understand and can remember. Grimley (2010) uses the phrase "by-pass the analytical mind" for this phenomenon. Another way to describe it would be a comprehension short-cut.

---

The Team loved it! For the first time, I sensed energy and engagement in the room around PERILL. Note the "PERILL Plus" apple tree diagram illustrated in Figure 3.2 is not what I originally walked into the room with that day. We began the conversation with a simpler version of the diagram, including a tree and six PERILL elements, but nothing else.

The Team created the model in Figure 3.2 through discussion, bringing up the impact of:

- Weather and storms (unforeseen environmental impacts, such as building moves, "hailstorms," leaf spot, system glitches, funding challenges).
- Apples falling off the tree that were left to rot (depicting work that failed or was not used).
- Producing red apples when the farmer wanted green (failure of stakeholders to provide good briefs, or failure to meet briefs).
- Worms and birds deliberately attacking apples and the tree (stakeholders out to sabotage).

The Team emphasised that precious resources were exhausted managing the impact of all these factors and they needed to be explicit in their model.

They also insisted that team resilience and wellbeing (Theory Break 4.1) needed to be added as another key element, as it was crucial in their context – and "PERILL Plus" was born!

I felt like a very proud mother that day. As I reflect on the experience now, not only had the Team finally embraced the HPT model, they had created their own bespoke model. The Team was genuinely leading their own development! This was one of my proudest moments working with the Team, and in my team coaching career to date.

## Readiness for team development and coaching

### Year One

When I met them at the beginning of Year One, every member of the Team described a step up from their previous role, leading significant system and process changes, managing delivery issues, and recruiting staff into the new Consulting Services structure – all at the same time. It was also evident that most had little experience of leadership development and were sceptical of potential benefits.

Workload and scepticism manifested as resistance – strong resistance. The Team did not want to invest in development. In particular, they did not want to take days out of their busy diaries to attend team development sessions. I know they spoke to Michael about it, and he worked hard convincing them to attend.

The Team were focused on "horizon one" work (Theory Break 7.5), and Michael and I wanted to focus on "horizon two" and "horizon three" work, for at least one day a month. While all parties had the best of intentions, conflict around this caused tension within the system.

### Years Two and Three

Over time, as they describe in Chapter Four, the Team grew to see the connection between development work, collaboration, honest communication, collective problem solving and better performance. By the middle of Year Two, the Team were fully supporting team development – with the exception of Tom (more later).

As I reflect back on this change in the Team's attitude, I can see that as the Team grew and learnt together, and trust and psychological safety increased, there was also a change in intervention modality (Theory Break 3.5). The Team's development activity in Figures 3.4, 3.5 and 3.6 shows a

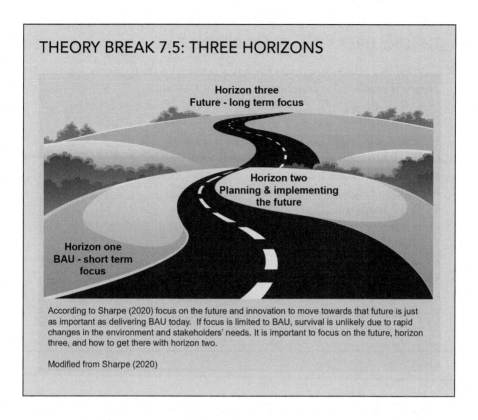

**THEORY BREAK 7.5: THREE HORIZONS**

Horizon three
Future - long term focus

Horizon two
Planning & implementing
the future

Horizon one
BAU - short term
focus

According to Sharpe (2020) focus on the future and innovation to move towards that future is just as important as delivering BAU today. If focus is limited to BAU, survival is unlikely due to rapid changes in the environment and stakeholders' needs. It is important to focus on the future, horizon three, and how to get there with horizon two.

Modified from Sharpe (2020)

more facilitative modality and the beginning of the Team's journey and more team coaching as time progressed. This reflects growth and maturity over time, and the Team's capacity to take on more uncertainty and responsibility for their own collective outcomes as they developed.

In Chapter Five, Michael describes change in the Team's maturity (Theory Break 5.3) from his perspective, and I could see it too. The Team had been operating at level one, "survival" mode in Year One, and I think they moved into "relationships" and "self-esteem" levels of maturity during Year Two.

## Overall reflection

While on the journey, and even now, I wondered whether the Team were actually ready for intensive development and team coaching in Year One, or, indeed, whether they were ready in Years Two or Three. Clutterbuck (2020) suggests certain criteria be considered before working with a team in this intensive way (Theory Break 7.6).

## THEORY BREAK 7.6: TEAM READINESS

Clutterbuck (2020) suggests criteria to consider to help assess whether a team is ready to be coached:

- Does the team see itself as a team; is there interdependence?
- If not, can/will/should it become a team?
- Are team members able to commit to open dialogue?
- Are there existing conflicts to resolve before starting?
- Is there a desire to experiment and change?
- Is the team too large?
- Is the team leader on board, and strong enough to handle challenges?
- Are there resources available to support change and actions taken?
- Does the team expect the coach to do the work for them?
- Does the leader expect the coach to become a surrogate leader?
- Does the team understand the coaching process; if not, will they try it?

While a useful list, I did not apply Clutterbuck's criteria with the Team at the beginning of Year One, or at any time during the three-year journey. If I had, answers to most questions would have been no. If we had have waited for Years Two or Three, when things were more "settled," we would have found that things were never "settled," and we would not have started at all.

Based on my experience with this case, I think Clutterbuck's team readiness criteria are useful considerations, but is it more about finding ways to mitigate areas of concern rather than waiting. My sense is a team is never ready, and in our increasingly complex and uncertain environment, there is never a good time to start. It is a "chicken and egg" situation, where some work needs to be done with a team to ready them for intensive development and coaching, and that happens by investing in development and coaching.

The trick is to do what the team can benefit from at the time – or Hawkins' (2022) concept of team maturity (Theory Break 5.3). Hawkins suggests the style and approach a coach uses with a team, or mix of modalities and interventions, should align with the team's maturity level. Although I did not formally make an attempt to assess the Team's maturity in this case and use that assessment to inform interventions and modalities used, I think I did subconsciously. And most of the time my intuition around appropriate interventions and modalities was accurate.

The context of team maturity also provides a rationale for why some interventions and modalities were more successful than others in this case. For example, facilitating a session focusing on the priority of deliverables during the "hailstorm" in Year One was successful, as the Team were in survival mode at that time. It also explains why focus on team purpose, using a coaching modality, gained greater traction in Year Three than it did early in Year One (more later).

## Team dynamics

### Year One

As I joined the Team in Year One, it was apparent that team members did not communicate well with each other or, as mentioned above, understand how their roles interrelated. Some tense relationship dynamics within the team did not help.

I was aware that Rosa and Drew did not seem to talk, even though their delivery processes were completely reliant on one another. Jane seemed to be afraid of Greg, and everyone had issues with Tom when he arrived. I was involved in some interesting dynamics as well, in particular with Taylor and Rosa (more later). The reason for all this tension was unclear, but the impact it had on the Team was crystal clear.

Lack of communication and tense relationships meant trust between team members was low, and with low individual trust in the system, team psychological safety (Theory Break 7.7) would be hard to establish and maintain. If team members were not talking to each other one-to-one, sharing meaningful and insightful conversations when together was a big ask.

As all team members seemed comfortable speaking with me, including sharing their concerns and complaints about each other, I found myself taking on the role of team counsellor and peacemaker; instead of clearing concerns with each other, they told me, expecting me to resolve their issues for them (more later).

As I took on the role/hat of team counsellor, I appreciated there were pros and cons. I am not suggesting that coaches should become team counsellors – the ICF (2020a) Code of Ethics specifically mentions that internal coaches need to take extra care managing their privileged role and potential conflicts of interest. However, I do suggest that circumstances provided the perfect environment for me to build trust with each team member. Those informal one-to-one conversations and coaching moments

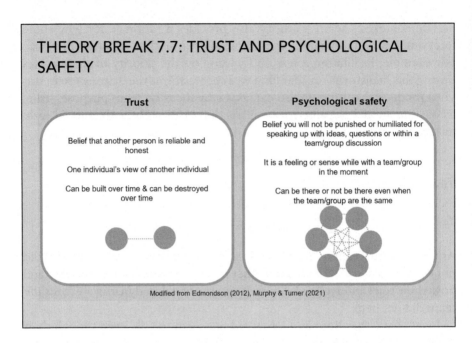

## THEORY BREAK 7.7: TRUST AND PSYCHOLOGICAL SAFETY

**Trust**

Belief that another person is reliable and honest

One individual's view of another individual

Can be built over time & can be destroyed over time

**Psychological safety**

Belief you will not be punished or humiliated for speaking up with ideas, questions or within a team/group discussion

It is a feeling or sense while with a team/group in the moment

Can be there or not be there even when the team/group are the same

Modified from Edmondson (2012), Murphy & Turner (2021)

was a significant benefit of being an internal coach (more later). As trust built, I was able to support team members to work through their relationship issues for themselves.

Another important team dynamic that played out during Year One was the "who's the boss" event, elaborated on from the Team's perspective in Chapter Four. I will not repeat full details here, but I do consider it a pivotal moment in the Team's growth journey. During that event, I witnessed team members challenge Michael and raise concerns in an open forum for the first time outside a development session – a great example of psychological safety and collective contracting in a real-world environment. The lead-up to the event also illustrated that in my role as Coach, I was part of, and disrupted the Team's system (Theory Break 7.8) – sometimes positively, and sometimes negatively.

## THEORY BREAK 7.8: COACH IS PART OF THE SYSTEM

Hawkins and Turner (2020) remind us that coaches are part of the system they work in and with. Coaches both influence and are influenced by systems they are part of. They all bring their own ways of thinking, interpreting and communicating, and are biased in what they are studying, curious about or interested in. All coaches have filters through which they see and influence everything they interact with.

I refer to contracting often in this chapter, a term drummed into me over and over when I began team coach training and supervision. The "who's the boss" situation was a great example of the importance of multi-stakeholders contracting within a CAS (Theory Break 7.9). The EMCC Team Coaching Competencies (2020) identify multi-stakeholder contracting and relationship management as a core standard for team coaches.

## THEORY BREAK 7.9: CONTRACTING IN TEAM COACHING

"Contracting is the process of agreeing boundaries and is a dialogue that establishes and then sustains a relationship," according to Turner, Lucas and Whitaker (2018).

Hawkins and Turner (2020) and Hawkins (2021, 2022) say that from their experience, contracting and re-contracting lies at the heart of STC. There are many types of contracts to consider:

- Business contracts – formal commercial agreements.
- Evaluation contracts – how progress will be tracked and measured.
- Process contracts – logistics of timing, responsibilities, session format and content, tools used, actions taken.
- Roles and boundaries – who is responsible and is not responsible for what, including what roles the team leader, team and coach play.
- Psychological contracts – expectations among parties.

Clutterbuck (2020) provides examples of common team coaching challenges resulting from insufficient contracting:

- Leader transferring responsibility to coach.
- Coach upsetting team by challenging them too hard.

- Coach upsetting the leader and team by taking over aspects of the team leaders role.
- Team assuming coach is there to solve their problems.
- Team assuming coach will do the work for them.
- Lack of clear responsibility for actions taken.
- Coaching work not relevant to team's needs at the time.
- Team assuming coach will know the answers.

## Year Two

Dynamics between team members and resulting trust between them appeared to improve during Year Two. Formal one-to-one coaching with Jane (more later) also helped the situation. One of the first things we worked on was her relationship with Greg – which improved considerably. While Tom was still completely anti-development, his concerns seemed less prominent in Year Two.

My sense was that trust and collective psychological safety was much stronger in Year Two, despite high movement in team membership during the year, described in Chapter Two. The Team seemed more open, challenged each other, contributed much more, and were very accepting of their new members.

## Year Three

Early Year Three, I sensed dynamics and trust between team members had shifted again. Although I was an external supplier of services at that time and no longer had visibility of what the Team were working on day-to-day, I felt they were in survival mode again, and had slipped down the team maturity hierarchy (Theory Break 5.3).

What I did experience first-hand was the de-prioritisation of team development. Team days were frequently cancelled, shortened or de-scoped, and I suspected other BAU team meetings and one-to-one time was de-prioritised the same way. I recall physically feeling a decline in trust and psychological safety in the room when I was with the Team – it was a strange and uncomfortable sensation.

At around the same time, I noticed team members were trying to hijack one-to-one time with me. As part of the monthly team development cycle, we were supposed to be talking about session content and feedback; instead, they wanted to talk about issues they had with each other – another sign that trust had declined.

How did I respond? Well, thankfully much better than my response in Year One – I kept the correct hat on this time! I successfully avoided the counsellor role and, instead, confronted them collectively in a team session.

I held up my coaching mirror (Theory Break 7.10) and I presented them with my hypothesis, something like:

> I am hearing that you are working really hard. As a result, you are spending less time together as a team and one-to-one and I know for a fact that team development has been de-prioritised. My hypothesis is that spending less time together has resulted in reduced trust and psychological safety, and that decline has encouraged you to work in a more siloed and individual way, reinforcing reduced trust and psychological safety. Ultimately, this pattern is decreasing the quality of your work and increasing your workload.

They agreed. Their responses included phrases like: "we have lost something valuable," "we want it back," "we have hit a bump" and "we need to invest more time together to get back to what we had." And they did! The Team committed to spending more collective time together, more one-to-one time, and regular team development sessions were back on track.

---

### THEORY BREAK 7.10: COACHING MIRROR

One of the roles of a coach is to hold a mirror for clients, sharing observations to help them gain insight. ICF Core Competencies (2019) say coaches need to "share observations, insights and feelings, without attachment, that have the potential to create new learning for the client."

More specifically, when working with teams, ICF Team Coaching Competencies (2020b) state that team coaches are expected to "Challenge the team's assumptions, behaviours, and meaning-making processes to enhance their collective awareness or insight. If harnessed properly, this can greatly enhance team performance."

---

After discussing the event with Tammy in supervision, I cancelled one-to-one pre- and post-team session discussions as insurance. I wanted to discourage the system from tempting me back into a team counsellor role.

Less opportunity to talk to me might encourage team members to talk to each other and resolve their own issues instead.

## Intervention (A) – Team development sessions

### Year One

Chapter Three describes the process and cycle of team development sessions in Year One, and Figures 3.4, 3.5 and 3.6 show intervention topics and delivery modalities used across all three years. I will not repeat details of the entire process here, instead picking up on points of interest or significant events.

### Flexible content

Agendas were set in advance, and I spent considerable time preparing content, researching, and briefing team members and Michael on topics. However, in reality, sessions did not follow the agendas, and were very fluid and dynamic. Planned content changed frequently leading up to a session, on the morning of a session, and often during sessions, depending on where the team was at and "hot topics" at the time. I knew the EMCC (2020) Team Coaching Standards specifically state that coaches must "adapt and experiment in order to support the team to maximise awareness and insight." But in honesty the EMCC guidelines were not my motivation. I could not see the point of sticking to an agenda that was agreed weeks in advance if other topics were more relevant and useful for the Team at the time. As I was part of the Team and working in their system alongside them every day, I had a very good sense of what was relevant and what conversations might be useful.

I tried my best to partner with Michael as agenda changes were made in the moment. Sometimes we talked during breaks in sessions, sometimes we stepped out of the room for a quick chat, and sometimes we openly contracted in front of the Team. I think we were role-modelling well in this area. An even better approach would have been to contract all changes in the room, with the entire Team collectively.

Due to the flexible nature of development content, the Team's development plan was more of a retrospective record of topics covered than an advance plan, as discussed in Chapter Three.

There was a downside to the highly flexible approach. A lot of pre-prepared collateral was never used. Initially, I assumed material would be recycled and used in later sessions, but in most cases the Team had moved on by the next session, and other topics took precedence.

## Flexible modality

In addition to flexible content, delivery modality (Theory Break 3.5) was fluid and constantly changing as well. I was aware that the ICF (2020b) Team Coaching Core Competencies state that coaches must "maintain distinction between team coaching, team building, team training, team consulting, team mentoring, team facilitation, and other team development modalities." I recall Tammy, my supervisor, challenging me on this point too. She suggested I make a call on modality when planning development content and explicitly indicate modality on agendas.

However, I did not take on her suggestion for two reasons:

- I was confident the Team and Michael had no interest in which modality was used; their priority was gaining benefit from content.
- If a particular modality was indicated in advance, it would likely change in the moment anyway, depending on what I thought was best for the Team.

I will explain what I mean. An activity may have been heavily facilitated to begin with, and if interesting topics were uncovered, I would likely switch to a team coaching modality to enable further exploration. Conversely, my intended modality may have been team coaching, but I would switch to facilitation or teaching if the Team were not in the right headspace for the intended conversation or were stuck.

## À la carte menu

An "à la carte menu" is a good metaphor to describe team session interventions and flexibility, refer to Figure 7.3:

- The Team's needs were considered in context of the system (a craving for apple pie).
- Topics were selected from options identified in the Team's draft development plan (menu), or "hot topics" in the moment (daily specials).

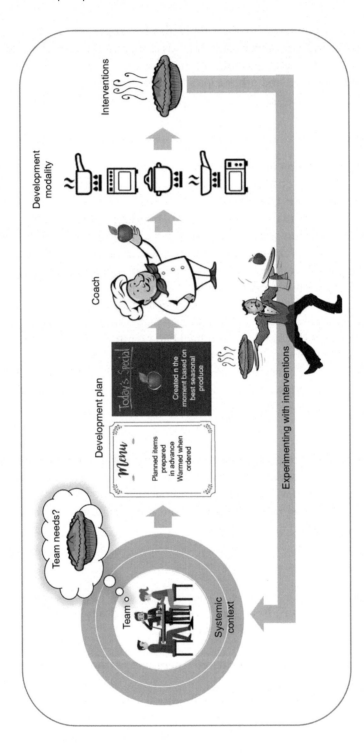

Figure 7.3: À la carte interventions

- I selected the modality that I thought would be most useful (poach, bake, fry, steam), or a combination of all.
- Resulting in the intervention (apple pie).
- If the intervention was successful, good; if not, another selection would be made from the menu (perhaps apple crumble), and we would try again.

## Psychological safety

The first team development session is vividly etched into my memory. Process-wise, everything went well, and, given it was the first session, everyone was well prepared although a little apprehensive, including me. As described in Chapter Three, the first part of team days focused on development activity, and the second part covered strategy. In this first session, the morning went well. We worked on fundamentals, such as team ground rules and getting to know each other better, all aimed at building psychological safety.

During the strategic part of the day, each member of the team was responsible for talking through their own assigned strategic initiatives. Unfortunately, some critique was given and/or interpreted harshly – with emotional responses. Although I heard emotional behaviour was common with this Team, it was the first time I saw it first-hand.

I was stunned, and even more surprised that I was left to find a way forward and get us back on track. From memory I suggested a break, and we juggled content so some team members could take a back seat for a while. We continued the day, but it was tense.

On reflection it would have been better to park the agenda and draw the Team's attention to the emotional event itself, and the application, or lack of application, of new ground rules (created two hours prior). However, I realise now I did not have capacity or capability to deal with the situation differently at the time. In that moment, I was in shock, and the lack of psychological safety in the room applied to me too (Theory Break 7.7).

My experience in that first session significantly impacted my impression of the Team, the Leader, the system, and the entire three-year time period I worked with the Team. It was also the catalyst for arranging professional one-to-one team coaching supervision. I was scared, out of my depth and I knew I needed help!

Strong emotions continued to surface in team sessions during Year One from time to time. Again, I did not have the knowledge or experience I needed to address behaviour openly with the collective Team, opting instead to talk to individuals during breaks or after team sessions to try to smooth things over. Looking back, not ideal, but at least the approach allowed us to move forward.

## Valuable interventions and challenging topics

The success of specific interventions within team sessions was mixed – not surprising given the "à la carte menu" approach described above. Some sessions resonated well, with great feedback from the Team, and some were less impactful. From my perspective, some of our more memorable and useful work in Year One included:

- Roles in team – small plastic construction blocks were used to build models representing roles and connections between roles in the team.
- Stakeholder analysis – identifying main stakeholder groups and their possible perceptions of the Team, using stakeholder persona and stakeholder radar (Mayfield, 2015) techniques.
- Positive Leadership (Cameron, 2012) – each member of the team committed to an area to work on and pairs assigned to hold each other to account.

As mentioned above, an area the Team struggled with early on was collective purpose. My first suggestion to work on purpose was met with staunch resistance. I recall Greg saying, "We have our ground rules, a Consulting Services purpose, Green Apple Co values and strategy, and all this collateral already. Why do we need a purpose for our team as well? It's all too complicated."

I was not getting support to continue with the topic from anyone else in the room, and as a result, the topic was parked. I made another attempt to work on purpose later in the year, and while some time was spent on it, there was no real buy-in, and the topic was parked again (more later).

## Broken commitments

As we progressed through team development sessions over the year, commitment to pre- and post-work deteriorated. Preparation and pre-reading were not done, and areas agreed to be actioned between sessions were not prioritised. I shared my observations with the Team several times, without much reaction. This development work was incredibly important to me; it was the focus of my professional life and future. I was very frustrated and felt the burden of the Team's success resting on my shoulders (more later).

## Year Two

Team sessions in Year Two ran similarly to Year One, with Michael taking a more active role during the year. In line with his decision to work on his leadership style, he was more invested in designing agendas and content prior to sessions and was a more active co-coach in sessions as well (Theory Break 7.14). I was enjoying Michael's increased enthusiasm, although the Team's lack of action outside of sessions continued.

In the latter part of Year Two, a new challenge emerged. Physical logistics became an issue – by that, I mean confusion around responsibility for securing venues, equipment, catering and such. As I was an external service provider, I assumed those matters were not my responsibility, yet I often found myself pulled into logistical issues at the last moment. I found the situation incredibly distracting and frustrating, which contributed to my energy drain (more later).

## Year Three

Ongoing challenges and frustrations I describe above, and energy issues I talk more about later, really made me wonder whether it was time to go. Circumstances were impacting me so severely that I wondered whether I was providing services in accordance with ICF Code of Ethics (2020a) and I questioned whether I was "fit for purpose" (Theory Break 7.11). My energy level was zero, and I was very close to walking away from the engagement.

## THEORY BREAK 7.11: "FIT FOR PURPOSE" COACH

Team coaching is complex and requires a multi-skilled and dynamic approach. Team coaches must ensure they are "fit for purpose" at all times. ICF Code of Ethics (2020a) states that coaches need to "recognise . . . personal limitations or circumstances that may impair, conflict with or interfere with . . . coaching performance."

More specifically, the EMCC (2020) team coaching standards state that self-care and resilience are required, and team coaches must "develop and implement appropriate processes to maintain resilience and self-care and the active management of . . . their own needs." The ICF Code of Ethics also states that coaches must "reach out for support to determine . . . action to be taken and, if necessary, promptly seek relevant professional guidance."

Supervision is often the first port of call and best approach to maintain competence, capability and capacity (Turner, Lucas and Whitaker, 2018), and build reflective practice and the self-awareness required for team coaching.

## Formal contracting

Before making a final decision on whether to stay or leave, I discussed the situation with Tammy. She suggested I consider the unique learning experience I was part of and balance that fairly with the frustration I felt.

She also suggested that amending the formal written contract between myself and Green Apple Co might help, including detailed expectations of team members, Michael and me. Although Michael agreed to change the contract, and we found common ground on details reasonably smoothly, I felt incredibly uncomfortable about it. To me, it felt like I had failed. The arrangement implied that professional trust between parties was so low that verbal contracting was not sufficient.

Despite my discomfort around formal contract changes, improvements were instant! Why had we not tried this earlier?

## Rotating leadership

Another change in Year Three was the decision to rotate leadership for development purposes amongst team members, as described in Chapter Three. The nominated leader in any given month was my key contact point in relation to agenda, content, pre-work and logistics. In addition, the nominated leader would be my co-coach in sessions. When Michael suggested the rotation concept, I loved it. It would be a great opportunity to practise shared leadership, and I thought more diversity of input would increase creativity and buy-in of content as well.

While great in principle, the rotation concept came with some challenges:

- Team members had different levels of experience, enthusiasm and capacity to be involved.
- Team members found the co-coach role in sessions difficult to maintain while contributing as a member of the Team as well.
- Michael took over the facilitation or co-coaching role when he found space to do so.
- The Team often deferred to Michael for decisions.
- Out of habit I often re-contracted session content with Michael rather than the nominated leader or the Team as a whole.
- There were differing views of priority, resulting in topics jumping around from session to session rather than building and reinforcing over time.

We persevered with rotating leadership anyway, with the intention of discussing the challenges listed above as content within sessions themselves. However, we never got the chance!

## Cancelled sessions

The first two sessions of the year went ahead as planned, and then, for the first time, sessions were either de-scoped at the last minute or cancelled. I spoke to Michael about it, and he said he was intentionally leaving all decisions around team development to the Team to make for themselves, including the call on whether to cancel sessions. Although I felt the Team were no longer focused on development, at least they were making that decision themselves – a silver lining from a challenging situation I suppose.

Although I understood the Team's rationale for cancelling sessions I was concerned about lack of continuity, the impact of "hailstorm No.2" that was playing out at the time, and the loss of psychological safety I was sensing as described above. It seemed pointless to me to continue working with the Team at all. I also felt that staying around while the Team imploded would adversely impact my professional reputation. Again, I was on the verge of leaving – admitting defeat.

I was very unhappy, but Michael assured me that he and the Team remained committed to the development journey; the only issue was capacity.

## Valuable interventions

Despite challenges with continuity, there were four intervention areas towards the middle and end of Year Three which were defining moments for the Team, and also significant wins in my team coach development journey.

- Trust and psychological safety (Theory Break 7.7)
  As discussed earlier in this chapter, by holding a mirror up, the Team recognised themselves that psychological safety had been lost and they wanted to invest in getting it back.

- Team purpose
  There was a third and successful attempt to develop team purpose. The difference this time was Michael's level of engagement on the topic, and he rallied the Team to co-create content.

- "PERILL Plus" HPT model
  In Chapter Three, and earlier in this chapter, I talk about the Team creating their own bespoke HPT model. The creation of this model was completely unplanned and led by the Team – a good example of their increased maturity, as well as mine.

- Good endings
  The "good endings" exercise which both the Team and Michael mentioned in Chapters Four and Five. It was the right intervention at the right time for the Team, Leader and for me. I expand on this next.

## Good endings

Soon after the Team's discussion around regaining lost psychological safety, Michael let us know his plans to leave Green Apple Co. As I was processing where the Team was at and what the change would mean, I was drawn to the work of Bridges' (2017) transition model (Theory Break 7.12) and the importance of "good endings."

I thought the best use of remaining team development time that year would be the creation of a team story, reflecting on the past, acknowledging hard times, celebrating good times, and marking Michael's contribution. I suggested the idea to the Team, and they loved it. In fact, they wanted to take it further, and insisted we use the full Bridges model and work on identifying

## THEORY BREAK 7.12: TRANSITIONS

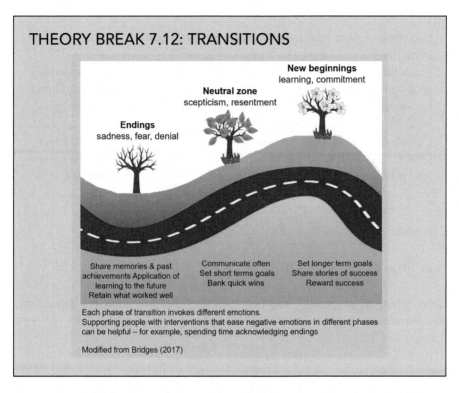

New beginnings
learning, commitment

Neutral zone
scepticism, resentment

Endings
sadness, fear, denial

Share memories & past achievements Application of learning to the future Retain what worked well

Communicate often Set short terms goals Bank quick wins

Set longer term goals Share stories of success Reward success

Each phase of transition invokes different emotions.
Supporting people with interventions that ease negative emotions in different phases can be helpful – for example, spending time acknowledging endings

Modified from Bridges (2017)

future development priorities as well. The Team was really getting to grips with leading their own development and demanding things from me – it was great!

From my perspective, those final few sessions in Year Three were some of the Team's and my best work. To prime the conversation I prepared a timeline in advance, consisting of major past events to spark memories, similar to Figures 2.9, 2.10 and 2.11. In the sessions themselves, the Team walked through that timeline, with each of them telling parts of the story most relevant to them, adding anecdotes and any missing information as they went along. My role was making sure that everyone had an opportunity to contribute, and everyone had said all they wanted to say. It was powerful work – a form of narrative coaching (Theory Break 7.13).

## THEORY BREAK 7.13: NARRATIVE COACHING WITH TEAMS

Drake (2010) explains that a narrative approach in coaching is useful as explicit verbal stories told indicate perception of yourself and also surface potential opportunities for development and changes in behaviour.

Drake goes on to say that in a team context, a narrative approach helps a team to "surface and sort through (both) their individual and collective stories as ways to address conflict, align their purpose, or shift patterns of engagement." There are other benefits as well, I think, as the process of collective storytelling is an opportunity to create increased trust and psychological safety, align what has been learnt together, and identify and agree on further opportunities.

## Co-coaching

### Year One

Co-coaching is recommended best practice in team coaching situations, recognising the high demands and stresses of working in a CAS (Theory Break 7.14).

### THEORY BREAK 7.14: BENEFITS OF CO-COACHING

Best practice team coaching is for coaches to partner together and co-coach. While this adds complexity to the system, it also brings many advantages. ICF Team Coaching Core Competencies (2020b) explain that the use of a co-coach

> will allow the team coach to be more present in the coaching session . . . It takes the pressure off the singular coach, given the significant amount of information emerging during team coaching sessions. A co-coach can help to observe team dynamics, team and individual behaviour patterns, provide alternative perspectives, and model team behaviour."

As mentioned above, Michael was essentially my co-coach in Year One, as he was involved in agenda setting, supporting content, and co-facilitating at times. We also spent time after sessions debriefing, reviewing team members' feedback, any challenges, and talking through changes to make going forward – at least, that was my interpretation of our agreement.

Unfortunately, my interpretation of our agreement did not always play out in reality. Michael was inconsistent, in that I never knew how prepared or engaged or physically and mentally present he would be in sessions until we were actually in sessions. The inconsistency I experienced was one of the factors contributing to tension in our relationship (more later).

Michael suggested several times we try using an independent coach for team sessions. I doubt his motivation was linked to the inconsistent support issue described above. I also doubt that he was aware of ICF recommended best practice. I think he just wanted my input as a member of the Team, and to do that, I needed to let go, or at least loosen the reins on the Coach role.

We experimented with another coach in the room in one session. It was a very uncomfortable experience for me – I remember being so focused on the other coach and her style, and what role I needed to play, I did not contribute much.

When I asked the Team for feedback on the experience, I recall Rosa saying, "It felt almost the same as you. She (external coach) was using very similar techniques and questions." The Team seemed comfortable enough with the experience, and Michael continued to offer support, but I pushed back.

Interestingly, co-coaching came up in supervision sessions several times, and I recall brushing it off as impractical, which was not entirely true. I was making excuses.

Looking back now, I recognise my resistance was driven by control issues. I had a lot at stake in the Coach role – I wanted to take credit for the "experiment" and did not want to share the glory and pain that came with it with anyone else. Unfortunately, I had put my own needs ahead of the best interests of the Team, my learning experience, and my health.

## Years Two and Three

The co-coaching situation in Year Two was very similar to Year One, with Michael effectively in the co-coach role. In Year Three, in line with the rotating leadership model, team members took turns in the co-coach role, as described above.

By Year Three, I had fully transitioned into an external coach mindset, and was working hard on growing my own business and client base. I did think about involving an external co-coach, but to be honest, I was focused on cashflow and not willing to share revenue at that point.

Another area I did not explore – and should have – was working with an internal co-coach. By Year Three, several of Green Apple Co's HR staff had completed some level of team coaching training. I think partnering with an internal coach would have been beneficial for them, me and the Team. In *The team coaching casebook* the editors (Clutterbuck, Turner & Murphy, 2022) comment on a chapter I contributed about this case saying: "We wonder how the scenario may have been different for this coach if an external (or internal) co-coach had worked alongside them."

Collaborating more with others and co-coaching is one of my personal development objectives, which I touch on again in Chapter Eleven.

## Intervention (B) – One-to-one formal and informal coaching of team members

### Year One

As described above, informal coaching was prevalent during Year One. As I was part of the Team, I attended all team meetings, met one-to-one with each member, and interacted with them in delivering other aspects of my role. There were many opportunities to work on development areas, suggest corrections in the moment, and role-model behaviours. This worked really well and was one of the most significant advantages of being both an internal coach and a part of the Team.

### Year Two

During Year Two, informal one-to-one coaching continued as I became an external service provider, as I still interacted regularly with team members.

Also, during this period, Michael asked me to work with Jane in a formal arrangement. She was struggling with expectations of her role, which impacted her ability to deliver on that role and build relationships with other team members. At first, I was hesitant, concerned that I would not be independent enough to serve Jane well. However, I agreed to try it, on the condition that we reassessed along the way.

To create as much formality as possible, I insisted that all parties – Jane, Michael and me – sign a formal internal coaching agreement, clarifying our respective roles and responsibilities. I also asked Michael to join sessions on occasion, to ensure we were all aligned and discussing Jane's progress.

As mentioned above, outcomes from the formal coaching programme were better than any of us anticipated. By the second session, Jane had shifted her mindset and was embracing ways to make her role work for her. I noticed that relationships between Jane and Michael, Jane and Greg, and Jane and other team members improved in parallel.

## Year Three

Once one-to-one pre- and post-team session meetings were cancelled partway through Year Three, as mentioned above, there was no opportunity for one-to-one conversation at all, apart from incidental interactions during development sessions themselves.

## *Outcomes*

## Year One

As we set off on our "experiment," I do not recall discussing how we would measure success or progress – not good methodology; all experiments should involve a baseline or control set and a predetermined measurement methodology!

Despite no formal KPIs, we did have two tangible measures available: The HPT assessment, measured at six-month intervals (refer to Figure 3.7) and engagement scores (refer to Figure 3.8). Neither measure increased in Year One, which disappointed me. I recall taking to Tammy about it in supervision. While I appreciated the environment was tough, and tried to reframe my expectations, it still hurt. Fortunately, verbal feedback collected from the Team was more positive – the Team include examples of their own feedback in Chapter Four.

## Years Two and Three

Improvements were more visible in Years Two and Three. Both Figures 3.7 and 3.8 show clear upward trends in measures – I was much happier!

Verbal feedback collected from team members in Years Two and Three are included in Chapter Four as well. Although most comments were consistently positive, I did notice a change in the type of content over time. Early in the journey, feedback seemed superficial, for example, "We have each other's backs." Later in the journey, feedback seemed more specific and meaningful, for example, "In the past, Michael shielded us from a lot of organisational politics, and now we shield and support each other and grow our collective reputation." Although I see a clear distinction now, I did not notice at the time, and consequently lost the opportunity to review my observations with the Team during the journey itself.

## Overall reflection

The concept of team maturity is introduced by Michael in Chapter Five (Theory Break 5.3). From my perspective, I observed an increase in the Team's maturity too. However, as indicated throughout this section, their maturity bounced around; it was not a nice tidy linear trend. I have added a graph to the team maturity concept in Figure 7.4 indicating my perspective of their maturity track. Note that in Year Three, my thoughts are based on what I could see and extrapolate from team development sessions, rather than seeing the Team first-hand in their BAU environment.

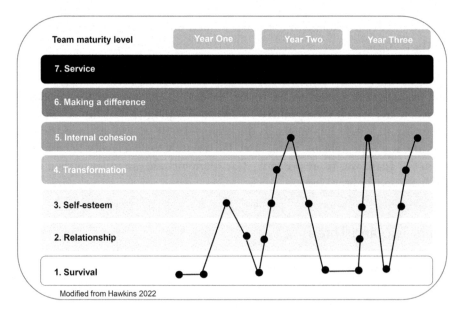

Figure 7.4: Coach's perspective of change in Team

We knew from the outset that the Team's development journey would take time and investing in tracking that journey would have made good sense. Hawkins and Turner (2020) offer a useful guide to measurement frameworks based on both tangible and intangible measures (Theory Break 7.15) that we could have used.

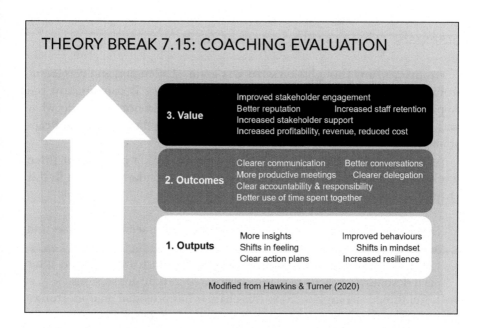

**THEORY BREAK 7.15: COACHING EVALUATION**

**3. Value**
Improved stakeholder engagement
Better reputation   Increased staff retention
Increased stakeholder support
Increased profitability, revenue, reduced cost

**2. Outcomes**
Clearer communication   Better conversations
More productive meetings   Clearer delegation
Clear accountability & responsibility
Better use of time spent together

**1. Outputs**
More insights   Improved behaviours
Shifts in feeling   Shifts in mindset
Clear action plans   Increased resilience

Modified from Hawkins & Turner (2020)

## Measurement possibilities

Unfortunately, we did not take the Hawkins and Turner (2020) framework, or any other measurement framework, into consideration – a significant opportunity missed.

Some simple things we could have done to enhance measurement include:

- Extending the HPT assessment to include a sample of stakeholders, providing a 360-view of scores.
- Assessing the "Consulting Services industry benchmark" more frequently, providing measures of change in functional processes and

efficiency (refer to Figure 4.4). Although used prior, this measure was not actively tracked during the period of this case.

- Formal collection of intangible measures from the Team and stakeholders, providing rich verbal 360 feedback. Most verbal feedback contained in this book was collected primarily for inclusion in this book, rather than a yardstick during the case period.

## Summary – Coach's perspective of Team

A summary of my thoughts on what was good, challenging and was learnt from my perspective of the Team and their journey is contained in the Appendix to Chapter Seven. As described above, I did not always do what was best for the Team, however, I did my best with the capacity and capability I had at the time.

As I reflect on the long list of learning areas, it strikes me that the three levels of learning I introduced in Figure 1.3 are particularly relevant in this chapter so far:

- Level one learning – for example, flexible team session agendas and adapting interventions in the moment.
- Level two learning – for example, feedback from team members after each development session was incorporated into future sessions.
- Level three learning – writing this chapter has provided an opportunity to ponder on my resistance to partner with an external co-coach.

As I write this book, my increased knowledge and experience with team coaching since leaving the Team has enabled me to interpret and gain insight from this story in ways I was not able to at the time. I discuss this more below, and Tammy talks about it even more eloquently in Chapter Eight as she talks through reflection and reflexivity.

## The Leader

I talk about Michael next, my boss, client and friend. My perspective of him within the system is illustrated in Figure 7.5.

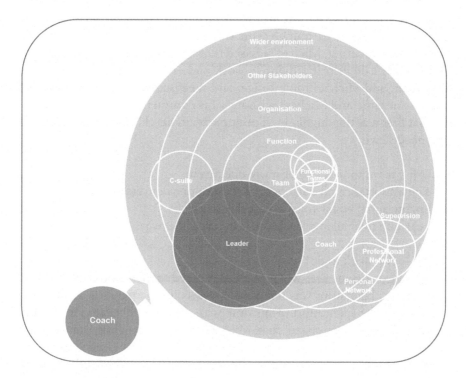

Figure 7.5: Coach's perspective of Leader

### Leadership style

Year One

Michael reflects on the importance of his leadership role in the Team's journey in Chapter Five (Theory Break 5.4) and I acknowledge that. After all, without Michael's sponsorship and support, this story would not exist. At the same time, from my perspective working with Michael was confusing and challenging.

### First impressions

Michael described himself as having high IQ and low EQ. My first impressions of him aligned with his self-view. He was extremely passionate about Green

Apple Co, Consulting Services and the Team. It was his passion and long-term vision to be world class that drew me to the Coach role in the first place. However, it did not take long to observe a "top-down" leadership style, little delegation, and retention of information and control.

I will never forget the first team meeting I attended, the day after I started. Michael spoke around 90 per cent of the time, leaving a few minutes for others to quickly run through their priorities at the end. In that same meeting, Michael advised that one-to-one conversations with him would be de-prioritised due to workload – to which I openly objected. The Team and Michael took notice, and we discussed the importance of one-to-one time and Michael withdrew his comment.

That first meeting highlighted multiple team development opportunities that needed work:

- Using team time together more effectively.
- The importance of, and effective, one-to-one conversations.
- Encouraging equal voice across the Team.
- Learning to challenge each other in respectful ways.

I had a lot of work to do!

I was also curious that while Michael seemed to like control and talking in meetings, his nature was reclusive. He was not particularly visible, and I understood he spent most of his time with the C-suite, located in another building. I also appreciated that Michael was under a huge amount of pressure from stakeholders both within and external to Green Apple Co. It seemed his relationship with his C-suite colleagues was mixed and quite tense at times too.

Michael was an enigma in many ways – a description I am confident he would endorse. On one hand, he was absolutely passionate and driven by his vision for the Team and Function, and on the other hand, his leadership style misaligned with that vision. It was clear that Michael needed to change his style if there was any hope of the Team moving toward their HPT goal, but in Year One he resisted that suggestion with great force.

Looking back now, there are things I could have done differently in those early days to support Michael's:

- Clearly communicated the misalignment of Michael's style and resulting implications with him and his boss, the CEO. Effectively enlisting CEO sponsorship.
- Insist Michael work with an external one-to-one coach in a formal way.
- Elicit support from Michael's C-suite colleagues.

I did talk to Michael about the misalignment of his leadership style –
constantly! On reflection, those messages were so frequent and mixed with
so much other information, it might have felt like nagging rather than a ser-
ious issue and genuine concern.

I talked to Michael about formal one-to-one coaching, offering to be his
coach – he declined. The notion of an independent external coach was not
pursued either.

I am also confident I would have received support from the CEO and
Michael's colleagues if I had asked for it. After all, it was clear right from the
start that they were expecting me to "fix him." However, at the time, it felt like
I would betray Michael's trust by involving others – I felt trapped.

## Accountability and responsibility

In line with Michael's "top-town" style, I observed and experienced confusion in relation to accountability and responsibility within the Team (Theory
Break 7.16). Michael seemed to be involved in everything, with "fingers in
many pies," resulting in confusion and inefficiency. I also thought Michael
was "too nice" at times – protecting and taking the blame for team members

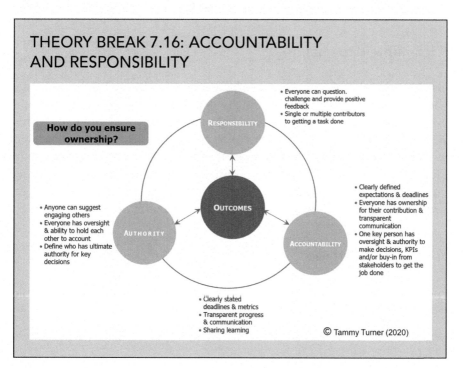

### THEORY BREAK 7.16: ACCOUNTABILITY AND RESPONSIBILITY

**How do you ensure ownership?**

**RESPONSIBILITY**
- Everyone can question, challenge and provide positive feedback
- Single or multiple contributors to getting a task done

**OUTCOMES**

**AUTHORITY**
- Anyone can suggest engaging others
- Everyone has oversight & ability to hold each other to account
- Define who has ultimate authority for key decisions

**ACCOUNTABILITY**
- Clearly defined expectations & deadlines
- Everyone has ownership for their contribution & transparent communication
- One key person has oversight & authority to make decisions, KPIs and/or buy-in from stakeholders to get the job done

- Clearly stated deadlines & metrics
- Transparent progress & communication
- Sharing learning

© Tammy Turner (2020)

when something they were responsible for went wrong. It was kind of him, but not necessarily the best thing for the Team in the long term.

At the beginning of Year One, it seemed that Michael was holding the roles of authority, accountability and responsibility for almost everything. Unless shared, he would never be able to delegate effectively and move out of the "top-down," hands-on cycle he was in. Although some attempts were made to clarify responsibility across the Team in Year One, I do not think there was full clarity and buy-in until the Year Two plan was created.

### Leadership vacuum trap

The Team talks about the "vacuum trap" (Theory Break 4.3) in Chapter Four, and Michael talks about it in Chapter Five, so I will not repeat details here. In short, I took on activities that would be expected of Michael – some were formally delegated, and some I took on unconsciously as gaps arose. While there were pros and cons to the situation, when Tom joined the Team and took on leadership responsibilities as well, the Team revolted.

While I think Michael took huge steps forward by sharing leadership with me and Tom, shifts in responsibility were not well communicated, and it took the "who's the boss" event, discussed above, to get the clarity we all needed.

### Commitment to change

Towards the end of Year One, Michael suddenly changed. It was like he had an epiphany overnight and finally decided to swim with the current rather than resist. During one of our team sessions near the end of the year, he made an open commitment to change his leadership style (refer to Figure 5.6). I do not know what triggered his sudden change – but I liked it! I was both relieved and proud, and I recall feeling as though the burden of changing Michael's style had shifted from me to him. Things were looking up, and I was looking forward to Year Two.

### Years Two and Three

Year Two began with great energy and Michael embracing his new leadership approach. While not perfect, and overzealous at times, it was great to see his commitment come to life. One of his key enabling initiatives was the Year Two plan, including very clear accountability and responsibility for strategic priorities amongst team members. The plan was shared across Consulting Services at a successful conference at the beginning of the year. I felt like we were finally on course and getting good traction – very exciting.

Unfortunately, later that same week, "leaf spot" hit, and most Year Two plan content was put on hold. Soon after, I left Green Apple Co as well. Although the Year Two plan was significantly de-scoped, and I no longer saw Michael working in a BAU context, I sensed his style was changing.

During Year Three, I had very little contact with Michael apart from team development days. I cannot comment on what his leadership style was like, but I sensed he was sustaining the more collaborative style I observed in Year Two.

## Overall reflection

I asked Michael to assess his own leadership maturity in Chapter Five, in line with Hawkins' (2021) model (Theory Break 5.6). My own thoughts on maturity differ slightly from his. While I agree that he was operating at "team manager" level at the beginning of Year One, I am less convinced of "team leadership" that year. While Michael articulated vision and long-term focus, I saw minimal evidence of that coming to life. In the context of Sharpe's (2020) Three Horizons (Theory Break 7.5), from my perspective he was operating within horizon one.

Evidence of "team leadership" and "team orchestrator" maturity levels became evident in Year Two, particularly at the beginning of the year. Michael was more collaborative, delegated more, communicated more, and the creation of the Year Two Plan provided clear accountability and responsibility across the Team.

I cannot comment on whether Michael reached higher levels of maturity in Year Three, as I only saw him for a few hours a month in team development sessions – a somewhat artificial environment where he may have been on his best behaviour. However, the Team were actively trying to share leadership within development sessions, so there was some first hand evidence of collaborative leadership.

## Intervention (C) – One-to-one informal coaching of leader

### Year One

Michael and I met frequently, sharing challenges and priorities, and I quickly became his lieutenant. As I was part of the Team, I spent time with him in normal day-to-day activity as well, so there was plenty of opportunity for informal one-to-one coaching. I would love to say the approach was something Michael and I planned and contracted together; however, it was not. It evolved organically as we spent time together and opportunities arose.

From my perspective, the ad hoc coaching experience was a constant battle. While I think Michael appreciated my input and took in much of what we talked through, I was fighting against resistance to focus on himself. I recall Michael saying in frustration, "Just tell me what I need to do [in relation to leadership], and I will do it." I had to break the news that cookie-cutter leadership models would not be effective in his circumstances – he needed to explore and create what would work best for him.

That conversation was the start of our work together on Michael's bespoke leadership model, which he talks about in Chapter Five (refer to Figure 5.6). The flexible leadership approach depicted in his model felt right to me at the time given the context and system. My encouragement of a bespoke approach was not based on a particular leadership philosophy I was aware of at the time. However, as I write this, I note work is being published in the area, notably *Real time leadership* (Noble & Kauffman, 2023).

I suggested a formal development plan, along with formal one-to-one coaching, would be a good way to explore leadership style options. Michael declined my suggestions, saying he preferred the ad hoc approach we had established and did not have the time or energy for a formal process. However, I suspected there might have been more to it:

- Perhaps he thought it was inappropriate for someone reporting to him to coach him (and he may have had a point).
- Perhaps he thought our already complex relationship would become even more complex (more later).
- Perhaps it was a control issue.
- Perhaps he was afraid of commitment or failure.

I sensed that control was a significant part of the challenge. In an interview about this case, Michael was asked what it was like having an internal coach as part of the team reporting to him. He replied with, "I was in a position where I had someone reporting to me with skills that I wanted to develop. It was challenging; it wasn't natural."

Despite Michael's resistance to do anything formal, I can only assume that his leadership epiphany, described above, was in some way influenced by the many ad hoc coaching and other conversations we had. I wonder if I had have made different choices earlier in the journey, such as asking Michael's boss for support, the epiphany would have occurred earlier in the journey. We will never know!

## Years Two and Three

There were fewer opportunities for one-to-one informal coaching in Year Two, and none at all in Year Three. I was not aware of any other ad hoc or formal coaching taking place in years Two or Three.

## *Relationship between Leader and Coach*

### Year One

So far, I have described Michael as a visionary, actively investing in change within the system. At the same time, his leadership style was inconsistent with that vision, certainly during Year One. There was a lot of frustration, confusion and tension in the system right from the start, and the relationship between Michael and me was both a product of and an aggravation to that tension.

## *System forces*

Michael and I supported each other. I wanted to help him be the best leader he could be, and he supported me with learning and career opportunities. I was his sympathetic ear, and he was my most supportive ally. We shared personal challenges and friendship as well. I think part of what drew us together was the lack of understanding and support I had from other parts of the organisation (more later), and he may have felt the same.

Our close relationship was obvious to others in Green Apple Co, reinforced by me taking on some of Michael's leadership activities, both officially and unofficially, as part of the "vacuum trap" described above. As mentioned above, Michael's boss, and others, used me as a go-between at times, expecting me to pass on messages and support him at the same time. System forces from all directions were reinforcing our connection and complexity in that connection.

## Transference

Rosa referred to Michael and me as "Mum and Dad" at times, and I really did feel like Michael's work wife. Although Rosa was probably joking, she was actually describing our relationship very accurately. Transference was in play on both professional and personal levels (Theory Break 7.17). On a professional level, Michael reminded me of previous bosses, as well as myself earlier in my career. On a personal level, he reminded me of my father in some ways, and also my brother. I cannot comment on characters I represented in Michael's life, but our relationship was riddled with transference and countertransference. Tammy expands on this more in Chapter Eight.

---

### THEORY BREAK 7.17: TRANSFERENCE

Lewis (2019) explains that transference stems from unconscious struggles causing inter- or intrapersonal issues between two people. Person A may unconsciously transfer their feelings and attitudes about an influential person or situation in the past onto Person B, who may have similar feelings. A positive example is anticipating unconditional positive regard, where any type of behaviour is expected to be accepted without consequence. A negative example is anxiety about rejection, where approval is constantly sought.

Countertransference relates to feelings evoked as a result of transference from another. For example accepting behaviour unconditionally.

Countertransference is not an impediment or negative as long as it is used constructively within the relationship. If unnoticed, it may result in different unhelpful responses or treatment to normal behaviour, such as giving a person more time than they would others or colluding with a person's reasons for avoiding the action they agreed to take.

---

Our friendship, and transference, impacted the way we perceived each other, our official roles, and the way we both operated within the system. More specifically, while I was comfortable working in partnership with Michael, I did not accept him as someone with authority over me, despite reporting to him in the organisational structure.

## Pros and cons

As the dynamic between us played out, clear pros and cons surfaced. A pro was the high level of openness and trust between us, where anything and everything was up for discussion without reservation or filter. I think Michael benefitted from being challenged and supported at the same time by someone who knew him well and appreciated context. I think, ultimately, the Team and the organisation as a whole benefitted from someone actively challenging Michael's thinking processes.

The high level of openness and trust between us was also a con. Naturally we disagreed at times, and due to role hierarchy, Michael had final decision-making authority. Sometimes he made decisions I was not comfortable with, or he behaved differently to what I thought we had agreed. While this is a normal part of organisational and professional life, because of our friendship, I took his alternative views and unexpected behaviour personally. It felt like a friend, or husband, or father, or brother, had betrayed me. As a result, our relationship and the system surrounding us was filled with tension. The diagram in Figure 7.6 is my attempt to draw the positive and negative forces in our tense relationship.

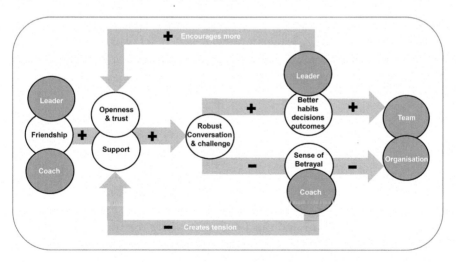

Figure 7.6: Impact of Leader and Coach relationship

Another con was the impact our relationship had on regular boss/ employee one-to-one conversations. Michael used a coaching style, which he was good at. I resisted. In fact, I recall literally squirming in my seat with discomfort during those conversations, wanting to escape the room. I am not exactly sure why, but suspect my reaction was a combination of:

- Our friendship and my discomfort in being coached by a friend.
- Struggling with the irony of being coached by someone who I perceived as causing many of my challenges.
- Transference, and my discomfort in being coached by a representation of my husband, father or brother.
- My control fetish, and I wanting to be the coaching SME in the Team.

Whatever the reason, our one-to-one conversations were a disaster.

While both Michael and I, and ultimately the Team and Green Apple Co, benefitted from our relationship in many ways, I found the tension it created in the system overwhelming. The impact of our relationship was a significant contributor to my energy struggles (more below) and the "stay or leave see-saw" I was on, mentioned previously.

In hindsight, I should have openly talked to Michael about the transference I noticed and the impact that our relationship had on the system. We should have set firmer professional and personal boundaries as well and contracted much more.

## Year Two

There was some relief at the beginning of Year Two, as Michael began actively working on his leadership style. But relief was temporary, and tension returned. Despite becoming an external service provider during Year Two, the dynamic between Michael and me was essentially the same as in Year One.

## Year Three

The notion of "firmer professional and personal boundaries" was finally realised in Year Three. Amendments to the formal legal contract included active avoidance of any personal relationship or communication between me and Michael, and me and the Team. Essentially, the friendship between Michael and I had ended too. Roles and boundaries were extremely clear – albeit awkward and unnatural, and sad.

While I mentioned earlier that changes in the formal contract were successful, and improvements were immediate, there was one example during Year Three where our new role clarity and firm relationship boundaries backfired.

In the section above relating to my perspective of the Team, I talked about sensing the Team had lost connection and psychological safety early in Year Three. When I first felt something was amiss, I shared my concerns with Michael – he assured me there was nothing to worry about. My alarm bells continued to ring, and I brought it up with him again, asking for his permission to raise what I was sensing with the Team. He said no, everything was fine, and I left it. I assume he was either in denial or was protecting the Team from something. What I did not know at the time was "hailstorm No.2" was beginning to build, and my sense the Team was in trouble was bang on.

I intentionally "left it," ignored my alarm bells, because of the awkward relationship between Michael and me. I did not want to rock the boat and push the matter further, jeopardising the relationship equilibrium we seemed to have finally found. Also, once I had asked his permission, I had no choice but to follow his wishes.

If I had have acted on my initial gut feeling and made the choice to raise concerns directly with the Team rather than talking to Michael first, the outcome might have been different. Perhaps the impacts of "hailstorm No.2" might have been mitigated in some way, resulting in less impact on delivery and less distress for stakeholders. This is a great example of how a seemingly small decision, by one party within a CAS, can have a significant impact on the entire system. More in Chapter Ten.

## Summary – Coach's perspective of Leader

A summary of my thoughts on what was good, challenging and was learnt from my perspective of Michael, the change he went through as a leader, and our complex relationship is contained in the Appendix to Chapter Seven. It was complicated, and as mentioned, the challenges between Michael and me significantly contributed to the energy crisis I suffered (more below).

While Michael described improvements in his leadership style in Chapter Five, I remain more sceptical. While I observed improvements at the beginning of Year Two, I am not sure whether further progress was made.

## The Function and Organisation

A Team's organisational context has a significant impact on how it operates. I have already touched on some aspects of Consulting Services and Green apple Co in this chapter, and I will use this section to fill any gaps. My perspective of the Function and Organisation within the system is illustrated in Figure 7.7.

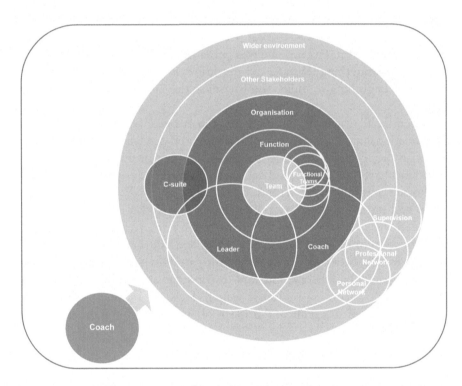

Figure 7.7: Coach's perspective of Function and Organisation

## Organisation culture

Year One

As described in Chapter Two, Green Apple Co's culture was "top-down" and siloed at the beginning of Year One. It would be difficult for any team or leader to have a fully collaborative style in that systemic environment. There were multiple streams of activity underway to change that culture, also described in Chapter Three. I ensured my work with the Team aligned with Green Apple Co's overall people strategy and culture implementation streams wherever possible.

One of the strategic enablement workstreams involved in-house development of online resources that staff, and managers could access themselves to support their own development. I worked closely with the HR team on this project, providing input as well as reviewing content created by them.

A library of good quality resources grew, and while this was a positive move, both Michael and I questioned whether the organisation's self-service approach would be effective as busy people are less likely to voluntarily access resources.

Within Consulting Services, I supported the rollout of new in-house resources as they were released – it was in people's faces rather than voluntary. I was in a good position to offer local support due to my involvement in creating content, and some organisation-wide content formed content of interventions I used with the Team. The opportunity to be close to HR and to influence and understand overall OD across Green Apple Co would not have been possible if I had been an external coach.

## Years Two and Three

As budget cuts became necessary in Year Two, one of the areas pared back was the culture change programme. Most organisation-wide initiatives were parked or de-scoped during Years Two and Three.

As an external service provider by this time, I was no longer involved in supporting organisation-wide OD work, and unfortunately my connection with overall people strategy and the use of in-house resources was lost. I only hoped and assumed that development content I covered with the Team in Years Two and Three remained aligned with overall organisational strategy and the Team would tell be if it did not.

## The Coach's role

### Year One

The HR function was very supportive of my role to begin with. I understood they were heavily involved in both designing my role and in my recruitment process. Erica, one of the HR managers, interviewed me. Once in the role, I worked closely with Erica and her team, and our relationship was strong, although, as mentioned above, I was disappointed there was less opportunity for me to learn from her team than I expected.

As soon as I began meeting people across the organisation, it became clear there was confusion around what I had been hired to do. Some key stakeholders, including C-suite members, thought I was there to "fix delivery systems and processes," and some thought I was there to "fix Michael." The lack of role clarity negatively impacted my reputation. I was continually passing issues to others or pushing back on requests, and as mentioned, Michael was refusing to "be fixed." It might have appeared I was disengaged, lazy or ineffective – not perceptions I was comfortable with.

Staff within Consulting Services were sceptical of my role at first too. I recall a member of staff saying, "Your role implies we are not doing a good job – we are told we are doing a good job, so what exactly are you here to change?" Thankfully, over time, as I formed my role, staff within the Function grew to trust, respect and appreciate the support I provided.

## Years Two and Three

In the early part of Year Two, Erica left Green Apple Co, and shortly after, I did too, and my connection with the organisation and HR dissipated and became tense. The new incumbent in Erica's role made it clear she did not support my ongoing work with the Team. I suggested she and Michael speak about her concerns – however, as far as I am aware, that conversation never took place.

## The Function and Organisation's role

Throughout this book it has been made clear that stakeholders were not involved enough in the journey. The C-suite, staff within Consulting Services, and representatives from across Green Apple Co, should have been involved all the way through – from establishing the Team's development goal, to prioritising development focus areas, supporting interventions as relevant, and co-creating a measurement framework.

As mentioned above, some stakeholder diagnostic work took place within development sessions, but stakeholders were never directly asked for input, nor were they ever in the room with us. Chapter Six includes comments from stakeholders expressing their disappointment in not being involved.

I think there were a few reasons why stakeholder input was not as prominent as it should have been:

- The environment and system were so complex and demanding to begin I did not have the headspace to involve more parties.
- Later, when I did want to get stakeholders involved, Michael pushed back on the suggestion. I suppose he wanted to protect the Team from negative feedback.
- Later still, when I convinced Michael to involve stakeholders in an online questionnaire, the timing was bad. The response rate was so low we could not use the data collected.

Looking back now, I know I should have pushed harder for stakeholders to be involved earlier. However, I am sharing responsibility for the omission with Michael and stakeholders themselves. I do not recall any stakeholder proactively asking to be involved over the entire three-year period I worked with the Team. The first time I heard that stakeholders felt ignored was reading their contributions to this book.

## Summary – Coach's perspective of Function and Organisation

A summary of my thoughts on what was good, challenging and learnt from my perspective of the Function and Organisation is contained in the Appendix to Chapter Seven.

The omission of direct stakeholder involvement in our journey was an error, and I hope the Team solicit more direct involvement from the Function and Organisation in future stages of their development journey. I know I have learnt from this experience, and I make a point of discussing stakeholders during the scoping stage in work I do with other teams in my current practice.

## The Coach

In this section, I talk through significant events that impacted my role, and me personally. Some were touched on earlier in this chapter and the perspective of me, reflecting on myself as Coach, is depicted in Figure 7.8.

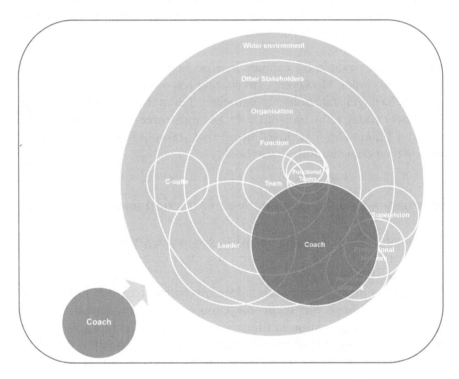

Figure 7.8: Coach's perspective of herself

*First Impressions*

Year One

At the very beginning of this chapter I said I was excited and optimistic about the "experiment" I was embarking on, and I knew the Team were new and needed my support. However, as I walked into Green Apple Co there was little or no pre-warning of:

- The "top-down" culture of the organisation.
- Michael's misaligned leadership style.

- Significant and messy change management processes in play.
- The low level of staff development investment and support across the organisation.
- Lack of opportunity to learn from internal OD.
- The significant impact environmental events would have.

Although surprises are expected in new roles, I was disappointed, and questioned whether I would be able to influence the system enough for the Team to gain any benefit from the "experiment" and my role at all. It was clear I was battling strong forces against change (Theory Break 7.18) and the road ahead would be extremely challenging for all of us.

## Relationship between Coach and Team

Year One

I talked about Team dynamics earlier in this chapter, and how I was part of the dynamic as well (Theory Break 7.8). As an internal coach in Year

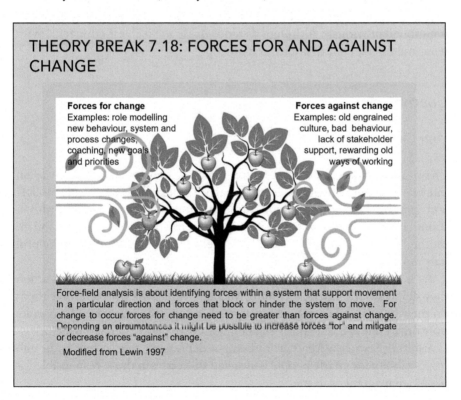

**THEORY BREAK 7.18: FORCES FOR AND AGAINST CHANGE**

**Forces for change**
Examples: role modelling new behaviour, system and process changes, coaching, new goals and priorities

**Forces against change**
Examples: old engrained culture, bad behaviour, lack of stakeholder support, rewarding old ways of working

Force-field analysis is about identifying forces within a system that support movement in a particular direction and forces that block or hinder the system to move. For change to occur forces for change need to be greater than forces against change. Depending on circumstances it might be possible to increase forces "for" and mitigate or decrease forces "against" change.

Modified from Lewin 1997

One, and part of the Team, I was even more integrated than most coaching scenarios would have allowed. On the whole, my relationship with each member of the team was good, even with Tom, who was firmly opposed to my work.

My role was quite different to other members of the team. Others had staff reporting to them, as well as delivery responsibilities, and I was in a support role. I am not sure if this was the reason, but I never really felt like a member of the Team, or like I belonged, and the support I gave others was not reciprocated. In many ways, even in Year One, when I was part of the Team, I felt like an external consultant.

## Years Two and Three

When I moved to an external role in Year Two, I did not notice much, if any, change in relationships between team members and myself. They were still calling me for advice from time to time, and we saw each other often.

During Year Three, in line with contract amendments made, I actively reduced contact with the Team outside of team development sessions, as mentioned previously. Although distance made me feel less connected with team members, I felt that trust remained.

## Coach's many hats

### Year One

I have already described some of the helpful roles, or hats, I wore as an internal coach in Year One – "formal coach," "informal coach," "role model" and "part of the team." I have mentioned some hats that were unhelpful in some circumstances too – "leadership vacuum trap." "work wife." "team mother," "team counsellor" and "Michael's friend." I add more unhelpful hats next.

As is normal in any organisation, staff issues arose at times, and when they did, team members, including Michael, would ask me to resolve them on their behalf. While providing support in this area was part of my role, over time I felt like the "mess cleaner" for every people-related issue across Consulting Services. Apart from being a depressing role, it felt as though responsibility for gnarly people issues had shifted from those responsible for people management to me.

I also inadvertently took on the ground-rule "enforcer" role. If a team member tripped up on a ground rule in a meeting, the rest of the Team, including Michael, would literally turn to me with the expectation that I would sort it out. Often I tried to, rather than supporting the Team to take collective responsibility.

The diagram in Figure 7.9 was created in a supervision session, illustrating my many hats, some helpful and some unhelpful at times.

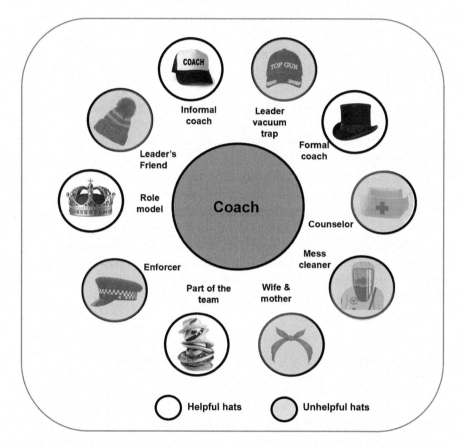

Figure 7.9: Coach's many hats

I think there are many reasons I slipped unhelpful hats on so easily:

- Like most coaches, I get energy from helping people – that is why I do what I do.

- Michael and the Team were under a lot of pressure, and I had more capacity than them.
- My role position description clearly stated I was there to support the Team and Michael with all people matters.
- Unclear, or lack of, responsibility – Michael shared his thoughts that, "It didn't really matter if we bought into the development work we are doing, because Helen was there to fall back on."
- Blind spots – sometimes I knew I was wearing an unhelpful hat, and sometimes it slipped on without me noticing.

The Team benefitted from me wearing unhelpful hats – at least in the short term. It relieved them of responsibility and released capacity. If I was dealing with staff issues and meeting with HR to find solutions, they did not have to.

As Year One progressed, I became increasingly aware I needed to shift some hats back to where they belonged. However, it was hard going as I had set an unfortunate precedence and Michael was encouraging the Team to delegate people matters to me.

As I reflect on my hat dilemma, another common analogy comes to mind about teaching someone to fish rather than giving them fish. In this case, teaching, supporting and coaching the Team to be their own "enforcers," "counsellors" and to clean up their own "mess" would have been a better approach right from the start. Note that ICF Team Coaching Competencies (2020b) state that one of the roles of a coach is to support clients to be self-managing, in effect making their own role obsolete (Theory Break 7.19).

### THEORY BREAK 7.19: TEACH A TEAM TO FISH

The ICF Team Coaching Core Competencies (2020b) emphasises that one of the purposes of team coaching is to help build a sustainable team that does not require the presence of the coach to maintain forward momentum. While the team coaching process may initially be directed by the coach, agreement should be reached as to how the ownership is gradually turned over to the team leader and the team as a collective.

Clutterbuck (2020) also explains that the aim of team coaching is to "build the team's capability to solve their own problems."

## Years Two and Three

As I moved to an external role, the opportunity to wear unhelpful hats gradually reduced. For example, as I was no longer physically present, it was impossible to "enforce" team ground rules in a BAU setting. Also, I was not able to clean up staff "messes" if I was not there.

By Year Three, I believe the correct hats were being worn by the correct people. Apart from team sessions, where I wore my "formal coach" and "role model" hats, the Team needed to fend for themselves.

## *Energy management*

## Year One

I have touched on energy a few times in this chapter already, and I expand more here. I have described many positives and opportunities related to my role in this chapter – and many challenges, disappointments and tensions as well. In addition to navigating a very challenging role, I was managing health and personal issues outside of work too, which also drained my energy.

I was doing many of the right things to look after myself and keep up my positive energy, including:

- Regular wellbeing activities – meditation, yoga, walking in nature and gratitude exercises.
- Intensive and ongoing team coaching training.
- Professional one-to-one and group team coaching supervision (more later).
- Support from my professional network.
- Support from family and friends.

I was able to keep balanced for the first few months in my role, but it did not last long. It felt like the Team, Michael and all of Green Apple Co were sucking energy out of me faster than I could replenish it. I recall talking about my "energy crisis" with Tammy in supervision, and I drew an energy system diagram, similar to Figure 7.10, with pipes feeding positive energy into my system, and larger pipes sucking energy out at a faster rate. I could literally feel my wellbeing and resilience decline day by day. Everything seemed harder, heavier and exhausting.

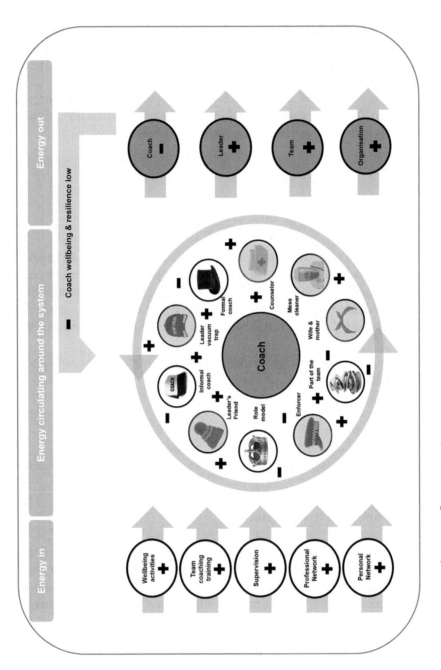

Figure 7.10: Coach energy flow – Year One

By the end of Year One, I was struggling to manage my emotions, and my mental health was suffering too. I questioned whether I could, or in fact should, continue with my role, and whether I was "fit for purpose" (Theory Break 7.11). Leaving played on my mind continually, the "stay or leave see-saw" referred to several times already.

## Year Two

In Year Two, despite moving into an external coach role, energy challenges continued. In fact, in many ways, I felt even more depleted. The cycle depicted in Figure 7.10 continued, health and family issues continued, and on top of that I had to manage the implications of transitioning to an external role, including rebuilding my own business (which was parked when I took on the role at Green Apple Co). I also had to deal with personal implications of other challenges in the wider environment, including "leaf spot" and new confusion around team session logistics mentioned above. The "stay or leave see-saw" was literally about to snap.

## Year Three

In Year Three, once formal contract amendments were in place, hats were worn by correct people, new routines in relation to my business were established, and I was working with other clients, I could feel my energy levels increasing, as depicted in Figure 7.11. I was feeling good and as though I had more capacity to see and manage the systems, I was in.

I was still thinking of leaving – although my motivation had changed. In Year Three, it felt like the Team had gone backwards and were no longer committed. As mentioned previously, several team development sessions were cancelled, they appeared to have lost connection and psychological safety, "hailstorm No.2" was playing out, and the awkward relationship between Michael and me was upsetting. I felt like I was wasting my time and energy with the Team, and it was finally time to admit defeat. As mentioned above, I also felt that continuing to work with the Team while they imploded would adversely affect my professional reputation. Michael assured me commitment was there, so I continued to sway on the "stay or leave see-saw".

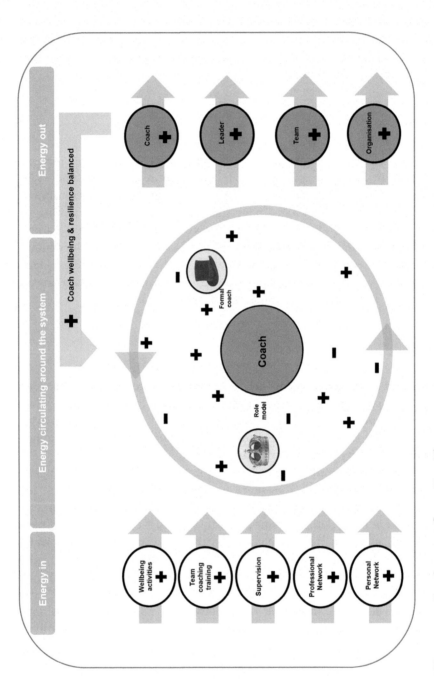

Figure 7.11: Coach energy flow – Year Three

## Coach development journey

As I reflect on my development journey over the three-year period of this case, the words that come to mind are difficult, challenging and highly rewarding! This chapter describes many of the successes and struggles I experienced during the "experiment." By living through and reflecting on experiences, I have learnt much more than I ever thought possible.

It was a complete coincidence that I started team coaching training at the same time I began the Coach role. I completed Practitioner level team coach training in Year One, and Senior Practitioner in Years Two and Three. This case created a serendipitous opportunity to apply what I was learning as I was learning it – level one and two learning (refer to Figure 1.3).

Now, as I write this book and have the opportunity to reflect on events again, I have gained further insight – level three learning, Figure 1.3. In addition to gaining experience and confidence as a team coach, by being part of this journey, I believe I have grown my:

- General coaching tool kit.
- Change management tool kit.
- Leadership development tool kit.
- Curiosity and creativity.
- Ability to think systemically and holistically.
- Resilience and patience.
- Self-awareness.

Megginson and Clutterbuck (2009) describe four levels of coach maturity (Theory Break 7.20). Although their model was developed with one-to-one coaching in mind, it is equally valid for team coaching scenarios. In Chapters One and Three I talk about the approach in this case being eclectic, in that it does not illustrate the application of a particular STC philosophy or approach. However, in applying the coach maturity model I would say I was mostly "process-based" at the beginning of Year One with hints of other maturity levels coming through. By the end of Year Three, my practice moved more into the "philosophy" and "systemic eclectic" areas, with hints of "model" and "process-based" work continuing as appropriate. Reflecting on it now the eclectic approach was unintentional to begin with, and grew to become very intentional over time.

This thinking aligns with comments I made earlier in this chapter about increased team coaching modality (Theory Break 3.5) as the Team matured. I believe that increased opportunity to apply team coaching came from changes in my own development and maturity as well. The Team and I grew into less structured and freer and fluid development experiences together.

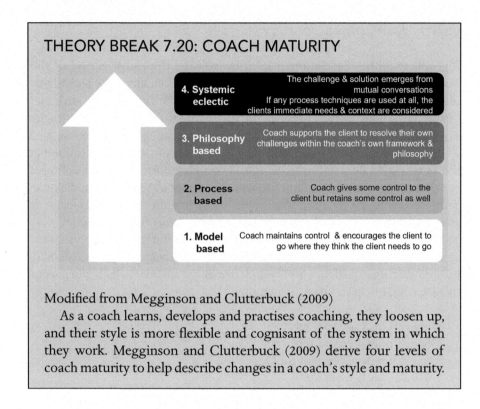

## THEORY BREAK 7.20: COACH MATURITY

Modified from Megginson and Clutterbuck (2009)

As a coach learns, develops and practises coaching, they loosen up, and their style is more flexible and cognisant of the system in which they work. Megginson and Clutterbuck (2009) derive four levels of coach maturity to help describe changes in a coach's style and maturity.

*Summary – Coach's perspective of herself*

A summary of my thoughts on what was good, challenging and what I learnt about myself on this journey is contained in the Appendix to Chapter Seven. My current team coaching practice is primarily built from my experience and learning in this case. More importantly, this case provided opportunity for significant personal growth and development as well.

## Supervision and Other Support

This part of the story is about my support networks. Simply put, without Supervision and Other Support, this journey would not exist – the "stay or leave see-saw" would have tilted towards leave, and I am sure I would have left within the first few months.

There are many types of coach supervision (Theory Break 7.21), and this chapter focuses on (D) professional one-to-one team focused, and (E) group team focused. Other Support refers to more informal support of colleagues in my professional network and friends and family.

No one in my Supervision and Other Support networks knew or had met the Team or Michael, and their only awareness of Green Apple Co was via news media. Therefore, their view of the system was formed by a combination of their own biases and my biases via what I shared with them – multiplied cognitive bias (Theory Break 1.3).

My view of Supervision and Other Support in the system is depicted in Figure 7.12.

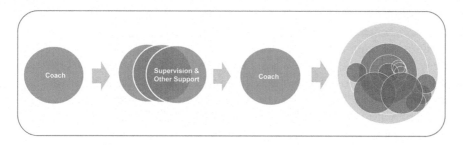

Figure 7.12: Coach's perspective of Supervision and Other Support

---

### THEORY BREAK 7.21: FORMS OF SUPERVISION

There are many forms of formal supervision with different focus areas, and each has their place. Some examples:

(A)  One-to-one individual focus – a professional supervisor with a coach who focuses mainly on one-to-one clients.
(B)  Group individual focus – a professional supervisor with a group of coaches who focus mainly on one-to-one clients.

(C) Peer group individual focus – self-managing group of peers using supervision techniques to support each other, and clients of coaches are mainly one-to-one.

(D) One-to-one team focus – a professional supervisor with a coach who focuses mainly on teams.

(E) Group team focus – a professional supervisor with a group of coaches who focus mainly on teams.

(F) Peer group team focus – self-managing group of peers using supervision techniques to support each other, and clients of coaches are mainly teams.

Of course there are informal ways of being supervised as well, by gaining advice and support from professional colleges.

## One-to-one team coaching supervision

### Year One

One-to-one team focused supervision came about through necessity rather than choice. As described at the beginning of this chapter, the first team session scared me – I needed help, and I needed it immediately. I knew Tammy was a professional team-focused supervisor, and arranged a programme with her, which Michael fully supported. Tammy and I met every three to four weeks throughout Year One.

Early sessions with Tammy focused on the behaviour of team members, my relationship with Michael and transference, the many hats I wore, and my energy crisis – effectively, the main points covered in this chapter.

The purpose of team coaching supervision is to support systemic thinking, doing and being (Theory Break 7.22), and through supervision, I am confident I grew in all three areas. Here are some examples of topics covered in each area:

- Systemic thinking – appreciating that a slow increase in engagement scores did not mean that development work was ineffective; the score was impacted by the entire system.
- Systemic doing – considering which development modalities (teaching, facilitation, or team coaching) were appropriate in which circumstances.

- Systemic being – acknowledging my energy impacted how I showed up and my ability to serve the Team's needs.

Tammy talks about these and other supervision topics in more depth in Chapter Eight.

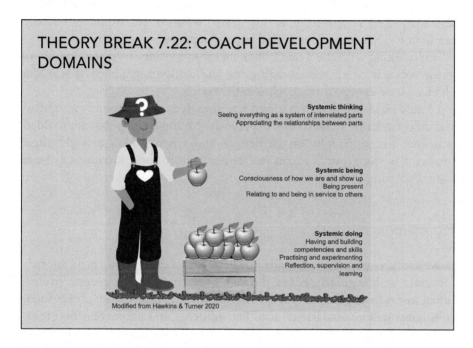

THEORY BREAK 7.22: COACH DEVELOPMENT DOMAINS

**Systemic thinking**
Seeing everything as a system of interrelated parts
Appreciating the relationships between parts

**Systemic being**
Consciousness of how we are and show up
Being present
Relating to and being in service to others

**Systemic doing**
Having and building
competencies and skills
Practising and experimenting
Reflection, supervision and
learning

Modified from Hawkins & Turner 2020

## Years Two and Three

One-to-one supervision continued throughout Year Two, and topics brought to supervision were similar to Year One – and covered in more depth. Role clarity continued to be a hot topic in Year Two, and as mentioned it was through supervision the idea of amending the formal contract came about.

During Year Three, as roles clarified and my energy system was more balanced, I decided to change my arrangement with Tammy to ad hoc supervision sessions if and when issues arose. I would say we met every two to three months during Year Three.

### Group team coaching supervision

My supervision group was formed with members of my team coaching training cohort. The group formed in Year One, with Tammy and David

Clutterbuck alternating the supervisor role. We met, and still meet, monthly. Group membership has changed over the years, with John, Jim and me remaining solid throughout. John talks about the experience of the supervision group from his and the group's perspective in Chapter Eight.

I often took challenges relating to this case to the group, and so they got to know the Team, Michael, and me well over the years. I found group sessions just as confronting as one-to-one sessions, yet supportive at the same time. That support extended beyond supervision sessions themselves. When working with the Team I often had weird visions of group members in the room with me, encouraging me and whispering advice. It was like I had a whole group of co-coaches in the room.

I found, and still find, the group learning dynamic extremely insightful and different from a one-to-one experience. Multiple perspectives provided rich and diverse insight on challenges and when others brought their scenarios to the group, I learnt just as much from their situations as I did from discussing this case.

## Professional network

I have a solid network of other coaches, team coaches and other professionals I interact with regularly, either through other supervision groups, professional association groups, or networking groups. Some of my professional colleagues are personal friends too. The influence and support of this group of people cannot be underestimated, and one of the main advantages was availability – advice and support was, and still is, just a phone call away. John talks about the experience from the perspective of being part of my professional network in Chapter Eight.

## Personal network

Many tears were shed in relation to this case – often over a wine or two with family and friends. Despite most of them not really understanding what I do, and why I got myself so entangled in this case, they were always available for a download, hug or laugh. It would have been blatantly obvious to them that I was emotionally impacted by the situation I was in, and, despite me ignoring their continual advice to pay attention to the "see-saw" and walk away, their support never faltered.

Rachael fits into both the professional and personal network categories, and she talks about the perspective of Other Support in Chapter Eight.

## *Summary – Coach's perspective of Supervision and Other Support*

A summary of my thoughts on what was good, challenging and what I learnt about Supervision and Other Support is included in the Appendix to Chapter Seven.

At the time this case was playing out, my decision to have intense and frequent one-to-one supervision, group team focused supervision, and rely heavily on professional networks, family and friends felt right. I was scared, stressed, and actively searching for advice and energy anywhere I could get it.

As part of the process of writing this book, I asked professional peers to review content. After reviewing an earlier version of this chapter, a colleague challenged my thinking around support and questioned whether I had rallied too much. She asked whether a break from living the story, repeating the story multiple times, and maintaining multiple support channels might have been more beneficial? She suggested that the extensive support I was working with may have encouraged rumination rather than relieving stress. I cannot say, but her comments made me question my choices – is there such a thing as too much support?

## Chapter Seven summary

This chapter is very personal, and I have openly shared struggles and emotions I experienced throughout this journey. Team coaching is hard, and although my circumstances were unique, and much of what I experienced was unique to the system I was in, my story also illustrates many common considerations, pitfalls and blind spots that team coaches, and indeed everyone working within CASs, can be faced with.

I asked the others contributing to this book to comment on the best, most challenging and most significant learning from this case, and I do the same:

- The best part was riding out the "stay or leave see-saw" and being in a position now to share my learning with you.
- The most challenging aspect was my energy crisis, which hindered my ability to see the system objectively and work through my challenges and choices.
- The most significant thing I learnt was appreciating that team coaching requires more than traditional professional development; it involves deep and continual personal growth and development too.

As I embarked on this journey, I assumed that the Team would benefit from the experience and that I would gain some knowledge too, but I had no concept of the significant and life-changing experience it would be. I am different, stronger, and more confident now than before the "experiment" began, and hopefully a more effective and valuable team and one-to-one coach too.

I talk about the application of learning from this case to my current and future team coaching practice in Chapter Eleven. Next up we hear from Tammy (my Supervisor), John (a member of my supervision group) and Rachael (a professional peer and friend) describing the last of the five perspectives covered in this book, Supervision and Other Support.

## References

Bridges, W. (2017). *Managing transitions: Making the most of change.* Boston: Da Capo Lifelong Books. https://doi.org/10.15358/9783800656561.

Cameron, K. (2012). *Positive leadership: Strategies for extraordinary performance.* Oakland: Berrett-Koehler.

Clutterbuck, D. (2020). *Coaching the team at work.* London & Boston: Brealey.

Clutterbuck, D., Turner, T. & Murphy, C. (2022). *The team coaching casebook.* London: Open University Press.

Drake, D. (2010). Narrative coaching. In E. Cox, T Bachkirova & D. Clutterbuck (Eds), *The complete handbook of coaching.* London: Sage. https://doi.org/10.4324/9781003089889-28.

Edmundson, A. (2012). *Teaming: how organisations learn, innovate and compete in the knowledge economy.* San Francisco: Jossey-Bass Wiley.

European Mentoring and Coaching Council (2020). *EMCC global team coaching accreditation standards framework.* Retrieved from https://emccglobal.org/accreditation/tcqa.

Grimley, B. (2010). The NLP approach to coaching. In E. Cox, T. Bachkirova & D. Clutterbuck (Eds), *The complete handbook of coaching.* London: Sage.

Hawkins, P. (2021). *Leadership team coaching: Developing collective transformational leadership.* 4th edition. London: Kogan Page. https://doi.org/10.1111/peps.12006_5.

Hawkins, P. (2022). *Leadership team coaching in practice: Case studies on creating highly effective teams.* 3rd edition. London: Kogan Page.

Hawkins, P. & Turner, E. (2020). *Systemic coaching: Developing value beyond the individual.* London & New York: Routledge. https://doi.org/10.4324/9780429452031.

International Coaching Federation (2019). *ICF core competencies.* Retrieved from https://coachfederation.org/credentials-and-standards/core-competencies.

International Coaching Federation (2020a). *ICF code of ethics.* Retrieved from https://coachfederation.org/ethics/code-of-ethics.

International Coaching Federation (2020b). *ICF team coaching competencies: moving beyond one-to-one coaching.* Retrieved from https://coachfederation.org/team-coaching-competencies.

Katzenbach, R. & Smith, D. (1993). The discipline of teams. *Harvard Business Review.* Retrieved from https://hbr.org/1993/03/the-discipline-of-teams.

Lewin, K. (1997). *Resolving social conflicts & field theory in social science.* Washington: American Psychological Association. https://doi.org/10.1037/10269-000.

Lewis, L. (2019). *Bluesky International ESQA/ESIA diploma for coach, mentor supervision.* C.2 11 November 2019.

Mayfield, P. (2015). Stakeholder strategy. In R. Smith, D. King, R. Sidhu & D. Skelsey (Eds), *The effective change managers handbook.* London: Kogan Page.

Megginson, D. & Clutterbuck, D. (2009). *Further techniques for coaching and mentoring.* London: Routledge. https://doi.org/10.4324/9780080949420.

Murphy, C. & Turner, T. (2021). *The importance of psychological safety in team coaching.* Retrieved from https://www.turner.international/resources.

Noble, D. & Kauffman, C. (2023). *Real time leadership.* Boston: Harvard Business Review Press.

Sharpe, B. (2020). *Three horizons: The patterning of hope.* United Kingdom: Triarchy Press Ltd https://doi.org/10.1007/978-3-319-91554-8_82.

Turner, T. (2020). Excellence in Leadership: Responsibility, Accountability and Authority (3 Factor RAA model). https://www.turner.international/_files/ugd/11f34b_6ae0f2d809c84c6bb97a2a3dbe7f066f.pdf [accessed 9 November 2022].

Turner, T., Lucas, M. & Whitaker, C. (2018). *Peer supervision in coaching and mentoring: A versatile guide for reflective practice.* London & New York: Routledge. https://doi.org/10.4324/9781315162454.

Appendix to Chapter Seven: Good, challenging and learnt – Coach's perspective

| Good | Challenging | Learnt |
|---|---|---|
| | Strategy enablement and change management | |
| Team's development goal, model & plan aligned with Green Apple Co's strategy (Y1). | Tangible measures were slow to improve (Y1). | Ensure Team's development approach is aligned with the organisation's approach & strategy. |
| Green Apple Co's organisation-wide people & culture change interventions. | No formal agreement or framework for measuring progress & success. | The "people" part of strategy enablement begins with leaders being in line with the goal. |
| Michael's inspirational vision of future for Team & Consulting Services, & his passion & investment in developing the Team. | Green Apple Cos culture interventions slowed down due to "leaf spot" (Y2). | Tangible evidence of growth & improvement may take time to emerge. |
| Tangible outcomes & positive feedback improved (Y2 & Y3). | | Have a structured progress & outcomes measurement framework. |

| Good | Challenging | Learnt |
|---|---|---|
| | Team development and coaching | |
| Investment in monthly team development days, with flexible content & flexible modalities. | "Top-down" & "siloed" culture of Green Communities (early Y1). | Even if the team is not "ready" to start team coaching, just start! |
| HPT assessment completed regularly to inform focus areas. | Gap in HR processes, resources & support (early Y1). | HPT goal & model ideally selected by the team – but initially the coach can select to get traction. |
| | HPT goal & model initially selected by me, not Team (Y1). | |

(continue)

(continue)

| Good | Challenging | Learnt |
|---|---|---|
| | **Team development and coaching** | |
| Michael's insistence that all team members attend development sessions (Y1). | Initial resistance of Team to invest in development (Y1). | Team development sessions:<br>• Decide up front on level of commitment to pre-work. |
| I supported the Team with formal & informal one-to-one coaching & advice (Y1 & Y2). | Team not recognising they needed to be a team (Y1). | • Ensure responsibility for logistics is clear. |
| Team eventually recognised long-term benefits of development (Y2). | Some team dynamics were challenging & trust & psychological safety ebbed & flowed. | • Align content with team maturity level. |
| Formal contract amended to clarify roles & responsibilities (Y3). | Unclear accountability & responsibility across Team (Y1). | • Align modalities with what feels right in the moment. |
| Shared leadership of team development (Y3). | Challenges with team development sessions, including commitment to do pre-work, responsibility of logistics, some interventions too advanced for Team's maturity level, cancelled sessions in Y3. | • Continually review & adjust the processes. |
| Team recognising "bump" in their journey & wanting to get back on track (Y3). | "Hailstorms," "leaf spot" & other environmental factors forced Team to focus on navigating storms & BAU, resulting in less development commitment. | Spend as much time as needed contracting roles between all parties & continually re-contract. |
| | Rotating leadership role for team sessions (Y3). | One-to-one formal or informal coaching and advice in parallel with team sessions embeds change. |
| | | Sometimes detailed written contracting of roles may be required. |
| | | Team dynamics, and hence trust & psychological safety, are fluid. |

| Good | Challenging | Learnt |
|---|---|---|
| | Stakeholders not directly involved in process or informed of progress. | Authority, accountability & responsibility of activity needs to be clear amongst leader & team. |
| | Team maturity zig-zagged; it was not a smooth journey. | Involve stakeholders throughout, including prioritising activity, progress & outcome measurement. |
| | | "Good endings" are a good investment. |
| | | The team development path is bumpy, team maturity is not linear, expect ups & downs. |

### Leadership development

| Good | Challenging | Learnt |
|---|---|---|
| I supported Michael with one-to-one informational coaching & direct advice (Y1 & Y2). | Michael's "top-down" leadership style was misaligned with strategic direction (early Y1). | If leadership style is not in line with team development direction, something needs to change. |
| Strong trust & friendship between Michael & me. | Michael's resistance to work on changing leadership style (Y1). | One-to-one formal or informal coaching & advice for leader is helpful to embed change. |
| Michael's commitment to change his leadership style (end Y1). | Michael's resistance to create formal development plan & formal one-to-one coaching. | |

(continue)

(continue)

| Good | Challenging | Learnt |
|---|---|---|
| | Leadership development | |
| Year Two plan helped clarify accountability & responsibility across the Team (Y2). | "Leadership vacuum trap" & "Who's the boss" events (Y1). | Elicit support from leader's colleagues, boss & others to help support change. |
| Michael had clear enablers in place to help support change in style (early Y2). | Most enablers of leadership change put on hold due to impact of "leaf spot" (early Y2). | Leader needs to create their own style that works for them & their team. |
| | I did not solicit support from C-suite or others to support Michael change. | The leader is accountable for their own leadership style – not the coach. |

| Good | Challenging | Learnt |
|---|---|---|
| | Coaching in general | |
| Being an internal coach & part of the team allowed me to provide focus & build strong trust. I was also able to experience the Team & Michael in context first-hand (Y1). | Being an internal coach & part of the team resulted in lack of role clarity & some unhelpful hats (Y1). | There are advantages & disadvantages of an internal coach versus an external coach – it is not clear cut. |
| Michael supported my development in team coaching. | Some confusion & scepticism around my role across Consulting Services & Green Apple Co. | Coach is part of the system & this has pros and cons – use pros to advantage. |
| HR High support of my role (Y1). | I felt the burden of the Team's & Michael's success rested with me (Y1). | Use or at least experiment with formal co-coaching. |
| I was involved in Green Apple Cos HR projects (Y1). | | |

| | | |
|---|---|---|
| Great opportunity to experiment with team coaching models & techniques as I was learning them. | I questioned whether I could influence the system enough to make any gains (Y1). | Contract & continually re-contract expectations & roles with the team, team leader, co-coach, HR, and other relevant stakeholders in the system. |
| Some of my many roles/hats were helpful. | Opportunity to experiment with external coach & formal co-coaching not taken. | Sometimes formal contracting may be required for role clarity. |
| Michael was effectively my co-coach (Y1 & Y2). | Sometimes I put my own professional needs ahead of the Team's. | Keep the needs of the client/team at the forefront of everything done & all decisions made. |
| My self-awareness & continual questioning whether I could/should continue with the role/engagement. The "seesaw". | Tension & complex dynamics between Michael & me – I took setbacks personally & it impacted the Team. | Take care with personal boundaries & watch for transference. |
| Change in formal contract improved role clarity for all (Y3). | My energy crisis compromised my ability to deliver services professionally (Y1 & Y2). | "Teach the team to fish" rather than fish for them. |
| My development journey was difficult & challenging & highly rewarding. | Changing from internal to external coach role reduced my ability to see the Team & Michael in context (Y2 & Y3). | Coach self-awareness & self-care is critical. Continually check if "fit for purpose." |
| Writing this book has added another layer of reflective learning – level three learning. | My discomfort in needing to formally contract roles & expectations (Y3). | Coaches need to build reflection in their practice & reflecting again sometime later is insightful – level three learning. |
| | | Learning from a complex case while studying team coaching at the same time is beneficial. |

(continue)

(continue)

| Good | Challenging | Learnt |
|---|---|---|
| | **Coaching in general** | |
| | Relationship between myself & HR became tense, & HR lost sight of what I was working on (Y2 & Y3). | The coach learns just as much from the experience as the team & leader. |
| | The stay & leave see-saw was constantly on my mind. | *Being a team coach means more than professional development, it involves continual personal development too. (Most valuable learning for Coach).* |

| Good | Challenging | Learnt |
|---|---|---|
| | **Coach support** | |
| Early recognition I needed professional supervision support. | I could not get the support I needed within Green Apple Co. | Supervision & support in team coaching is critical, & different types are useful. |
| I found different types of formal supervision helpful. | Some messages received in supervision were confronting & emotional. | Coaches should tap into all support networks they have, professional & personal. |
| Informal support of professional colleagues & friends & family is important. | There may have been too much support – inhibiting ability to have a break & see the system objectively. | Consider the right level of support – not enough versus too much. |
| Team coaching supervision gave me positive energy. | | |

# Supervision and Other Support perspective

**8**

*Tammy Turner and Helen Zink*

---

## HOW TO READ CHAPTER EIGHT

I am Tammy, Helen's supervisor, and I will explain how Chapter Eight fits into the book.

The five system elements covered in this book describe their own versions of their development story in Section B. This includes thoughts on whether the approach and interventions used in this case, as described in Chapter Three, were useful, what was good, what was challenging, and what was learnt from the experience. Using a movie analogy, Section B involves five "parallel plots", whereby the same story is narrated by different characters, with each character describing themselves and the other main characters in the movie.

Chapter Eight is one of the parallel plots – Supervision and Other Support's perspective of the story and three different voices narrate this chapter:

- Me, Tammy: Speaking from a professional supervisor's perspective, and the primary supervisor across the three-year timeframe this case covers.
- John: A member of Helen's team coaching supervision group, representing the entire supervision group, including Jim, Fred and Amy – all of whom have contributed to this book.
- Rachael: A professional peer and friend of Helen's, speaking on behalf of her professional network, family and friends, including

---

DOI: 10.4324/9781003367789-10

Anna, Robbie, Heather, Kirsten and Keith – all of whom have contributed to this book.

As there are different authors and voices within this chapter, each section begins by clearly identifying which of the three voices above they represent.

The top diagram in Figure 8.1 illustrates my view of Helen as Coach in the reflective space of supervision. I can only see Helen and myself directly, as I have never met the Team, Michael or anyone in Green Apple Co. The bottom diagram illustrates John's, Rachael's and my view of the system via Helen in the Coach role. John, Rachael and I can see the entire system, but our view is via Helen's view. Our thoughts in this context are formed through Helen's biases as well as our own. As such, we only comment on Helen and ourselves in this chapter, as comment on the Team, Michael or Green Apple Co would involve compounding biases.

Content for this chapter comes from answers to questions Helen asked of us for inclusion in this book, notes from supervision sessions, Helen's memory, and John's, Rachael's and my own memories.

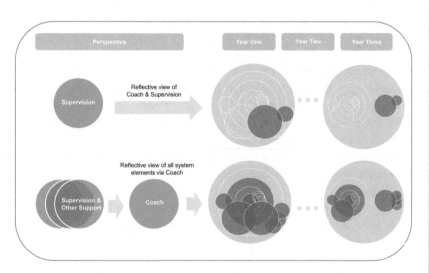

Figure 8.1: Supervision & Other Support's perspective of system

## Supervision

**Author Tammy Turner**
**Written in the voice of Tammy, as Helen's Supervisor**
I was Helen's professional supervisor throughout the time period this case covers. Although the elements in Helen's case are unique to her, given the systemic nature of organisations, the dynamics and challenges exist in all organisations and teams. It is a privilege to publish the sensitive content this chapter covers. It involves real people doing a challenging job under difficult circumstances, and I encourage you to read the chapter with empathy to enrich your learning.

Please note the term "client" used in this section can mean an individual, the team as a whole, or the organisation, depending on context.

### Overview

Supervision is a systemic field and looks at all elements within an organisational system. The foundation of supervision is reflective practice – "The ability to step away from your work and identify patterns, habits, strengths and limitations in your work and/or within the system you work in" (Turner et al., 2018).

To prepare for supervision, the coach/supervisee reflects on their own coaching portfolio and each of their clients' wider systems. Their reflections may include:

- Examining themselves, their feelings and insights.
- Interventions, tools and techniques they have used.
- Additional data used to understand the client, such as 360s, other diagnostic tools, and input from the client's manager, their peers or their sponsors.
- How the client, groups or teams have responded to interventions.
- Parallel process, transference and countertransference.
- Other systems, ecosystems or systemic factors that may be impacting on the client or team.
- The impact of change.

Reflecting on these various elements within the system creates insight for the coach in the form of a supervision case, which they bring to a supervision session.

The case is then examined by the supervisee and supervisor in an individual session and/or other supervisees in a supervision group. During a supervision session, the supervisor in the background uses a framework such as the Hawkins and Turner Systemic Model of Supervision (2020) (Theory break 8.1) to help navigate the systemic aspects arising as part of the reflective process. The framework can also support a supervisee in reflecting on systemic aspects within the organisation they are coaching. The coach takes enhanced awareness, gained from collective reflection, back into the client system to enhance overall outcomes and support themselves in their role.

In this case, Helen gathered reflections and shared them with others in both professional individual and group supervision. During supervision sessions, we explored the client's ecosystem and various elements comprising my perspective of the field, as illustrated in the second diagram in 8.1.

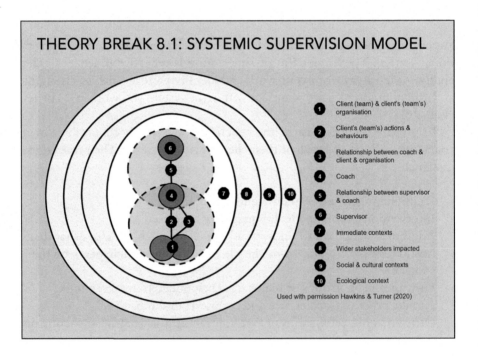

THEORY BREAK 8.1: SYSTEMIC SUPERVISION MODEL

1. Client (team) & client's (team's) organisation
2. Client's (team's) actions & behaviours
3. Relationship between coach & client & organisation
4. Coach
5. Relationship between supervisor & coach
6. Supervisor
7. Immediate contexts
8. Wider stakeholders impacted
9. Social & cultural contexts
10. Ecological context

Used with permission Hawkins & Turner (2020)

## The Coach

Throughout this engagement, Helen, in her role as Coach, is a central element in the system supporting organisational change. In this section,

I discuss the various roles she undertook within the organisation to impact growth, through the lens of what she brought to supervision sessions. As a result, I describe what I noticed in the reflective space of supervision across her journey.

## Context

It is important to recognise that a coach is part of the system, regardless of whether they are internal or external to the organisation (Theory Break 7.8). As soon as a coach begins to scope the engagement with the client, or take the job, they bring their own biases, background, training, preferences and ways of being into the system. The coach's personal life, energy levels and familial history impact their ways of "being" with a team and consequently their capacity to be neutral. A coach's way of being is brought into team coaching unconsciously and impacts the system in which they work. Supervision can help illuminate ways of being and support the coach through challenges that may arise.

As an experienced one-to-one coach, Helen had already been a part of a regular peer supervision group prior to Year One. Helen came to professional team coaching-focused supervision after the first team coaching session with the Team in this case. It sounded like a challenging session.

We first met during ICF peer supervision training, which I hosted some years before. There, I emphasised the importance of both peer and professional supervision for complex engagements, and she felt professional supervision would support her growth and development in her new role.

It was my understanding that Helen's job description and employment contract included terms relating to leadership and team development – the same team she was a member of. As an experienced consultant and executive coach, Helen said she was "excited" about her new role, despite the role not being well defined and not having much previous organisational design or team coaching capability. In her dual role, Helen began to get to know the Team both as co-workers and client. During individual interviews, she gathered information about where each person thought the Team's development was at, and how she could support them. She also collected Michael's hopes and objectives for the year ahead.

In our first supervision session, we established our verbal supervision agreement through contracting, and we also co-designed the second team coaching workshop based on what she knew at the time and from the data she had compiled. She said she left feeling equipped to run the second team meeting.

Michael had committed to support Helen. However, like many senior leaders, my impression was he was largely unavailable due to competing organisational priorities and running the day-to-day business. I also hypothesised he might have some blind spots about the Team and where they needed to develop. The way Helen described Michael's behaviour, data she collected in individual interviews with the Team, and pronounced emotion displayed during the first team session, all indicated cracks in the system – which I look at later.

Given the complexity of her circumstances, Helen committed to ongoing reflective practice to increase her capacity, and ultimately developed her team coaching maturity. As a team coach, Helen aligned with the EMCC (2020) Team Coaching Competencies, which specifically states that coaches must "develop and implement an appropriate team coaching-focused supervision and reflective practice plan for their own development." Helen also began Practitioner team coaching training shortly after she started her new role, and opted to use the Team in this case to practise and develop her skills and write her essay for the programme. In tandem, she started regular peer-learning groups with the programme cohort as well as continuing with her peer-supervision group and individual professional team focused supervision with me.

The Practitioner programme was well timed. It provided Helen with the flexible methodology and structure required to coach the Team in developing collective agreements and envisioning their future – grounding them more solidly as a team. Helen chose to use the PERILL model (Clutterbuck, 2020) to define the Team's purpose and engage their key stakeholders and influencers, sparking their opportunities for growth. The Team realised that through enhanced listening and leadership skills, developed as part of the team coaching engagement, they created psychological safety and interpersonal support. Helen often came to supervision excited about co-creating a generative environment for this Team and being a part of their advancement.

After completing team coaching training, Helen joined a professional supervision group with the same Practitioner learning group in which David Clutterbuck and I alternated the supervisor role. She also continued one-to-one professional supervision, and tapped into support from family and friends, which Rachael talks about later. This may seem like a lot of support, but the complexity of the assignment and her capacity were key factors in this choice.

## Supervision topics

### Year One

The threads that ran through all professional individual supervision sessions were the multiple roles Helen was playing. We reflected on the various "hats" she wore in the context of:

- Ethics and her boundaries within the various roles.
- The expectations Michael and the Team had of her.
- Expectations she had of herself.
- Organisational factors.
- Her capacity and health.
- Relationships and tasks defined within her job description.
- Agreements in her employment contract.

ICF (2020a) Code of Ethics specifically mentions that internal coaches need to take extra care managing conflicts of interest. To ensure ethical conduct and psychological wellbeing, we discussed if Helen could, or should, be coaching team members, her boss, or the Team, which included her peers. We also talked about how she was managing various conflicts of interest both in her role as Coach and as a team member, as well as a friend, work colleague and other parts of the system illustrated in the bottom diagram of Figure 8.1.

We used the Karpman Drama Triangle (Karpman, 2014) (Theory Break 8.2) several times to look at the pattern of victim, rescuer and persecutor. When tensions were high, the Leader responded by taking it out on the Team, becoming a persecutor. In turn, this allowed Helen to become the rescuer and the Team to become victims. The Team then became even more dependent on Helen as a protector from Michael, effectively creating a family dynamic of Michael as Dad and Helen as Mum. When Michael felt under-resourced or unsupported by the organisation, he moved into a victim role, and Helen rescued him. When Helen moved into role of persecutor, Michael then became the rescuer. The pattern of Michael and Helen moving between roles in the triangle illustrates how a typical drama triangle dynamic works.

We also explored Helen getting caught in a parallel process (Theory Break 8.3) both in her day job and during team coaching sessions. By the end of Year One, she was able to understand the parallel process in the context of this case, and why it was important in team coaching.

## THEORY BREAK 8.2: KARPMAN DRAMA TRIANGLE

Commonly used in therapy, the drama triangle is a tool used to frame up human interaction, conflict and drama. As this is a systemic dynamic, the roles are not fixed and move between the players as the situation warrants. Each of the characters encourages and reinforces the other roles, resulting in unhelpful outcomes for all. The characters in the triangle are:

**Persecutor** – controls, blames others, and becomes defensive when challenged. Encourages rescuers to help them and under pressure often moves to victim.

**Rescuer** – feels obliged to come to the rescue to save others and feel frustrated if their attempts to rescue are not successful. If the persecutor moves to victim, often the rescuer will move to persecutor.

**Victim** – convinces themselves and others they are helpless and unable to resolve the situation despite their best efforts. If persecutor moves to victim, and rescuer moves to persecutor, victim often moves to rescuer.

In a drama triangle, people tend to have a habitual role, learned from their own family dynamics. Also, despite having a favoured role, people often rotate across all three positions.

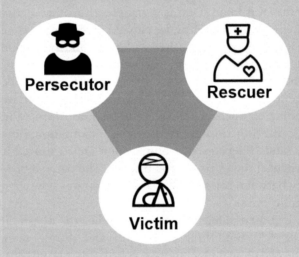

Used with permission Karpman (2014)

## THEORY BREAK 8.3: PARALLEL PROCESSING IN TEAM COACHING

Parallel process originated in a therapeutic context and relates to similarities between a client's experience (individual or team) and that of the coach (Turner, 2022). The coach might respond to a situation as if it were their own circumstance or behave in a way highly influenced by their past. The key issue is the coach's ability to maintain neutrality and act in the best interests of the client.

An example of this is a team coach who grew up in a family where it was not polite to interrupt. During a team coaching session, the team coach might interrupt the team leader who gets angry for the interruption and the team coach loses their confidence. If the coach brings this situation to supervision, they can explore the pattern safely.

Once the coach understands this pattern and when this parallel process arises again, they can draw attention to it by asking, "What are the team's shared agreements about interrupting?" and it can become a shared learning experience for the team.

### The "hats"

A major breakthrough came during a supervision session where we explored the various "hats" that Helen wore in the organisational system. Helen is a visual person and was viscerally able to experience how she moved into and between various roles she played in the organisation by which hat she was wearing. This became a foundational piece of the supervision work throughout the three-year journey, and is used extensively throughout this book (refer to Figure 7.9).

What Helen came to realise, particularly in Year One, was that because her job description was not clearly defined, and her "Coach" role evolved from expectations of herself and others, she ended up being all things to all people. To simplify, Helen discovered that three of the "hat" categories helped her to move more easily between her ways of being: Formal coach, informal coach and role model. When she was not in one of these three roles, lack of clarity triggered emotional responses which manifested as losing confidence, falling into the pattern of rescuer, frustration and sometimes tears.

By pausing for reflection and meditating when triggered, Helen described how she was able to observe herself in the moment "wearing hats" and to manage herself better as a result. With this awareness, Helen said she tried to stay clearly in the team coach role during team coaching sessions and supported the Team to deepen their learning and interdependent accountability.

Helen learned more about contracting in the context of a CAS (Theory Break 7.9) in the team coaching Practitioner course. She introduced the Shared Outcomes model (Turner, 2014) (Theory Break 8.4) to the Team as a framework for contracting. Contracting also helped to engage team members around their expectations of Michael and each other. Over time, contracting became part of the Team's and Helen's DNA, supporting the system to better stay out of the parallel process and maintain role clarity.

---

### THEORY BREAK 8.4: CONTRACTING AND SHARED OUTCOMES

The shared outcomes concept (Turner & Hughes, 2022) focuses on above-the-line behaviours to enable successful contracting conversations between parties. Ultimately, the objective is the creation of shared outcomes, with clear accountability and responsibility for parties involved. (See Theory Break 7.9 for contracting and multi-stakeholder contracting and Theory Break 7.16 for accountability and responsibility).

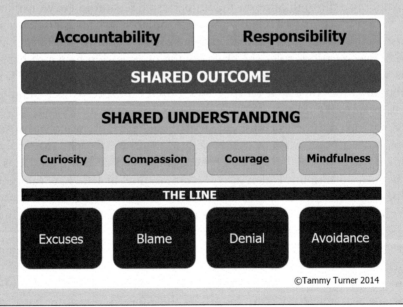

©Tammy Turner 2014

## Transference

Transference (Theory Break 7.17) was a constant feature in Helen's work and in supervision. There were many intersections of transference – between Michael and Helen and vice-versa, team members and Helen, Michael and team members, and Helen and me.

Due to the link between transference and family dynamics, transference is a pattern that perpetually arises, and when the supervisor has the training to do so, it can be worked on in professional supervision. It is important to understand that transference is a common occurrence in the workplace, is often underpinned by unspoken agreements and assumptions, and driven by historical familial roles and patterns. In Helen's supervision, the transference we discussed most often was the relationship between her and Michael and how it impacted her and the Team.

Helen often brought examples of herself and Michael in team meetings or individual and team coaching sessions to reflect upon. She noticed that while she needed to add value to the organisation, she was also conflicted with unclear boundaries, lack of role definition and work challenges – resulting in anxiety for both her and the Team. She also talked about the care she had for Michael. These factors encouraged him to talk about both personal and work-related challenges in coaching conversations, which is not uncommon. However, in any organisational context, this can create extra complexity and amplify conditions for transference.

Through supervision, Helen realised that when tensions were high, the Team related to her and Michael as mother and father. They did not stay a cohesive team and instead aligned with either Mum or Dad. We also discovered a father and daughter, or husband and wife type of relationship was common in one-to-one meetings between Michael and Helen. This created a tricky power imbalance that made muddy role clarity even murkier. By understanding the transferential dynamic between herself and Michael, and continually reflecting on it in individual professional supervision, Helen was able to more easily see her family of origin issues which encouraged transference and contributed to the dynamic. She shared that she was better able to stay in her defined role(s), which contributed to a more constructive working relationship with Michael and the Team particularly in Year Three.

## Personal system and resilience

As in any new job, the toll of learning new things, building relationships and delivering is more draining than when it is familiar. In addition to adjusting to a new role, dealing with a particularly complex system, unclear roles, and transference during this period, Helen also had some health and personal issues. As time progressed, Helen also described that she had less and less internal support as Michael and team members assumed that she was well integrated into her role. This combination meant that Helen's wellbeing and resilience were low by the end of the first year. She was struggling and lacking in capacity. The content of sessions related to her feeling like "the energy was being sucked out" of her. We discussed a wellbeing plan and who within her personal and professional networks could scaffold her during this particularly difficult period. The energy diagram in Figure 7.10 came from these supervision discussions.

As illustrated, despite good activities to pump energy in, it was not enough to top up the energy output required. As an internal coach and part of the team, Helen was not able to ever have a break from the Team to reset, as would be the case with an external coach, or an internal coach with multiple internal clients. Green Apple Co was under pressure, and Helen's pattern of rescuing and wanting to constantly be of service by supporting her coachee/teammates and coachee/Leader, who played victims in the drama triangle (Theory Break 8.2) by constantly asking for her help, left her lacking in support for herself from typical sources within the organisation.

One thing that could have supported Helen, particularly at this time, was the introduction of an external co-coach (Theory Break 7.14). Benefits might have included:

- Having an outside observer of team dynamics.
- Sharing responsibility of seeing and working in the system.
- Sharing design and delivery.
- Taking pressure off day-to-day work to support wellbeing.

I also speculate that the transferential and drama triangle issues within the system may have been eliminated or minimised by bringing in an external team coach as a circuit breaker. However, by this stage, Helen's capacity and decision making was compromised, and she told me she did not think the organisation would support this recommendation and chose not to broach it with management.

In lieu of having a co-coach, supervision became frequent support, helping Helen to better understand the dynamic between herself and Michael, fraught with emotional turmoil. In desperation, Helen talked about leaving the role and Green Apple Co. We explored whether she was actually "fit for purpose" and able to meet clients' needs (Theory Break 7.11).

She scheduled in some time off and tried to have better boundaries while she was at work. Ultimately, she moved out of the organisation to become an external coach in Years Two and Three.

## Year Two

During this period, Helen moved from an internal to an external role. The transition of coach, team member and colleague relationships were constant features in supervision during this year. Although Helen's role as external service provider was agreed, and a formal written contract outlining outcomes and payment schedules of her engagement was defined, role definition and responsibilities continued to be a challenge. Helen described many instances of lack of clarity, re-contracting, followed by a period of clarity, and the cycle repeating itself. The expectation that "things would be different now" because she was no longer an internal coach pervaded the system. Helen continued to bring self-judgement, frustration and persistent energy drain as themes from her reflective practice into supervision.

In my view, the challenges continued because neither the client system, nor Helen's pattern of pleasing, had changed. In her new role of external individual coach, Helen was caught up in trying to help stressed previous colleagues blaming others, the organisation and/or their manager for issues. Due to her previous history, Helen lost objectivity, and team members unconsciously knew how to pull her into a drama triangle and engage her as a rescuer. In her capacity as external team coach, she tried to help Michael by supporting the Team with collective decision making. When they did not enact this, Michael became frustrated, and Helen was again caught in a drama triangle, indicating the system had not changed much, if at all.

At the same time, Helen's working environment during Year Two meant she was less able to connect with personal and professional networks. This contributed to the continuation of personal and health issues. Again, the conversation around being "fit for purpose" arose, as Helen had a sense of "hanging on" rather than doing the best for the client and herself. As a result, Helen was still considering ending the contract with the client.

## Coach boundaries

Though Helen had left the system, her pattern of being conscientious, rescuing and being overly responsible continued to follow her into her role as an external contractor, ultimately limiting the system's growth. She was outside of the system now, but many familiar patterns still existed. With my support, she turned attention to herself and realised she was not as strong as she needed to be in setting and maintaining clear boundaries.

An example was Michael, who was going through difficulties at home. His collegiate friendship with Helen blurred boundaries of being an individual coach, a team coach, a friend, current or ex-work colleague and an external service provider. Helen used the Shared Outcomes model (Theory Break 8.4) to review the psychological contract around expectations in the relationship, reach shared understanding and define shared outcomes. Through reflection, Helen was trying to work through how she could support Michael professionally without losing the human compassion for her previous boss, now client.

Another example was on-boarding a new team member who was desperate for guidance. Paralleling the situation when Helen first started, this new team member had little support, and Helen fell straight into the trap of rescuing him. In supervision, we were able to use her "hats" analogy to uncover "which 'hat' she was wearing" and "which 'hat' her client, situation and/or system was asking her to wear." Using the metaphor of the "hats" helped her to gain perspective and self-awareness.

From a new vantage point, Helen became an observer of herself moving into various roles within the Karpman Drama Triangle (Theory Break 8.2) and transferential dynamics she contributed to. All of these factors were amalgamated into the triangulation diagram, Figure 8.2, which was created and worked through in supervision. Once again, by using a visual diagram, she was able to better understand how to hold her boundaries and go back to something she was now quite capable of – contracting (Theory Break 7.9).

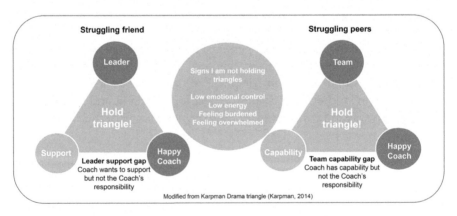

Figure 8.2: Coach drama triangle

This skill allowed her to identify what she needed in the moment, understand what the other party needed, negotiate, and try to come together with a shared agreement.

However, in Helen's view, shared agreements, or at least what she understood to be shared understandings, were not upheld. She reported still being frustrated by the lack of role clarity. In a supervision session near the end of Year Two, it was suggested that amending the "formal written contract" would ensure all parties were clear. This seemed to be a major revelation for Helen. Using her foundational contracting skills bolstered her confidence to re-negotiate and re-write the formal written legal contract that supported the working relationship heading into Year Three.

## Year Three

Changing the formal written contract was seemingly just an administration activity, but the outcome was palpable. Helen reported an immediate shift in her energy (refer to Figure 7.11). By defining the scope of the contract and articulating the delivery expectations of all parties, both Helen and Michael's role clarity improved. Consequently, the Team benefitted as well, and during Year Three, Helen told me that the Team began to coach themselves, taking more responsibility for themselves and their impact on the organisation.

At this stage, Helen was in the midst of Senior Practitioner team coach training, and she had her peer-learning group to call on for support. She also continued with peer supervision and professional group team coaching supervision. All this combined meant she was more externally resourced despite continuing environmental challenges. She had other team coaching engagements, her family and health issues improved, and her overall capacity increased. It appeared that with more autonomy, Helen's dependency and control within the organisation also decreased. Although she did not report this, I noticed her confidence had increased and her way of being was more consistently buoyant.

Toward the end of year three, Helen told me that Michael was leaving Green Apple Co. This created a cascade of challenges for her to work through, including:

- What that meant for the future of the Team.
- How her work with the Team would be impacted.
- Whether and how she should support Michael.
- What roles she would play as the organisation came to terms with the announcement.

Helen brought her whole self to these sessions – raw emotions, three years of systemic understanding, compassion for Michael and the Team, as well as a resolve to support them through change without that tipping into over-responsibility. Through active reflection and many types of support, Helen was able to segue herself out of Green Apple Co at the end of Year Three, and successfully use her learning to support Michael in doing the same, while supporting the Team to embrace a New Leader. Some of the work she did with the Team at the end of Year Three was specifically around how they would farewell Michael and induct the New Leader.

## Coach development journey

This case is an excellent example of human and professional elements coming together in a CAS and what is required of coaches to deliver organisational coaching. As evidenced, Helen was and is dedicated to ongoing personal and professional development, which was crucial in her ability to navigate complexity within the CAS in this case. However, it is important to underscore that the case we are focusing on for the learning purposes of this book is not exclusively about Helen, despite her being a central element within it.

As the system was dynamic, system elements, such as the Leader, the Team, individual team members, Helen's friends and family, "hailstorms," "leaf spot," economic and many other environmental factors, informed this case and impacted on each other. Helen is not in isolation from these elements. Instead, the elements within the system inform and respond to each other. For example, when Helen was fully present and delivering work, the Team benefitted from it. When the Team was having a difficult time, Helen felt it, and this feeling might have decreased her presence and ability to deliver the work. In professional supervision, we explore these factors and interdependencies to support the practitioner and the system in which they are working to enhance overall outcomes.

As a new internal coach with high expectations of herself and from others, a tendency toward pleasing, and the transferential factors outlined above, Helen resourced herself well. Her combined support infrastructure assisted her in developing competence, capability and capacity (Broussine, 1998), and she was able to professionally and ethically deliver her work at a particular point, in line with her coach maturity level. In short, she employed a continuous reflective learning cycle (Kolb, 1984).

In practice, Helen reported that the quality of her delivery increased, she was able to address emotional outbursts in team sessions, more nimbly step out of parallel process, and better address counter-transference issues, particularly in relation to Michael. In supervision sessions where Helen was internally buoyant, she creatively came up with new models to support her next challenge, laughed when she told stories of rescuing again, and reflected deeply about patterns she noticed about herself in relation to other clients as well as this case.

Despite the multiple challenges faced and overcome in this case, Helen seemed to advance her capability within her role to better support the Team. Through her three-year journey of understanding, defining and staying within the functional role of team coach, applying her multiple visual models, receiving support from friends, family and colleagues, and through reflective practice and supervision, Helen scaled from being a mostly models-based team coach to a philosophy-based team coach (Megginson & Clutterbuck, 2009) (Theory Break 7.20).

Within this CAS, it seems the Team also advanced and matured. They benefitted from Helen's role-modelling team coaching and were able to apply models, team agreements, and other development-plan content to work with and across Green Apple Co differently. As a result of Helen's dedication to her reflective practice, and elements within the system being open to and applying agreed changes, the collective system improved.

## Self-reflection

This case is a perfect example of complexity within organisational coaching and team coaching. Professional supervision is required for everyone who is formally looking at the system. As a professional supervisor, I too am in supervision, both for my client case work and for supervision of my supervision work.

When working with Helen in relation to this case, I noticed that I could get caught in a parallel process at times, by feeling how she, the system, or people within the system were drawn into the Karpman Drama Triangle (Theory Break 8.14). For example, during a supervision session, I might feel protective of Helen and be aware of whether I was colluding with her, or her manager, or being tempted to "feel sorry" for her, rather than simply having human compassion. If I noticed these issues arising, I put them back into the conversation, by saying something like, "I'm noticing I'm getting drawn into the frustration you feel. Where is that in the system for you?"

If I felt I was colluding or was unable to see a pathway forward because I got caught in the system complexity myself, I took that to my own supervision. In reliving this case while writing it, I am struck by how much we covered. I find it encouraging that the co-created nature of supervision can create richness and depth of awareness and opportunity to advance both the coach and the organisation as a result.

## Summary – Supervision

A summary of thoughts on what was good, challenging and what was learnt from the Supervision perspective of this case is included in the Appendix to Chapter Eight. In this case, Helen was both an internal and external coach, part of the team she was working with in a complex and challenging environment. Although exaggerated by challenging circumstances, the areas highlighted in Appendix Eight are common across many team-coaching scenarios. The most significant reflection from a Supervision perspective is that it takes a village to build and support a coach's capacity and maturity.

## Group supervision

**Author Helen Zink**
**Written in the voice of John, speaking on behalf of Helen's group supervision members**

I am a member of Helen's team coaching supervision group. As part of gathering input for this book, Helen collected written contributions from Jim, Fred, Amy and myself, which I draw from in this section.

Helen, Jim, Fred, Amy and I were in the same cohort of Practitioner and Senior Practitioner team coaching training. As Tammy mentioned above, we continued to work together as a supervision group between and after formal training courses. While some of us participated in one-to-one, team-focused supervision in addition to group supervision, including Helen, we all agree the shared learning experience we create when together has a unique and important place in our development. We have been fortunate to have both David Clutterbuck and Tammy working with us throughout, alternating in the supervisor role.

As Tammy explained above, sometimes we bring real cases to supervision, relating to teams we are working with, and sometimes we work through topics of common interest.

One of the curious things about the experience is that we emulate a team within sessions themselves, in that sometimes we disagree, sometimes we experience psychological safety and sometimes we lose it, and we invest time contracting what we will work on and how we will work together. We learn in two layers – the content of supervision cases we discuss and navigating the dynamics of working together. The complexity and layers involved are a little mind-blowing at times, yet a great illustration of dynamics within CASs.

Helen consistently brought cases relating to the Team to supervision, which benefitted all of us. Amy contributed, "I had the privilege of learning from Helen's case studies, and as a trusted colleague, I was invited to offer observations and reflections about the issues that Helen was working through." Fred added, "My role was a peer, a sounding board, another perspective. I was also a fascinated observer of the process we were experiencing!" As I read through the reflection notes from Jim, Fred, Amy, while preparing for this book, I noticed common themes coming through – role clarity, energy, system dynamics, Helen's development journey and our collective development journey as a supervision group. I expand on each next.

*Group Supervision topics*

*Role clarity*

I think much of the material Helen brought to supervision focused on, or at least included, challenges relating to role clarity within the Team. Amy thought, "The focus of topics were internal relationships between p articipants, the blurred lines of role and accountabilities of managers in the workplace, and the wholesale structural and process changes to core functions at the same time." Fred added, "Helen initially tried to please everyone, and she struggled to find a balance between her role as a coach and as an employee. Occasionally, she was drawn into rescuing behaviours in order to help the Team progress." Jim's reflections were similar – "Helen's challenges related primarily to different aspects of contracting and re-contracting." I think we helped Helen see that some of the roles she took on were not her responsibility and offered other ways to see her role and the system.

*Energy*

It was evident the challenges Helen was experiencing impacted her deeply, which affected her wellbeing and energy. In her contribution to this book, Amy referred to a group session where we were asked to "acknowledge the pain in Helen's system and share our sense of that pain." I remember it being an extremely powerful session. Fred's input also included comments on energy, saying that "despite the challenges Helen was experiencing and the impact on her, she was extremely resilient and determined throughout." Jim contributed that he "admired Helen's passion and energy, and her belief that she could make a difference from inside." I sensed that too – she was not going to give up on this Team without a fight. We tried to help Helen create more realistic expectations of herself and her ability to influence the stubborn system she found herself in – hopefully relieving some of the pressure she felt.

*System dynamics*

I believe Helen brought a strong sense of system dynamics and complexity to our group sessions with content she contributed. Fred recalled discussions about "transitioning from being part of the team to purely coaching the team, and how that impacted dynamics in the system for both Helen and the team." Amy's notes for this book included content on how working through Helen's challenges collectively helped her appreciate "how much we project our own reality into a system," and how "we as coaches can mirror resistance in the system by, for example, trying to fix the team or save the team leader."

## Coach development

Over time, I saw Helen's confidence and knowledge around team coaching grow. Jim also reflected my view in his notes, saying, "I gradually saw Helen mature and become confident in her role as a team coach." Amy wrote a similar comment in her contribution, specifically around the important skill of contracting. "Helen is now masterful at contracting and has commendable clarity around roles and expectations. She describes holding space for the team to thrive, whilst also sitting apart from them to be of service to all members and the team as a whole." We feel privileged to be part of and witness Helen's development journey.

## Peer group development

Helen was not the only beneficiary of the material she brought to group supervision. Jim, Fred, Amy and I benefitted too. Amy's said, "The challenges and topics were relevant and common for many teams and organisations, which made them very immediate and relatable to everyone in the room." Fred added that the "systemic challenges Helen and the team faced always brought practical real-life scenarios to supervision for discussion", and "Helen helped the entire group to group grow their competence and confidence with team coaching because of her willingness to bring real cases to each session." Jim contributed that "the situations helped the group see things from multiple perspectives, notice the tensions and explore possible pathways." I think that, over time, we got to know the Team well, and we all gained significant value from the generosity and vulnerability of cases Helen shared over a considerable period of time. Our collective and individual growth benefitted from the story of the Team in this case and our collective group supervision process.

## Summary – Group supervision

I believe Helen was able to develop through scenarios she brought to supervision sessions related to this case, and based on our input into this book, it is clear that Amy, Fred, Jim and I developed as well. As Tammy mentions above, the learning Helen experienced was fed back into the system for the benefit of the Team in this case and the entire system, including us. Learning we experienced from this case also fed into our work with our clients and their systems too.

Professional group supervision is a powerful learning experience for all involved, and we feel privileged to support your learning, too, by contributing to this chapter. A summary of our thoughts on what was good, challenging and what was learnt from Group Supervision is included in the Appendix to Chapter Eight.

# Other Support

**Author Helen Zink**
**Written in the voice of Rachael, speaking on behalf of all Other Support networks, professional peers, family and friends**
I am a colleague in Helen's professional network, as well as a friend. Content in this section is based on written contributions Helen collected from Anna, Robbie, Heather, Kirsten, Keith and me, for inclusion in this book.

I have known Helen for many years, long before her involvement with Green Apple Co, and I know her well. We often share war stories around clients and other professional interests. We are personal friends as well and support each other emotionally. My view, as well as Anna, Robbie, Heather, Kirsten and Keith's view of the system, is illustrated in the bottom diagram in Figure 8.1. Our view of Helen within the system is formed via Helen's perspective, and our comments in this section include a combination of her biases and our own.

## Benefits of Other Support

### Year One

I remember when Helen first started her role with Green Apple Co; she was very "excited," describing it as her "dream job." Sadly, it did not take long for her stories to be filled with frustration and complexity. Over the time period this book covers, my role was, and still is, to support Helen in an informal way. We had many conversations about the Team, Michael and Green Apple Co over a wine or two, and many of those conversations were emotional – including tears, frustration and laughter. It was clear Helen's involvement with her employer, later client, was very important to her, and she took many of the challenges she was faced with personally – I think too personally. Helen also said she felt very lonely in her role, and she turned to me and others in her network to talk things through and download. Keith, one of Helen's close friends, wrote in his contribution to this book,

> When Helen and I talked about her experiences with Green Apple Co, it felt like two parts downloading, three parts empathy and one part entertainment. Some of her stories were surprising and amusing at the same time – obviously amusing for me because I wasn't living them, but it was good we could laugh about it.

A family member, Kirsten, described her role in a similar way, writing, "I feel my support and occasional questions reinforced and clarified Helen's ideas and thinking . . . like a sounding board . . . an opportunity for her to hear her own words out loud."

## Year Two

Year Two was hard for Helen, and for all of us. We were dealing with the implications of "leaf spot," and Helen was working through the added complication of transiting from an internal coach role to an external role. I recall a telephone conversation we had when she first left her role – she was understandably emotional. In addition to adjusting to the change and finding her feet in relation to her new circumstances with the Team, she needed to rebuild her own coaching business and gain other client work, all during a "leaf spot" crisis. It was a hard time for her, and hard for all of us in similar professions. I was building a relatively new coaching business at that time too, so we had plenty to share and gain from each other's experiences and ideas.

## Year Three

By year three, Helen seemed more settled with her new business, had multiple clients, clear service offering and seemed to have found her groove.

Her stories about the Team were less emotional by then too – there was more separation between her work and herself as a person. I noticed a change in my role during this time as well. I felt our topics of conversation were more balanced and rounded. Anna, one of our mutual colleagues, wrote in her notes that, "We became more like professional peers – people to bounce business and client ideas off." I was and still am there when Helen needs me, and she is there for me too – mutual sounding boards, professional advisors, business advisors and sympathetic ears.

As a coach myself, I am very aware that coaches are whole people, and everyone within a coach's professional and personal network is part of their system and brought into a coaching engagement via the coach (Theory Break 7.8). For example, Helen had many conversations with me about the Team and how to tackle particular challenges, and our conversations most likely impacted the way she thought about those challenges, which in turn impacted how she framed up conversations with the Team, which impacted the Team's work on that topic and the outcome. Outcomes in turn impacted the wider organisation and hence the entire system.

## Support topics

When Helen and I spoke, we covered, and still cover, a wide range of topics. In relation to the case this book covers, there were several recurring themes relating to role clarity, energy levels and alignment with the system. Some of her stories I could relate to very well, as I had had similar experiences myself, and some were new, giving me an opportunity to learn as we discussed and worked through challenges together.

## Role clarity

It seemed that Helen was in a very unusual situation, especially in her first year working with the Team. It sounded like Michael and the Team wanted to delegate development and people leadership to her, and she was trying to do the opposite, by encouraging them to step up and take responsibility themselves. To me, it felt like the Team and Michael were on a completely different page to Helen; in fact, I am not sure they were even reading the same book. It is no wonder she described so much tension and friction.

It felt like the role Helen took on was not well thought through from the onset, and it was never really clarified – certainly not in Years One and

Two. One of our colleagues, Robbie, wrote in his notes that "Helen talked about wearing several hats in relation to the Team – coach, consultant, team member – and several hats in relation to Michael – sponsor, coachee and friend. There were certainly significant and challenging boundary issues to navigate." Anna, also part of our network, added, "Helen's relationship with Michael was tricky and troublesome at times, with him being overly reliant on her and expecting more than was perhaps appropriate for her role. I did not envy the situation Helen was in."

## Energy

Another important theme coming through in our discussions was energy and Helen's mental health. The tension and frustration she faced every day was clearly taking a toll. Anna highlighted an important area – "In a couple of instances, the demands Helen was juggling ran the risk of having significant impact on her physical and mental health, and I wanted to support her as she navigated this." Robbie added that "preserving wellbeing within Helen's role as team coach was a common theme of discussion." I, along with everyone in Helen's support network, was concerned for her wellbeing and suggested many times that she leave the engagement over the three-year period. Helen shared with me that her family were giving her the same advice – leave! I suppose we all felt the anguish she was going through was not worth the impact on her health; Helen's health was more important than any Team or any role.

## Part of the system

As I reflect on the situation Helen was in, I also sensed she was not only part of the system, but also completely engulfed by it. Whatever happened to the Team and Michael happened to her too – I think partly because she was so personally invested, and partly because she was so physically close to the Team. Heather, one of our peers, wrote, "Helen described a lot of back-and-forth progress, linked to psychological safety within the Team. It felt like Helen was going up and down with the Team at the same time, especially at the beginning."

## Summary – Other Support

A summary of what we found good, challenging, and what was learnt as members of Helen's Other Support network is included in the Appendix to Chapter Eight. A benefit of Helen sharing her challenges with me, and others in her professional network, family and friends, is that we are on tap, only a phone call away. Sharing concerns with us is a completely unstructured support tool, so our feedback and advice is unstructured as well. We are often quite blunt and unfiltered. The advantage of using us for support is that we are closest to her and know her better than anyone. I often recall Helen saying, "That is just what I needed to hear," and, "I have been thinking about what you said – it's like you are saying out loud exactly what is going through my head." Kirsten summed it up well in her reflection – "I know Helen is passionate about her work. As a family member, with no real understanding of the challenges involved, I listen and encourage with love. That's our job!"

## Chapter Eight Summary

**Author Tammy Turner**
**Written in the voice of Tammy, as Helen's Supervisor**
Back to me, to summarise this chapter. Within the industry, organisational coaching challenges everyone within the system to expand their capability and capacity to match what the CAS requires. We are still on a journey of understanding what is required to best support coaches, leaders and those who work within organisational CASs. I have a perspective on this which informs my biases in this chapter, and I expand on that in Chapter Eleven. This book, involving a three-year case, highlights the benefit of reflecting with others. It is through collective reflective practice that coaches build capability and capacity to meet systemic challenges – as Helen did in this case.

As part of writing this chapter, Helen asked what I thought the best, most challenging and greatest learning areas relating to support in this case. In consultation, we agreed:

- The best aspect was the choice of appropriate levels of support.
- The most challenging was applying insight gained from supervision with the Team and Michael, particularly during times when her energy was low.
- The greatest learning was that it takes a village to support a coach's capacity and maturity.

Though it may seem like too much support, I believe Helen resourced herself appropriately both based on the complexity of the assignment and her capacity to maximise her reflexivity (Theory Break 11.3).

> It is the various forms of reflective practice (both formal supervision and informal reflection and support) that help coaches develop their artistry and their unique signature as a practitioner . . . Reflective practice is not . . . about ticking a box. It is about facilitating a deeper understanding of how we each work
>
> (Turner et al., 2018).

As a result of Helen's commitment, her coaching maturity, reflective capability and capacity increased. In turn, her ability to both reflect in the moment and more ably self-manage and nimbly meet team coaching challenges increased.

A coach's supervision and less formal support experiences help inform and shape how they develop, the approaches and methodology they use, their preferences, and ultimately who they are as a coach. This is particularly relevant in early stages of their career. In Chapter One, Helen talks about multiple levels of learning and continuous learning cycles (Figure 1.3). Helen shared with me that, without a doubt, the formative stages of her development within this case, including team coach training, and Supervision and Other Support she tapped into, have defined her as a coach and her preferences in her current team coaching practice.

How a coach comes into "being" is also forged by peer relationships and with collegiate feedback. Together, both formal and informal support networks have a profound impact on a coach and, in turn, the impact the coach has on the wider system. Collectively, a coach, their system(s), their clients and their clients' system(s), their supervisor's systems, and, via group supervision, other coaches and their client(s) as part of the coach's wider systemic field, are all impacted. The concept of the coaching ripple effect (O'Connor & Cavanagh, 2013) (Theory Break 4.4) applies in both coaching supervision and informal support contexts as well as with clients. It is for this reason that a considered approach to reflective practice, peer and professional supervision, and other support networks, is crucial to the longevity and sustainability of the coaching industry, which I reiterate in Chapter Eleven.

This is the last of the perspective chapters. Section C which follows, changes tack by combining and comparing all five perspectives covered in this section, creating a more wholistic view of the CAS – meta-reflection.

# References

Broussine, M. (1998). *The Society of Local Authority Chief Executives and Senior Managers (SOLACE): A scheme for continuous learning for SOLACE members.* Bristol: University of the West of England.

Clutterbuck, D. (2020). *Coaching the team at work.* London & Boston: Brealey.

European Mentoring and Coaching Council (2020). *EMCC global team coaching accreditation standards framework.* Retrieved from https://emccglobal.org/accreditation/tcqa.

Hawkins, P. & Turner, E. (2020). *Systemic coaching: Developing value beyond the individual.* London & New York: Routledge. https://doi.org/10.4324/9780429452031.

International Coaching Federation (2020a). *ICF code of ethics.* Retrieved from https://coachfederation.org/ethics/code-of-ethics.

Karpman, S. (2014). *A game free life. The new transactional analysis of intimacy, openness, and happiness.* San Francisco: Drama Triangle Publications.

Megginson, D. & Clutterbuck, D. (2009). *Further techniques for coaching and mentoring.* London: Routledge. https://doi.org/10.4324/9780080949420.

O'Connor, S. & Cavanagh, M. (2013). The coaching ripple effect: the effects of developmental coaching on wellbeing across organisational networks. *Psychology of Well-Being: Theory, Research and Practice.* 3:2. https://doi.org/10.1186/2211-1522-3-2.

Turner, T. (2014) The importance of contracting: Using the shared outcomes model [pdf]. Available through: https://www.turner.international/_files/ugd/11f34b_752289ef72904c2f99521f72e8f22ec8.pdf [accessed 7 December 2022].

Turner, T. (2022). *Parallel process in team coaching.* GTCI course material.

Turner, T., Lucas, M. & Whitaker, C. (2018). *Peer supervision in coaching and mentoring: A versatile guide for reflective practice.* London & New York: Routledge. https://doi.org/10.4324/9781315162454.

Appendix to Chapter Eight: Good, challenging and learnt – Supervision and Other Support's perspective

| Good | Challenging | Learnt |
|---|---|---|
| | Coach support | |
| Helen was already familiar with peer supervision before embarking on professional team coaching supervision. | Topics covered in supervision were confronting at times. | The coach is part of the system & both impacts & is impacted by it. |
| Helen recognised early that she needed professional supervision support. | Common themes:<br>• Ethics.<br>• Role boundaries & hats.<br>• Energy & resilience<br>• Transference.<br>• Parallel processes. | The value of professional supervision with complex clients & situations. |
| Both professional one-to-one & group team supervision were used to illuminate the CAS. | | Both one-to-one & group supervision have their place & are beneficial. |
| Formal team coaching training took place in parallel with supervision. | Helen's vulnerability in front of professional peers while learning & under difficult circumstances. | Everyone involved in supervision is part of the system too – via the coach. |
| Helen created visual bespoke models – to help keep herself on track. | Using advice given by less experienced peers can be risky. | Everyone involved in group team coaching supervision benefits from the experience. |
| All involved in group team supervision learnt from Helen's contributions. | Setting appropriate boundaries with newer peers in supervision who do not know you well. | Increased competence, capability & capacity comes with practice & support. |
| Ad hoc informal support is easy to access & multi-faceted – sounding board, professional advisor, business advisor, sympathetic ear, friend. | Applying learning from supervision & training with the Team & Michael. | Creatively designing tools for reflective practice can be fun & rewarding. |
| Informal support of professional colleagues & friends & family is important as they know better than anyone. | | Coaches should tap into all support networks they have, professional & personal for emotional support. |
| | | It takes a village to support a coach's capacity & maturity. (Most valuable learning for Supervision and Other Support). |

# Section C – Insights

# Comparing perspectives – similarities 9

*Helen Zink*

---

## HOW TO READ CHAPTER NINE

I am Helen, the Team Coach in this story, and this is how this chapter fits into the overall book.

The three chapters in Section C combine the five perspectives in this book, highlighting further insight and illustrating the power of perspective taking (Theory Break 1.4) – meta-reflection.

In Chapter Nine, the first of the meta-reflection chapters, I review and narrate similarities in what was good, challenging and learnt across all five perspectives (refer to Figure 9.1). I divide similarities into themes of:

- Strategy enablement and change management.
- Team development and coaching.
- Leadership development.
- Coaching in general.
- Coach support.

This is the "plot twist" in the movie analogy, where it becomes clear that the parallel plots, described by five different characters in Section B, are in fact telling the same story and share many similarities.

Content for this chapter is collated from content in Chapters Four to Eight, in Section B.

---

DOI: 10.4324/9781003367789-12

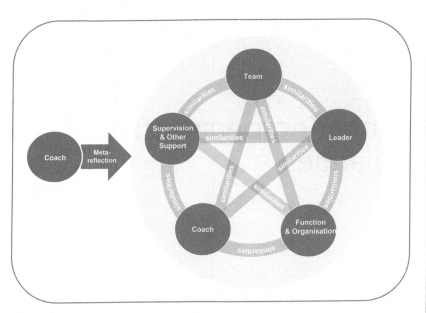

Figure 9.1: Meta-reflection similarities

Up to now, this book has told five different versions of the same story, and those versions of the story have been kept separate.

Now I combine common level one, two and three learning (Figure 1.3) from all five perspectives for further insight. Spoiler alert – there are many similarities in what each perspective found good, challenging and what they learnt from the experience. Most differences relate to alternative emphasis or priority rather than complete disagreement between parties. Areas where there was disagreement are covered in Chapter Ten.

## Strategy enablement and change management

### Strategic alignment

The first common learning is recognition that team development and coaching is a strategic enabler and change lever. As is the case with any other strategic enabler, alignment with overall strategy is critical. In this case, Michael intentionally invested in developing the Team as a critical lever to move Consulting Services towards a strategic goal of "being world class." As part of Jane's input to this book, she said, "It was not clear why we were doing the development work at first, but it became clear. The change we wanted to see needed to start with us."

Although Michael used a simplified change model, he consciously considered all of McKinsey's "Seven S's" (Peters & Waterman, 2006) (Theory Break 5.1). As Year One began, changes in strategy, systems and processes, structure and staff were already in play, and focus began on the "soft S's" of shared values, style and skills – the starting point for this case.

Another important learning was alignment between development work the Team undertook with the overall people strategy of Green Apple Co. This included alignment with organisation-wide intervention streams, such as the culture change programme, C-suite and senior leader development programmes and encouragement of coaching culture. This reinforced the work I was doing with the Team, provided consistency for all of us, and helped embed growth and learning.

### Change management

During Year One, the Team's development plan was managed by me, with Michael's endorsement. However, it was managed to a large extent in isolation from other change taking place across Consulting Services and Green Apple Co. Given team development and coaching was acknowledged as a critical change lever in this case, more thought should have been given to robust change management disciplines, described by Sally in Chapter Six.

In Chapter Four, the Team talk about their initial resistance to focus on development work – seeing it as an annoyance and another distraction from BAU activity. The Team's overall change journey would have been more effective if it had been integrated with other significant system and process changes taking place at the same time – part of an overall change programme. In addition to helping to convince the Team that development would be beneficial, integrated planning and prioritisation may have mitigated loss of service delivery during "hailstorms," or perhaps prevented the storms entirely.

In Chapter Five, Michael reflects that additional resource could have been added to the Team at the start of Year One, to add volume and focus for system and process changes taking place that year. If that choice had been made, it would have made sense for me to work closely with the incumbent in that role to create and manage the integrated change plan recommended above.

To be effective, the integrated change plan suggested would need to meet stakeholders' needs in addition to the Team's needs. The best way to ensure stakeholders are happy is to involve them throughout the process, from establishing team development goals and priorities, to creating options and solutions, to measurement of progress. In Chapter Six, Sally specifically highlighted this as a critical learning area and suggested the Team's development programme should have had C-suite sponsorship with formal governance in place, including progress and risk reporting.

Formal governance and risk management may have mitigated or at least increased visibility of impending "hailstorms," resulting in more informed balance between change and BAU activity. Although we cannot predict what would have happened, we can predict that the CAS would have evolved into a completely different outcome.

## Strategy enablement

All perspectives agreed the capability and capacity of the internal HR team to deliver people-related strategic enablers was resource-constrained during Year One. In Chapter Five, Michael talks about the limitation being a significant consideration in creating the Coach role, my role. Michael, the Team, and HR all agreed the Team would benefit from dedicated development focus and an internal resource – at least in Year One.

*Measurement framework*

Throughout Section B, the absence of a formal measurement framework was mentioned as a significant omission in this case. Chapter Six also suggests that the Function and Organisation should have been involved in creating said framework and contributed to the measurement of results as well. With more 360 input on progress and outcomes, I suspect this story would have unfolded very differently. As the saying goes, "You get what you measure."

Another common learning area was the importance of intangible measures. All five perspectives mentioned the importance of how they felt within the process, as expressed in written and verbal feedback at the time, or later as they contributed to this book. Michael went so far as to say that "tangible measures are good, and what can be measured should be measured," but more importantly he could "feel the change."

This case also highlighted that a significant delay in seeing results come through in tangible measures did not mean that work done was ineffective. In a CAS, many factors are in play, and the static scores in Year One were actually a good result, given the particularly complex environment the Team were faced with – patience is required!

## Team development and coaching

*Team development and coaching*

Although the choice to use team coaching and one-to-one informal coaching as interventions in this case were lucky opportunities, rather than intentional strategic choices, all perspectives agreed they were appropriate for the environment and beneficial for the overall system.

Despite the Team not "being ready" or supporting investment in their own development at the beginning, over time, all perspectives, including that of the Team, agreed they were benefitting from the experience.

It was clear to all that the impacts of environmental events, such as unplanned building moves, "hailstorms," "leaf spot," multiple structure changes across Green Apple Co, funding issues and other challenging environmental factors, were a significant distraction for the Team and their ability to maximise benefits from the development experience. Figures 2.9, 2.10 and 2.11 show a repeating pattern of some progress, an environmental event, some progress, another environmental event, and so on, throughout the three-year timeframe this case covers. Each setback pushed the Team down the maturity scale (Theory Break 5.3), and energy was required to build up again. Although unpleasant and frustrating, the experience provided the Team with great opportunity to build collective team resilience (Theory Break 4.1) as emphasised by the Team.

## HPT goal and model

The HPT goal and the PERILL (Clutterbuck, 2020) (Theory Break 3.2) model used in this case were chosen by me and adapted to align with Green Apple Co's own in-house model. Given the maturity of the Team at the beginning of Year One, all parties, including me, considered it appropriate for me to make those choices on the Team's behalf.

However, there were implications. All agreed the Team's understanding and buy-in did not rally occur until Year Two. And it took until Year Three for them to fully embrace PERILL. When they finally did buy in, their enthusiasm was so strong they effectively created their own version of the model – "PERILL Plus," Figure 3.2.

The main learning here is that appreciation of models, which may seem like abstract and theoretical concepts to a team, can evolve over time, and tweaking and adapting models is an effective way to get alignment and buy-in from both the Team and Organisation.

## Team readiness

The Team did not meet suggested team coaching readiness criteria (Theory Break 7.6); however, Michael made the decision to start at the beginning of Year One anyway. In retrospect, all perspectives agreed he made the right decision at the time. In Chapter Seven, I emphasise that if we had waited for the Team to be "ready," the journey would never have started at all.

This case illustrates that matching interventions and modality with the maturity level of the Team (Theory Breaks 3.5 and 5.3) is more important than a team's "readiness," It may be necessary to begin with simple, highly facilitated content to build "readiness," with more team coaching interventions introduced over time. I explained modalities and team maturity more fully in Chapter Seven.

## Team dynamics

All perspectives agreed that team dynamics were challenging at times. Some complex dynamics which existed before Year One were carried into this Team, and new challenges occurred when I joined, and later when Tom joined as well.

While some complexity in team dynamics is not unusual, an interesting observation in this case is noticeable alignment between dynamics in the Team and collective psychological safety (Theory Break 7.7).

The Team also noticed a direct relationship between psychological safety and the amount of time they invested in connection and development. The key learning here is that psychological safety is extremely fluid, and if it is lost, intentional investment in connection may encourage it to return.

## Intervention (A) – Team development days

One of the main learnings all perspectives agree on is the value of regular team development days. The Team learnt the hard way that once a pattern is formed, investment should continue, even when capacity is stretched and the temptation to focus on BAU is high. As shown in this case, a pattern of cancelling team sessions in Year Three led to noticeable loss in psychological safety, a dip in maturity, and a significant "bump" in the Team's development journey.

This case highlights learning areas related to approach and logistics as well:

- Balance flexibility versus structure
  A team coach's bias may be flexibility, but that may not suit all members of the team and could inhibit learning for some. I suggest a team coach continually contracts the appropriate balance with the team, providing some structure for those who need it, while leaving enough discomfort to create a learning edge for all.
- "Pure" team coaching is rare
  Moving between modalities of teaching, facilitation and team coaching (Theory Break 3.5) is normal and expected, and as shown in this case, coaches should use their intuition to assess which is best in which circumstance.
- Manage feedback and avoid moderation
  Including feedback from a team in future sessions is great. However, in this case, Michael moderated content, meaning some topics I thought would benefit the Team were never raised. Remember the client is the team (Theory Break 7.1) and their needs should come first. In this case, I believe the Team would have been willing to experiment more and push themselves harder than Michael gave them credit for.

- Harness the gift of learning from mistakes
  Similar to the point above, the opportunity to focus on mistakes and learn from them was moderated in some instances. For example, the first "hailstorm" was not used as a learning gift or fully explored within the team development programme – I think part of the reason it repeated.
- Get the housekeeping right
  Contract roles and responsibilities with all parties involved, including commitment to pre-work and follow-through on actions, physical logistics, and aligning frequency and timing of sessions with other commitments.
- Coaching sessions mirror real life
  What happens within team development sessions is a reflection of what the Team does outside the session. In this case, the cancellation of team development sessions mirrored lost connection within the Team back in the office. A coach is in a unique position to reflect back what they see in a team, share their intuition, and role-model and raise possible growth areas within sessions.

## Intervention (B) – One-to-one formal and informal coaching of team members

It is not common for an internal team coach be part of the team they are working with. However, in this case, having someone on hand within the team providing informal and formal one-to-one coaching and advice, in parallel with team development, helped embed change. This was one of the most significant benefits acknowledged by all in this case.

Ways to replicate similar benefit in other scenarios might be establishing peer-coaching pairs within a team, or across an organisation, or, if available, formal internal or external one-to-one coaching for team members.

## Responsibility and contracting

A challenging obstacle to overcome in this case was Michael holding all accountability, responsibility and authority (Theory Break 7.16) for the Team at the beginning of Year One. As he changed and began sharing responsibility with me, and then Tom, it was not communicated well, resulting in confusion and frustration.

The creation of the Year Two plan improved clarity of roles significantly, including clear documentation of delegation and responsibility.

There are several learning points related to this area highlighted in this case:

- Share responsibility.
- Clarify who has accountability and responsibility – formal documented plans are helpful.
- Communicate accountability and responsibility well with all stakeholders.
- Continually contracting between team members and stakeholders to clarify roles and accommodate changes.

Team coaching is a great way to establish clear accountability and responsibility within a team and a good way to practice multi-stakeholder contracting as well (Theory Break 7.9).

## Bumps in the journey

The Team, Michael and I recognised a significant "bump" in the Team's development journey in Year Three. I was extremely concerned by the drop in psychological safety I observed, as well as a sense of lost commitment. However, Michael and the Team were not at all concerned. They talked through the "bump," acknowledged it, and, with my support, created a plan to get back on track. It was the Team who normalised the situation for me by emphasising that ups and downs on a development path should be expected.

## Team resilience

The Team themselves emphasised the importance of team resilience in this case. In addition to adding team resilience to their bespoke HPT model, they also acknowledged that participating in team development increased both their individual and collective resilience. That in turn facilitated more team development and resilience – a continuous loop of reinforcement (Theory Break 4.1).

## Stakeholders and support

Stakeholders were effectively absent in the Team's development journey in this case – acknowledged by some perspectives more passionately than others in Section B. As mentioned above, and in Chapter Six, Sally argues the Team's development programme should have been managed as a formal integrated change programme with C-suite sponsorship.

An added benefit of involving stakeholders in the journey would have been better psychological contracts (Theory Break 6.2). If involved, stakeholders might have expressed more sympathy and support of the Team's predicaments and when times were tough.

## Gaps in the system

The Team and Michael mentioned one of the most significant things they observed was the gap created between team members and managers reporting to them. As the Team developed and stepped up, the layer below did not, pulling the Team back into detailed activity and habits they were trying to break – in effect holding the Team at a lower maturity level than their capability.

The main learning here is the importance of taking a systemic view of development, appreciating that the impact of change in one part of a system, including positive change, might negatively impact other parts. In this case, more work on "soft S's" with the next layer down would have benefitted the Team and the entire system.

## Ripple effect

All perspectives observed and agreed the Team's development work in this case had a wide ripple effect (O'Connor & Cavanagh, 2013) across Consulting Services and the entire organisation (Theory Break 4.4). I also suspect that benefits were felt much more widely than discussed in this book. Michael mentioned the personal impact the journey had on himself and members of the Team; I benefitted personally too.

I did not ask stakeholders external to Green Apple Co whether they noticed any change in the Team over time timeframe of this case. However, if I had, I think they would have observed positive change too.

## Good endings

The "good ending" exercise late in Year Three was recognised by all involved, including me, as a valuable and cathartic exercise. It is helpful to acknowledge significant events or changes in circumstances, such as the team leader leaving, as it allows a team and individuals to grieve loss and process change. The "good endings" work was a great example of how the right intervention at the right time can have benefits far beyond original expectations.

## Leadership development

### Strategic alignment

The alignment of a leader's leadership style with the trajectory of the team's development path might seem "a given" when embarking on a journey such as this. However, as this case shows, leader alignment should not be assumed.

It took a year for Michael to fully acknowledge the significance of his role as leader in the change programme (Theory Break 5.4) and role model and make a commitment to change his style. In particular, Michael and I agreed that the delay significantly impacted the Team's development growth, and more emphasis on alignment at the very beginning of the journey would have changed the story for all involved.

### Correct leadership style?

HPT theory suggests a leader's style needs to be what the team requires to perform at their best in their particular circumstances (Theory Break 3.2). Not a set list of "correct" attributes. Through this journey, Michael came to that realisation himself. He discovered he had several leadership styles, and all were useful in different situations.

The key learning was Michael's self-awareness and his increasing ability to recognise which style was most appropriate in any particular circumstance. Michael was also conscious that the leader as coach approach (Theory Break 5.2) he applied in Year Three was highly beneficial. The Team and staff across Consulting Services and Green Apple Co agreed, noticing he became more supportive and guiding – exactly what they wanted and needed.

### Intervention (C) – One-to-one informal coaching of team leader

Everyone mentioned the benefit of support I provided Michael, through one-to-one informal coaching and direct advice in Years One and Two.

Being an internal coach and part of the Team provided ample opportunity to provide Michael with on-tap support.

## Tension between team leader and coach

All observed the friendship and supporting relationship between Michael and me. They were also aware that our relationship had pros and cons. The most significant pro was on-tap support I provided Michael, as mentioned above. The most obvious con was tension between us playing out in public at times, particularly during Years One and Two and others' reactions to it.

## Overall reflection

This case provides a good example of how leadership style can shift, even a very stubborn one. All perspectives agreed bumps along the way should be expected, and changing style takes time. Michael also pointed out that working on professional change, the way he did, can have significant personal benefits for leaders as well.

# Coaching in general

## Internal versus external coach

Many pros and cons of my situation as an internal coach were highlighted in this case, particularly during Year One. Internal coaching is a complex situation to manage (Theory Break 3.4), and this case provided good evidence of common internal coach challenges related to role clarity, "leadership vacuum traps," and relationship dynamics.

Pros were evident as well, in particular the opportunity for informal one-to-one coaching and on-tap advice. Being part of the Team allowed me to support the Team to embed development activity in real-life situations. It also enabled me to experience the Team's system and feel their environment and challenges first-hand. The result being relevant interventions addressing "hot topics" the Team faced in real time.

The jury is still out on whether internal or external coaching is more effective – it is not clear cut. Either way, this case illustrates the importance of contracting, role clarity and experimentation with co-coaching options.

## Coach character

As described in Chapters Three and Seven, I was not specifically employed as a team coach or one-to-one coach for this engagement. Rather, the roles evolved from my own biases, experience, training and possibilities I brought to the engagement. Fortunately, my characteristics and approaches, including team coaching and a flexible and systemic mindset, were suited to the circumstances, and all perspectives agreed on this point.

If a person with a more structured and process-oriented approach had been appointed to the role, the team development process would have been very different for all involved. While I am sure the Team would have bene-fitted, particularly early on, I shudder to think what would have happened as relentless environmental impacts played out requiring constant adaption.

The key message is to carefully consider the type and magnitude of team change envisaged and the environmental context and employ a coach who is motivated by, and has characteristics that align with, the team's situation and system. As Tammy emphasises in Chapter Eight, the coach is ingrained within the system (Theory Break 7.8), and what they personally bring to the system significantly impacts everything that happens.

## Coach roles/hats and contracting

Throughout Section B, challenges with role clarity are highlighted and during Year One, that lack of clarity contributed to:

- Challenging team dynamics.
- The "leadership vacuum trap" (Clutterbuck, 2017).
- My unhelpful "hats."
- Implications of not "teaching the Team to fish."
- Misunderstanding and tension across the wider organisation.
- Tense and complex relationship between Michael and me.
- My energy crisis.

In Years Two and Three, there were more challenges with role expectations as I moved from an internal to external position. Logistics surrounding team development days also became an issue, and the rotating nature of leadership responsibility for development sessions was not a smooth pro-cess either.

There are several learning points related to coach role clarity highlighted in this case:

- Investment in contracting is critical. The Team, and all parties involved, will benefit from contracting and re-contracting roles and expectations throughout the journey (Theory Break 7.9).
- Verbal contracting may not be enough in some situations, and formal written contracts may be useful.
- Ensure relevant stakeholders outside the Team are aware of the scope and mandate of the coach's role.
- Maintain strong relationships between the coach and the organisation, normally via HR.

I am aware that the unusual nature of my situation in this case exaggerated the impact of coach role clarity, boundaries and the need for continual contracting. However, I think my experience highlights areas to keep front of mind in every coaching scenario.

## Co-coaching

An area not explored enough in this case was working with a co-coach – due primarily to my resistance. Michael, Tammy and I agree that working with an independent external co-coach or an internal co-coach would have changed my experience, and ultimately the experience of the Team and system (Theory Break 7.14).

Working in partnership with someone else would have provided opportunity to experiment with different ideas and approaches, and I might have felt less burdened and alone as well. Perhaps I would have been less reliant on Michael for support and friendship, and there might have been less tension in our relationship as a result.

## Coach development

I cannot emphasise enough the significant development experience this case provided me. Michael and those involved in my supervision networks attest to my growth too. While an extremely difficult experience, working with this Team and this system helped emphasise the importance of self-awareness and self-care, reflective practice, supervision, and support from all my professional and personal networks. All these factors are recognised as important considerations in team coaching development, and sufficient support is a requirement of EMCC Team Coach Accreditation Standards (2020) and ICF Team Coaching Competencies (2020b).

I also need to mention that similar to Michael's experience, my involvement in this journey resulted in significant personal growth. Now, as I write this book, the development opportunity provided by this case is shared even more widely across other systems – the gift that keeps on giving, that ripple effect again (O'Connor & Cavanagh, 2013).

## Coach support

Those most interested in my development and wellbeing (Michael in Year One, my Supervision and Other Support networks, and of course me) all agreed that having the support I needed was critical for the duration of this case, and most of that support came from outside Green Apple Co even when I was an employee.

Key insight around coach support highlighted in this case includes:

- The dual benefit of one-to-one and group team-focused supervision, as each is different and has its place.
- Everyone involved in group supervision is part of the system too.
- Everyone involved in group supervision benefits from the experience and takes learning back into their own areas of work and their clients' systems.
- Tapping into informal support networks is valuable – it takes a village to support a coach's capacity and maturity.

## Chapter Nine summary

This chapter illustrates many similarities across all five perspectives. Most differences reflect alternative emphasis or priority rather than disagreement between parties.

As there was so much learning within this case, I asked representatives of each perspective to identify the most significant thing they learnt. Their responses are included at the end of each chapter in Section B, and also summarised in Table 9.1.

That seemingly simple question has provided yet another layer of insight and the power of perspective-taking (Theory Break 1.4). Each area identified something different as their core learning point, and some chose themes I did not expect or did not even know about prior to working on this book.

Table 9.1: Key learning from each perspective

| Perspective | Key learning |
|---|---|
| Team | The value of team & individual resilience & appreciation that investing in collective development builds it. |
| Leader | The importance of leader as coach activity, based on EQ-centred leadership. |
| | The magnitude of personal change that took place. |
| Function & Organisation | Missed opportunity to find a way to support the Team & each other through change across the whole organisation. |
| | Integrated change programming & formal governance. |
| Coach | Being a team coach means more than ongoing professional development; it involves continual personal growth & development too. |
| Supervision & Other Support | Many support networks are involved – it takes a village to support a coach's capacity and maturity. |

The Team chose the importance of collective resilience and realisation that their collective development journey contributed to their individual and team resilience – a more reflective and considered response than I expected.

Michael talked about the importance of one-to-one leader as coach conversations he had with team members, and how he felt those conversations helped team members embed change in a tailored way. I had no visibility that this was a significant activity in Year Three, nor of the importance he placed on it.

The response from the Function and Organisation was more predictable, in that I was aware they felt forgotten, as I describe more fully in Chapter Seven.

My greatest learning of deep professional and personal change would not be a surprise to Michael or parties involved in Supervision and Other Support, but I am reasonably confident the Team would not have expected that answer from me.

The response from Supervision and Other Support was not a surprise. However, after working on Section B of this book, it is clear that some parties were not aware of my support networks, and if they did know, they did not fully appreciate the purpose of professional supervision.

In Chapter One, I talk about perspective-taking (Theory Break 1.4), and I emphasise that no individual perspective is better or truer than another. As a practising team coach working in the field of social sciences, this chapter is a good reminder that a team's individual and collective views are unlikely to be the same as each other's, or their stakeholders, or mine.

Rather than seeing different perspectives as an annoyance that slows down team process, I suggest intentionally using them as an opportunity. This chapter is a great reminder to harness the power of perspective-taking, hopefully resulting in more insightful knowledge, decisions and outcomes.

When I work with teams, I believe part of my role is to help them understand, navigate and take advantage of different perspectives amongst themselves, and across their stakeholder groups. If opinions are not particularly diverse, I encourage them to artificially inject different perspectives into the system to facilitate stronger exploration and debate, for example, by assigning thinking hats (De Bono, 1985).

Whatever your role is in relation to teams, whether you are a team member, coach, team coach, leader, HR professional, change manager, academic or consultant, I encourage you to embrace the power of perspective-taking too.

In the next chapter I pick up on genuine differences between perspectives and the implications of difference and choice within CASs.

## References

Clutterbuck, D. (2017). *The leadership vacuum trap and how coaches and mentors can avoid it*. Retrieved from https://www.coachingandmentoringinterna tional.org.

Clutterbuck, D. (2020). *Coaching the team at work*. London & Boston: Brealey.

De Bono, E. (1985). *Six thinking hats*. New York: Little Brown and Company.

European Mentoring and Coaching Council. (2020). *EMCC global team coaching accreditation standards framework*. Retrieved from https://emccglobal.org/ accreditation/tcqa.

International Coaching Federation. (2020b). *ICF team coaching competencies: Moving beyond one-to-one coaching*. Retrieved from https://coachfederation.org/ team-coaching-competencies.

O'Connor, S. & Cavanagh, M. (2013). The coaching ripple effect: the effects of developmental coaching on wellbeing across organisational networks. *Psychology of Well-Being: Theory, Research and Practice.* 3:2. https://doi.org/10.1186/2211-1522-3-2.

Peters, T. & Waterman, R. (2006). *In search of excellence: Lessons from America's best-run companies.* New York: Harper Business.

# Comparing perspectives – differences

# 10

*Helen Zink*

## HOW TO READ CHAPTER TEN

I am Helen, the Team Coach in this story, and this is how this chapter fits into the overall book.

The three chapters in Section C combine the five perspectives in this book, highlighting further insight and illustrating the power of perspective taking (Theory Break 1.4) – meta-reflection.

In the previous chapter, I reviewed similarities in what was good, challenging and learnt across all five perspectives. In Chapter Ten, I review and narrate the same information, this time highlighting differences between perspectives, refer to Figure 10.1. I identify differences in categories of:

- Strategy enablement and change management.
- Team development and coaching.
- Leadership development.
- Coaching in general.
- Coach support.

A key insight in this chapter relates to tension held in a system, and the impact of choices. If points of difference had been shared with relevant parties and resolved at the time, the story described in this book would have been different for everyone.

DOI: 10.4324/9781003367789-13

Using a movie analogy, this is the "climax" of the story, where the five main characters in the movie compare notes and realise they have different opinions on some matters. They argue and debate whether different choices made would have changed the plot and outcome of the entire movie.

Content for this chapter is collated from content in Chapters Four to Eight, in Section B.

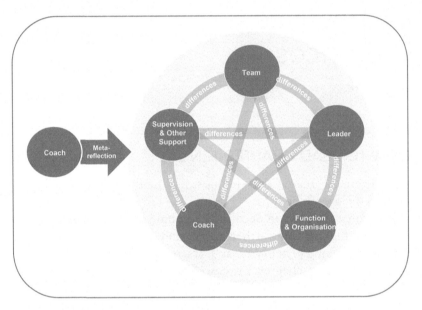

Figure 10.1: Meta-reflection differences

The previous chapter highlighted many similarities in what each perspective found good, challenging and what they learnt from the development experience. Most differences in opinion relate to alternative priority or emphasis rather than outright disagreement between parties. However, some differences were more significant and did create tension in the system, and these tension points are covered next.

## Strategy enablement and change management

### Formal change management

Soon after I started in the Coach role, it was clear there was a lot of change taking place simultaneously – structure, process and system changes, and "soft-S" changes were all being implemented at the same time. I raised concerns around gaps in formal change management several times during Year One, and Michael downplayed it.

In Chapter Six, Sally also suggested formal change management processes and C-suite sponsorship would have been a better approach. Sally may not have raised her thoughts at the time and I am unsure of the level of discussion within the C-suite on this matter, but there was certainly tension between Michael and me on this point.

### Continued use of external coach – Year Three

In Year One, HR fully supported my internal coach role. However, as I moved to an external role in Year Two, tension began to increase. By Year Three, HR was completely unsupportive of my work with the Team. Michael was aware of HR's views but argued that the Team wanted to continue to work with me. To complicate the situation further, HR raised their concerns directly with me, despite my suggestion that it was an issue between them and Michael. Was there tension? Absolutely! A triangle of tension between HR, Michael and me!

Figure 10.2 illustrates tension in the system relating to strategy enablement and change.

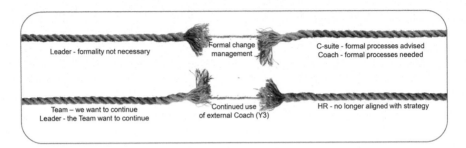

Figure 10.2: Differences – strategy enablement and change management

## Team development and coaching

### Team resistance – Year One

There was clear disagreement between the Team and Michael in relation to investing time in development in Year One. The Team argued they did not have capacity and did not understand the benefit of the investment, and Michael argued that team development was a critical enabler of overall strategy. As I explain in Chapter Seven, I am now an even stronger advocate of Michael's view. There is never a "good time" to begin a team coaching journey – just do it!

### Group versus Team – early Year One

At the beginning of Year One, both Michael and me were taken aback when the Team told us they were not a team, and argued that there was little relationship between their roles. Michael and I were puzzled, as we saw direct dependency between their roles. Understanding role inter-dependency became an immediate priority development, and it only took one intervention for the Team to see closer interconnection and align their thinking.

### Structure versus flexibility

The Team's views on the fluidity and flexibility of their development plan and development session content was divided. While some appreciated that agendas needed to be flexible to align with circumstances, others preferred structure and fixed agendas. While appreciating the Team's view on this, Michael and I very much favoured the flexible approach.

## Stakeholder involvement

Stakeholders were considered in some development activities; however, they were not directly involved and were never physically in the same room in development sessions. As a result, staff within the Function and Organisation felt they had been ignored, as described in Chapter Six. I knew that stakeholder involvement needed to be higher, but Michael pushed back. I suspect Michael was moderating content – protecting the Team from criticism.

As I mentioned in Chapter Seven, Michael and I cannot take full responsibility for lack of stakeholder involvement. I was not aware how strongly they felt until collating input for this book. Yet, I do not recall one stakeholder asking to be involved over the entire three-year period.

## Pace of change – Year One

Stakeholders, in particular the C-suite, expressed that while they saw improvements in the Team and Michael, change did not happen fast enough. Some also mentioned the "hailstorm" was the only reason change occurred at all.

Part of me agrees with the C-suite, and during Year One, I questioned whether I would be able to influence the stubborn systemic forces in play. Another part of me knows that change takes time, and given the exceptionally challenging environment, sluggish movement in the tangible measures we were tracking in Year One was actually a positive result.

## Cancelling sessions – Year Three

The cancellation of team development sessions in Year Three split the Team. Some supported cancellation, as they wanted to work on BAU and urgent delivery matters, and some were disappointed. Interestingly, Michael did not support sessions being cancelled – but he intentionally left the decision to the Team to make.

Although I was happy the Team made the decision rather than Michael, I was concerned about loss of continuity and connection amongst team

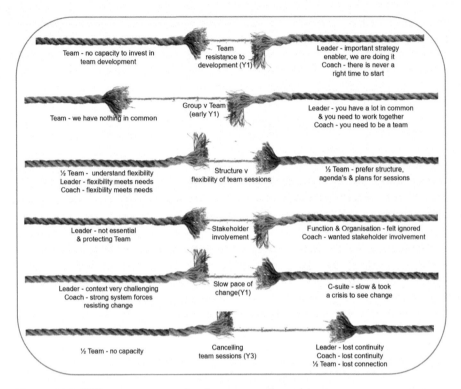

Figure 10.3: Differences – team development and coaching

members. Differing views on this point caused considerable tension, and in Chapter Five, Michael suggests my engagement in the process was negatively impacted as a result.

Figure 10.3 shows tensions within the system relating to team development and coaching.

## Leadership development

### Leader resistance – Year One

There are several differences in opinion in relation to Michael's leadership development, the most fundamental being his resistance to work on his own leadership style in Year One. The Team, C-suite, and I were all telling him he needed to change, as his leadership style was out of line with his own strategic vision, and a risk to the organisation. There was a huge amount of tension in the system on this point, and it took until the end of Year One for Michael to acknowledge change was required and focus on himself.

## Purpose of Coach

I have included this topic in this section, as some stakeholders thought the primary purpose of my role was to focus on and support Michael. I heard this from many across the Function and Organisation, including the CEO. Michael, on the other hand, believed my role existed for the Team, not him, a contributing factor in his initial resistance to work on himself. My view was split, in that I needed to work with both the Team and Michael individually as Leader.

## Formal development

In line with Michael's resistance to focus on his leadership style in Year One, he also resisted working on a formal development plan and formal one-to-one coaching. He said he preferred the informal approach we had established, despite my suggestion of more structure and accountability.

## Leadership feedback – Year One and Year Two

In Chapter Five, Michael comments that while the informal coaching and advice I provided was very helpful, the frequency and volume of it was overwhelming at times. He suggested a more consolidated approach might have served him better.

I did not know he felt this way until I read his contribution to this book. There is some irony here, as in my view, the development plan and formal one-to-one coaching I suggested, which he resisted, would have given him the consolidation and structure he was looking for.

## Two-tier Team – Year One

The two-tier Team issue was the result of Michael sharing leadership with Tom and me, and not others in the Team. While the matter was addressed – at least to some extent – it was not dealt with immediately, resulting in a period of tension between the Team and Michael. Michael articulates the impact of that tension well in his comments in Chapter Five.

## Team focus on Leader – Year Two

Michael felt uncomfortable being the focus of team development sessions towards the end of Year Two. In Chapter Five, he explains that content needed to focus on the collective Team, rather than him.

While I was aware of and could see his point of view, I disagreed. My motivation was to support the Team in finding ways to support Michael, and the Team told me they could see the value and were up for it. Their feedback on those sessions was extremely positive. Despite my view and the Team's view, we moved focus away from Michael, at his request, in Year Three.

Figure 10.4 summarises tensions within the system related to leadership development.

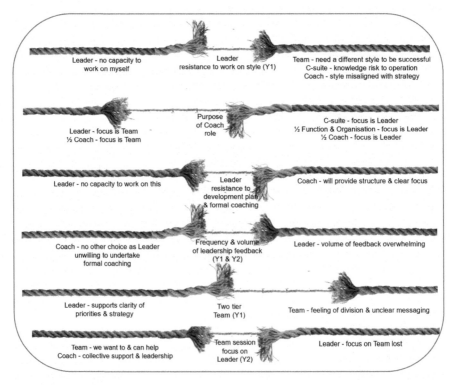

Figure 10.4: Differences – leadership development

## Coaching in general

### Coach roles/hats – Year One and Year Two

As I described in Chapter Seven, the many roles/hats I wore, particularly in Year One and Year Two, were contentious areas. Michael and the Team were comfortable with and encouraged me to wear unhelpful hats (refer to Figure 7.9) such as "team counsellor" and "mess cleaner," resulting in reduced responsibility and more capacity for them. I knew my role was to "teach the Team to fish" (Theory Break 7.19), but it was hard to argue when my position description and Michael reinforced unhelpful hats. The tension around my roles/hats was a significant contributor to my energy crisis (refer to Figure 7.10).

### Use of co-coach

Michael, Tammy and I all talk about an opportunity missed with co-coaching. Although Michael and Tammy were very supportive of the idea, they did not know of their alignment on this point, nor did I tell them. My motivation to pass by the co-coach opportunity was driven by a desire to retain control.

### Formal contracting – Year Three

Formal changes to the written contract between myself and Green Apple Co at the beginning of Year Three helped clarify the roles and responsibilities of all parties. The idea came from Tammy in supervision, and Michael supported it as well. However, despite an improvement in dynamics, I was uncomfortable the contract change was required at all. To me the situation implied lack of trust and misalignment with my professional and personal values, and ultimately a feeling of failure.

### Coach tenacity

In Chapter Five, I say that the "stay versus leave see-saw'" was on my mind throughout this case. Michael wanted me to stay, partly to preserve his reputation I think; it would not look good if his Coach and confidant walked out. Tammy also encouraged me to stay to enable me to reap as much benefit as

I could from the amazing development opportunity. My family and friends were on the other side of the see-saw, concerned about my health and well-being, and encouraging me to leave.

There was tension between many parties on this point, but the most significant tension was within me. My head told me to stay and maximise the learning experience. My head also told me to leave and save myself from anguish. My heart told me to stay because I was emotionally invested in the Team, in Michael and in the experience – and my heart won!

## Moderation of session content

Michael protected the Team from many things, including me! As discussed in Chapter Five, he effectively vetoed some interventions and discussions I thought the Team would benefit from. In hindsight, I should have talked to the Team directly about controversial topics and let them make the choice whether to explore further or not. As mentioned in Chapter Five, in my view the Team were able to handle much more than Michael gave them credit for.

Figure 10.5 outlines the most significant tensions in the system relating to coaching in general.

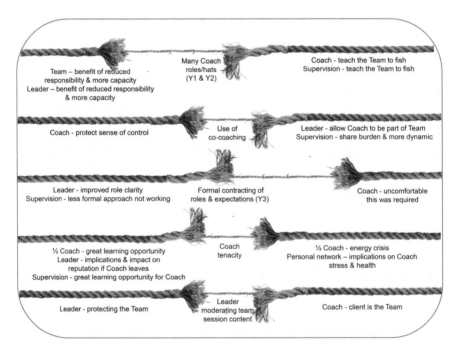

Figure 10.5: Differences – coaching in general

## Coach support

### Professional supervision

An interesting difference relating to professional supervision became evident while working on this book. As described in Chapter Five, it was clear very early in the journey that I needed professional support, and part of that support came from professional one-to-one and group supervision. As Tammy explains in Chapters Eight and Eleven, the purpose of supervision is to build a coach's reflective practice, identify patterns and habits, and appreciate self as the main instrument of change in a coaching engagement. Professional coach supervisors are very experienced coaches with many years of supervision training under their belts.

In Chapter Five, Michael's rationale for supporting my request for supervision was not quite the same. From his viewpoint, supervision compensated for support I would normally have from him in a boss–employee relationship. Supervision would have been needed even if dynamics between Michael and I had been more typical of a boss and employee. Michael did not have the professional knowledge or experience to play a team coaching supervision role.

### Level of support

In Chapter Five, I mention that the process of pulling this book together included professional peers reviewing content. One of those peers asked me whether I might have rallied too much support in this case. As I reflect now, I am conflicted. Half of me thinks I did the right thing, and the other half thinks my peer was right. Perhaps more breaks from being in the system every day, and talking about the system with supporters, would have been beneficial.

Figure 10.6 shows tensions relating to coach support.

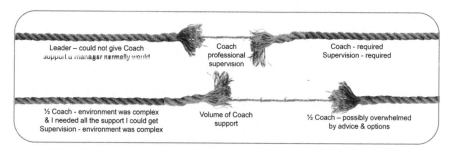

Figure 10.6: Differences – coach support

## Importance of choices

With more clarity of differences between perspectives and tensions in the system, you may be wondering, so what? Why have I put effort into identifying these differences, and what insight can be gained? I use a version of the Johari Window (Luft & Ingham, 1955) in Figure 10.7 to help frame up the rest of this chapter.

The horizontal axis in Figure 10.7 represents the level of awareness parties had of differences within the system. Options being:

- All relevant parties, or system elements, knew about the difference in opinion.
- One, or some, parties knew about the difference in opinion, and some did not.
- No one knew about the difference of opinion during the case period; the difference became evident sometime later, for example, when reflection on and contributing to this book.

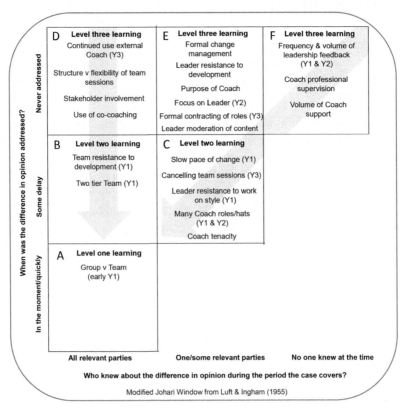

Figure 10.7: Awareness and timing of differences

The vertical axis relates to the timing of action taken to address differences in opinion. Options being:

- The issue was addressed immediately, and adjustments were made in the moment.
- There was some delay in addressing the issue, but it was addressed within the three-year timeframe this case covers.
- The issue was never addressed – however, experience gained from this case can be applied in other circumstances.

Combining three levels of awareness and three timing options creates six possible combinations, A to F.

I have taken the areas of difference/tension identified in the first part of this chapter and plotted them across the six combinations, which I expand on next. I also consider the implication of different choices in each combination.

A   *Known by all relevant parties and addressed in the moment/quickly.*
There was only one difference in this category, relating to the Team not identifying as a Team. The issue was addressed immediately.
However, what if Michael and I had chosen not to act then and there, and the Team made connection between their roles much later in the journey, or not at all?

B   *Known by all relevant parties but some delay in addressing differences.*
The two areas of difference in this category are the Team's initial resistance to development and the two-tier team.
What if Michael had listened to the Team, not insisted they attend development sessions, and delayed the start until they had more capacity? Well, as it turned out, they never had more capacity, so would the development journey have begun at all?

C   *Known by one/some relevant parties and some delay in addressing differences.*
Several differences fall into this category, and I will focus on Michael's leadership style for illustration.
What if Michael had decided to work on his leadership from the beginning of Year One as he contemplated in Chapter Five? Or what if he never had his epiphany at all and thus never focused on his leadership style?

D   *Known by all relevant parties and never addressed in this case.*
This is an interesting category, as everyone knew about the differences, and no one took action to resolve them.
Using stakeholder involvement as an example, what if I had invited stakeholders to team sessions in Year One? What impact would that have had on priorities and the trajectory of the entire development journey?

E   *Known by one/some relevant parties and not addressed in this case.*
    This is the most populated category, with many significant choice points. Using an example – what if I had made the choice to approach the C-suite early on, insisting that an integrated change management approach was necessary? How would they have responded? How would their response have impacted the "hailstorm(s)"? How would interaction with the C-suite have impacted my relationship with Michael? Would I have lost trust? Or worse?

F   *Not known during the case period and therefore never addressed.*
    Using the example of volume of coach support to illustrate. I cannot go back in time and reverse the level of support I tapped into in this case. However, I can consider more carefully the appropriate level of support I need in future circumstances.

The common thread across all six combinations is pondering on the implication of choices within a CAS, characterised by complexity, interrelationships and unpredictable outcomes (Cavanagh, 2006). Just one alternative choice made in relation to an area of difference or tension would have changed the entire system dynamic and outcomes for all involved. Every choice matters, whether big, or seemingly small – choices whether to:

- Share a difference of opinion with another party or keep quiet.
- Push points of view harder, or let it be.
- Do something or do nothing.
- Address something now, later or never.

## Chapter Ten summary

This chapter highlights differences in what the five perspectives in this case found good, challenging and what they learnt. It also highlights that differences are present, significant, and can be held in the system as tension, even when there is otherwise complete alignment of overall goals and intervention approaches.

Viewing differences between perspectives also illustrates the importance of choice points, system complexity and unpredictability of outcomes. Just one different choice made by one system element would have changed the entire story.

As Helen (no relationship to me) approaches the train in the movie *Sliding Doors* (Howitt, 1998) she chooses to run and catch the train in one scenario and waits on the platform for the next train in the other scenario. The movie illustrates how a seemingly small, split-second, unconscious decision can have momentous implications on many people's lives.

Team coaching helps teams understand and build comfort in working with system complexity, difference and tension, and the importance of choice points. Exposing, sharing, actively seeking, and explicitly debating differences and choices are great habits for teams, and all of us, to build.

This chapter is a little complex in itself and I trust this meta-reflection highlights the complexity of teams and CASs in insightful ways. The next chapter covers more choice points – choices each perspective has made on how they intend to apply what they have learnt from their experience in this case to their respective futures.

## References

Cavanagh, M. (2006). Coaching from a systemic perspective: A complex adaptive conversation. In D. Stober & A. M. Grant (Eds). *Evidence based coaching handbook: Putting best practices to work for your clients.* New York: Wiley.

Howitt, P. (Director). (1998). *Sliding Doors* [Film]. Intermedia Films, Mirage Enterprises, Miramax.

Luft, J. & Ingham, H. (1955). The Johari Window, a graphic model of interpersonal awareness. *Proceedings of the Western Training Laboratory in Group Development.* Los Angeles: University of California.

# The future

**11**

*Michael the Team Leader,*
*Tammy Turner and Helen Zink*

---

## HOW TO READ CHAPTER ELEVEN

I am Helen, the Team Coach in this case, and this is how this chapter fits into the overall book.

The three chapters in Section C combine the five perspectives in this book, highlighting further insight and illustrating the power of perspective taking (Theory Break 1.4) – meta-reflection.

Specifically, Chapter Eleven looks to the future, where I, and voices representing the other four system elements, describe our intentions to apply learning from this case to new situations. In a movie analogy, by this point the main story line of the movie is over, and as characters describe their hopes for the future, there is also a sense that their journeys are not done. Perhaps the door remains open for another movie – a "sequel"?

Chapter Eleven is narrated in six voices, representing five system elements:

Jane – a member of the Team, representing all members of the Team.
Michael – the Leader.
Sally – a member of the C-suite and CPO, speaking for stakeholders within the Function and Organisation.
Helen, me – as Coach.

---

DOI: 10.4324/9781003367789-14

Tammy – my Supervisor.

Rachael – speaking for my Other Support networks, professional peers, family and friends.

As there are different authors and voices within this chapter, I begin each section by clearly identifying the author of that section and which of the six voices above they represent.

Content for this chapter is sourced from specific questions I asked of team members, Michael, representatives across Consulting Services and Green Apple Co, Tammy, members of my professional network, family and friends, and my own thoughts.

**Author Helen Zink**

**Written in the voice of Helen as Coach**

So far, this book has focused on five different perspectives looking back over a three-year journey together. Within Section B, each system element described insight gained in the moment as events unfolded (level one learning), insight gained soon afterwards (level two learning), and insight gained now, as writing this book provided another opportunity for reflection (level three learning; refer to Figure 1.3). Wisdom acquired from the story in previous chapters is based on past experiences and layers of reflection on those past experiences.

Now focus turns to the future, and how the same five system elements intend to apply learning from this case to their future work, life and development journeys.

## The Team's perspective of the future

**Author Helen Zink**
**Written in the voice of Jane representing all members of the Team**
In this section I pick up where I left off in Chapter Four and talk about our collective future. As we begin Year Four, we have a New Leader join us, George, and hopefully a New Coach on the way as well. Our new system is illustrated in Figure 11.1.

In Chapter Four I described the positive way we ended Year Three, including clear plans for our future development as a collective Team. The "good endings" work we focused on prior to Michael's departure

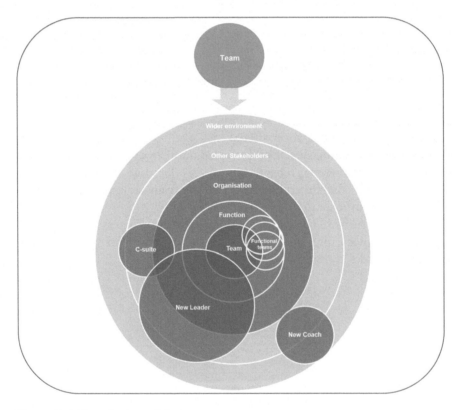

Figure 11.1: Team's view of their new system

provided an opportunity to clarify our thoughts and our priorities going forward, which included:

- Re-setting the strategy for Consulting Services.
- Focusing on the next level of team managers below us.
- Building better patterns of learning within our team and across Consulting Services.
- Continuing our team development journey, including focusing on our relationships, connecting as a team and maintaining psychological safety.

Figure 11.2 is one of the outputs from that "good endings" work and a visual representation of our collective commitment for the future.

To enable continued focus on relationships and connection, we intend to continue our pattern of monthly development sessions – they work well for us. We appreciate the opportunity to step out of day-to-day activity and focus on how we work together. A comment from Greg articulates our thoughts very well: "We are committed to continuing regular development days – we feel these days are the glue that hold us together." Although we

Figure 11.2: Team's future development

will no longer be working with Helen, we look forward to working with a New Coach, who will support us through our next development phase. In addition to monthly team days, we will ensure regular one-to-one conversations continue, both with George and between ourselves.

Stepping into Year Four is a critical time for us, as in many ways we need to reform ourselves. In addition to George joining us, Ethan has left the Team and been replaced by Ruth. We expect George, in particular, will bring new ideas which will influence our development in different ways. I suspect we will need to revisit our team fundamentals in our early days with George and Ruth, such as our ground rules, and refresh our team agreement – refer to Figure 4.4 for our current team agreement.

Helen shared this quote from Hawkins (2019) with us from time to time during our development sessions. "The HPT team development journey should never be seen as a place of arrival . . . The environment, subsystems and interrelationships between them are constantly changing." We think it suits our story perfectly – the world we live and work in is complex. The messy and challenging journey we experienced over the last three years clearly illustrates the significant impact environmental factors have on best-laid plans.

We are looking forward to our future as a Team, and we feel the investment we made over the last three years has been a key factor in our survival and resilience to date. We hope our environment is less challenging going forward, enabling us to take a more consistent long-term view of all that we do, including our development. Our thanks go to Michael for providing the opportunity for us to take this amazing ride.

## The Leader's perspective of the future

**Co-authors Michael (the Team Leader) and Helen Zink**
**Written in the voice of Michael**
I am now the Leader of a New Team in a new role. As I closed off Chapter Five, I left advice for other leaders embarking on a similar journey – advice I am taking on board myself now as I apply it to my new situation. In this section, I talk about the Team and my hopes for their future, my own plans and my thoughts on Helen's opportunities.

### The Team's future

As I reflect on the Team, I am proud of all we achieved over our three-year journey, and our increase in leadership and team maturity. We shifted our way of operating from a traditional, technically focused service delivery model to a contemporary EQ service delivery model. This enabled us to navigate unexpected environmental changes successfully and better align our service delivery approach with our stakeholders' needs. I believe an EQ-centred leadership style is required for successful leadership in the future and the consulting profession. I valued being part of a team that, eventually, fully engaged in the team development process and recognised the benefits.

I know the Team would like to continue their development journey, supported by a team coach. My hope is that they follow this through and continue to learn and grow together, building on what they have already achieved. As highlighted by events over the three-year time period this book covers, the environment the Team operated in changed more rapidly, significantly and unexpectedly than anyone would have anticipated. Unfortunately, I expect this will be the new normal for the Team and all of us. The best way for the Team, and any team, to maintain and build their capability and collective team resilience is to invest and continually reinvest in their development.

The "good endings" exercise we completed together near the end of Year Three, just before I left Green Apple Co, summarised specific areas of development opportunity for the Team to work on. In my view, focusing on the team managers (next level of leaders reporting to team members), and then the whole Consulting Services function is the next biggest opportunity. Once the capability of team managers improves, the Team will finally be in a position to reap the full rewards of the development work we undertook, and the whole Organisation and system will benefit.

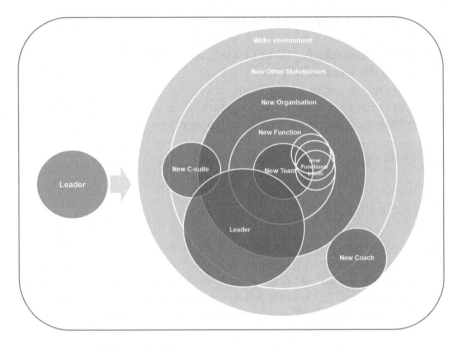

Figure 11.3: Leader's view of his new system

## The Leader's future

In Chapter Five, I talked about the significant benefits our collective development journey had on me. I was not expecting to be impacted to such an extent myself, yet the work we did led to the most significant and rapid change in my skillset of my career as a leader. Both my professional and personal EQ improved, creating a great foundation for my new role and future roles. As I navigate this new phase in my career, lead a New Team and a New Function, and integrate into a New C-suite and New Organisation, the lessons I learnt over the last years are forefront in my mind. Figure 11.3 illustrates my new system.

The Appendix to Chapter Five includes an extensive list of things I learnt about leadership development and coaching over our three-year journey. The area's most relevant in my new role are:

- Applying my own bespoke leadership model (Figure 5.6).
- Communication.

- Agreeing upfront roles, expectations and ways of working with all stakeholders.
- Supporting a culture shift from technically focused service delivery to EQ lead service delivery.

I am also acutely aware that ongoing one-to-one time with my team members in a leader as coach role (Theory Break 5.2) is one of the best investments I can make.

Helen shared emerging research with me on the importance of incoming leaders having good quality conversations early on in their induction (Theory Break 11.1), which solidifies the priorities I identified above.

## THEORY BREAK 11.1: INCOMING LEADERS

Clutterbuck (2022) is undertaking research in the area of incoming leaders, including identifying what activities support and/or hinder the success of leaders as they step into new roles. This research is in its infancy, however, anecdotally, Clutterbuck believes a critical factor is the quality and nature of conversations the leader and the team have in the first days and weeks. Conversations about who they are, how they like to work, expectations of each other, what they bring to the relationship, and agreements on how they will learn together. In other words, contracting.

In Chapter Five, I talked about areas of learning in relation to team development and coaching. Those of particular relevance as my New Team and I embark on our development journey are:

- Finding the right team coach with appropriate experience (if we decide to use support).
- Beginning the development journey immediately, even if the New Team does not seem ready.
- Ensuring roles and expectations of the New Team, myself (and the New Coach if we use one) are clear.
- Offering one-to-one coaching for individual team members in parallel to team development to help embed change.

No doubt strategy enablement and change management will become part of my focus in the near future too. In Chapter Five, I indicated important considerations supporting this – in particular, the vital part people play in strategy implementation, and the powerful impact of aligning intervention streams.

## The Coach's future

I would like to comment on Helen's future as well. I know she has learnt a lot about teams and systems from our time together, and I am proud that she gained personal insight during the process too. Helen helped us understand and adapt HPT and EQ leadership principles to our needs, and brought them to life in partnership with us, for the benefit of the Team, ourselves as individuals, and our entire system. I believe one of her greatest strengths is the ability to merge theory and practice.

What Helen has learnt during her three-year journey with us has undoubtedly benefitted her career. Her current clients are reaping the rewards of this right now, and her future clients will benefit even more as she continues to learn and develop her discipline. By way of the coaching ripple effect (O'Connor & Cavanagh, 2013), Helen's work with her current clients will also benefit their respective teams, functions, organisations, stakeholders and wider system elements.

## Collective future

My hopes for the future are wider than myself, the Team, and Helen, as discussed above. More importantly, I hope learning from our collective journey enables other leaders, teams and organisations to benefit from a more informed and less experimental version of this team development and coaching journey. This book demonstrates the importance of taking what has been learnt to a wider audience, so that many more will benefit from our hard work and insight – again, the ripple effect.

I would also like to emphasise that the process we went through was not a short-term stand-alone team development exercise. The process involved complete reengineering of the way we thought, operated as a team, led others, and delivered services to our stakeholders. It was hard, but the benefits were substantial. As I have said already in this book, please take what is useful from our insights and apply it where it works – whether you are a leader, team, internal or external team coach, academic, HR professional, consultant, or you work with or are part of any team. Good luck – it is worth it!

## The Function and Organisation's perspective of the future

**Author Helen Zink**
**Written in the voice of Sally a C-suite member and CPO representing stakeholders within the Function and Organisation**

I just have a few words to say, on behalf of Consulting Services and Green Apple Co, about our future role. Figure 11.4 illustrates our view of the Team's new system.

I could sum up our thoughts about the future in two words – involve us! The reflective process of contributing to this book has highlighted implications of omitting direct input from staff across the Consulting Services function, the C-suite and other stakeholders within Green Apple Co. After all, as I emphasised in Chapter Six, we are the Team's stakeholders and have a vested interest in their development priorities – we are the reason they exist.

Recognising our omission, we now have an opportunity to rectify the situation. Our views, priorities and perception of progress should be

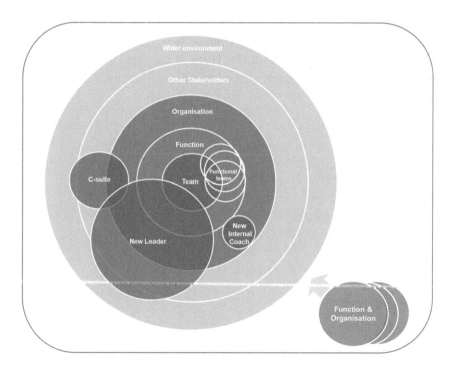

Figure 11.4: Function and Organisation's view of new system

forefront in the Team's mind as they continue their development work together, and I will ensure that happens.

In Chapter Six, we suggest the C-suite should have sponsored the Team's development work, as well as the overall change programme they were leading, including systems and process changes. Given the magnitude of change the Team were working through at that time, and implications of that change on us, a formal change management approach should have been used, including regular progress and risk reporting.

At the stage the Team are at now, given their significant progress, C-suite sponsorship may not be necessary or beneficial at his point. I think regular updates on priorities and progress against those priorities will be sufficient going forward. However, if the Team embark on significant system, process, structure and/or people development initiatives in the future, C-suite sponsorship is essential. I will insist it happens with this Team and all other teams within the Organisation going through significant change.

Figure 11.4 indicates a New Internal Coach working with the Team and supporting their development. Increased capacity and capability within our internal HR function enables this approach, and it will also ensure the Team's development priorities are aligned with the rest of Green Apple Co's people development strategies. As the HR function is my responsibility, the approach will also enable me to keep closer tabs on what the Team is working on. Everyone across Consulting Services and Green Apple Co looks forward to partnering with the Team as they and all of us continue our development journeys.

## The Coach's perspective of the future

**Author Helen Zink**
**Written in the voice of Helen as Coach**
My final words in Chapter Seven were about personal growth and the amazing opportunity this case provided for professional and personal development. I am different, stronger, more confident and more self-aware than I was before the "experiment" began. In this section, I discuss my thoughts and hopes for my own future, and also my wishes for the Team and Michael going forward.

### The Team's future

As I parted ways with the Team at the end of Year Three, I was grateful we had the opportunity to experience the "good endings" exercise together. One of the main outputs from that work was the Team's future development priorities, illustrated in Figure 11.2. My hope is that the Team truly embed their learning, and the benefit of our incredible journey comes through now and in the future, in all they do, how they work together and how they lead others.

The Team mentioned many times that regular team development off-sites worked well for them. I hope they continue to enable their development work in a form that meets their needs. I also hope more members of the Team take the opportunity to experience formal one-to-one coaching, as it was so valuable for Jane. More experience with one-to-one coaching will also influence team members' ability to take on the important leader as coach role (Theory Break 5.2) with their own staff, resulting in more coaching ripple effect (O'Connor & Cavanagh, 2013) across Consulting Services and Green Apple Co.

Although I have only spoken with George briefly, my hope is that he supports the Team to continue leading their own collective development in a way that works for them. In my view, the Team are able and willing to lead themselves.

There is some risk that George may not be familiar with HPT concepts and team coaching. He may take a less collaborative approach, perhaps driving development himself in a more traditional, individual-focused, "top-down" way. If that does happen, it would be interesting to observe how the Team react, and how their reaction influences their respective teams, the Consulting Services function, and their entire system.

## The Leader's future

Reflecting on Michael over the three years I worked with him, I observed a shift in his self-awareness and ability to take on feedback and learn. I think many systemic influences contributed to his shift, including:

- My support with informal one-to-one coaching and advice.
- The Team's collective development journey.
- Support from the Team and his C-suite colleagues.
- C-suite development activity underway at the same time.
- The culture change programme across Green Apple Co.
- Changes in his personal life.
- And possibly other influencing factors I am not aware of.

Now, as Michael moves to a new role in a New Organisation, my hope is that he is able to maintain and build on what he has learnt. Change is hard, and maintaining change is even harder, especially if he finds himself in an environment where system forces, and his new team's maturity level, entice him back into old, ingrained habits, such as "top-down," hands-on activity, and limited delegation.

My hope is that Michael seeks support from others to help keep himself on track. That support might come from his new boss, new colleagues or his wider support network. In this regard, I strongly recommend he takes the plunge and works with a one-to-one coach in a formal way. I also encourage Michael to use the services of a New Team Coach to support his New Team, as he begins working with them and they navigate their own HPT journey.

## The Coach's future

I am now focused on a completely new system and working with several new teams in their respective systems, as illustrated in Figure 11.5. As I mentioned throughout Chapter Seven, the experience of working with the Team in this case was pivotal in developing my team coaching career and my current practice.

Through the process of writing this book, I have had the opportunity to reflect on my journey again, in a deeper and more detached way – the level three learning experience I described in Chapter One and illustrated in Figure 1.3.

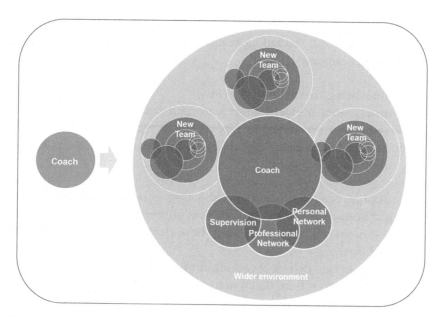

Figure 11.5: Coach's view of her new system

Above, Jane said the Team's development journey will not end after Year Three, and neither will mine. An important principle for team coaches is ongoing development (Theory Break 11.2), and Hawkins and Turner (2020) say the development cycle should never end. As I acknowledge life-long learning, I thought it would be useful to share my future development focus areas in the context of Hawkins and Turner's (2020) principles of systemic thinking, doing and being (Theory Break 7.20).

My "systemic thinking" development areas:

- The team is the client (Theory Break 7.1) – being aware that choices I make should benefit the collective team, rather than the team leader, an individual member of the team, or myself.
- Role clarity – being clear with myself around what I will do as team coach and what is the responsibility of the team or others in the system.
- Boundaries – ensuring conversations and relationships with clients do not become personal.

My "systemic doing" development areas:

- Partnering and collaborating with other practitioners – which may be in the form of co-coaching (Theory Break 7.13), co-facilitating, teaching, or writing.

- Contracting and re-contracting with all stakeholders continuously (Theory Break 7.9), including team sponsors and HR representatives within organisations.

My "systemic being" development areas:

My primary area of focus is self-care and self-awareness. I have not repeated, nor do I ever want to repeat, the energy crisis I described in Chapter Seven. To maintain my ability to be "fit for purpose" (Theory Break 7.10), I am focusing on:

- Relationship boundaries – the distinction between professional and personal boundaries mentioned above is important here too.
- Time boundaries – maintaining boundaries between work and personal time.
- Space – ensuring I do not overcommit myself and allowing space in my diary and time to reflect, digest and just think or "be."

The next section covers Supervision and Other Support, which are also critical in facilitating my ongoing self-care and self-awareness.

---

## THEORY BREAK 11.2: SYSTEMIC TEAM COACH DEVELOPMENT

Hawkins and Turner (2020) and Hawkins (2021, 2022) emphasise the importance of systemic principles in STC and the importance of ongoing development. The following apple orchard analogy helps explain their key points:

- Initial training – like attending horticultural school. It allows you to understand common techniques and some of the possible challenges ahead.
- Learning by doing – by planting some apple trees, you discover and negotiate the pests and viruses present and how much water and fertiliser is required to grow them. You learn from your successes and mistakes.
- Learning cycles – as you reflect on growing those first trees, you learn and apply new insight to growing the next trees you plant. (Essentially the same level one and level two learning illustrated in Figure 1.3).

- Working together – partnering with other orchardists helps spread knowledge, best practice and risk.
- Learning community – meeting regularly with other orchardists to share experiences creates a learning community that benefits all and builds collective knowledge.
- Supervision – working with a growing advisor with more experience than you, providing support and advice, is critical.
- Lifelong learning – as your orchard reaches maturity and is fruiting well, you need to be planning and planting the next set of trees. Your learning never stops.
- Whole person – the experience of running an orchard is more than physical or professional. Growth impacts you at the core and is personal.

## Supervision and Other Support's perspective of the future

*Supervision*

**Author Tammy Turner**
**Written in the voice of Tammy as Helen's Supervisor**
I remain Helen's professional supervisor post-case and begin this section by talking about the importance of ongoing supervision. Rachael follows me and talks about Helen's personal support from professional networks, family and friends. Our Supervision and Other Support view of Helen and her new system is depicted in Figure 11.6.

Although Helen is not actively engaged with the Green Apple Co any longer, she still attends professional individual and group supervision and peer supervision, as well as reaching out to her personal support network on an as-needed basis for her current clients.

Since working with Helen in supervision, I have observed her reflective practice increase, and topics brought to supervision relating to other clients are less emotional and personal. This indicates an increased ability to reflectively observe her own work. According to Helen, the systems she is coaching in now are benefitting from her services, and she has noticed a positive impact on individuals and teams within them.

This is unsurprising. Anecdotally, I see this trajectory in many long-term supervisees with commitment to reflective practice. Bachkirova (2016)

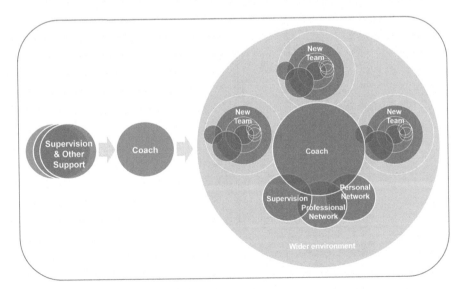

Figure 11.6: Supervision and Other Support's view of new system

emphasises the importance of reflective practice to develop the coach as an active member of the systems they work in. She argues that the interventions used by a coach are contextual based on factors such as:

- The clients' situation.
- The clients' psychological background.
- The coach's psychological background.
- Understanding of circumstances in the moment.

All of which make the coach the main instrument of coaching (Bachkirova, 2016).

If "Self of the Coach," as Bachkirova (2016) phrases it, is the main instrument of change in a coaching engagement, then reflective practice is critical – in particular, reflecting with others. It is only through the multiple perspectives of group reflection that coaches build the capacity and maturity required to understand "self," including:

- Their biases.
- What has shaped their current philosophies.
- Psychological underpinnings in the way they relate to others.
- How they integrate training and techniques.
- How they integrate industry standards.

Using this book as a case study of reflexivity (Theory Break 11.3), I could postulate that the years Helen has spent reflecting on her work in various forms – individual, professional, individual and group supervision, and peer support – have enhanced her ability to simultaneously be within a system and notice the system and interdependencies of relationships within it.

Note that Helen's commitment to "being a better coach" was and is self-directed, not an industry standard. Both the EMCC (2020) team coaching standards and ICF (2020b) competencies suggest team coaches consider supervision. Currently, supervision is only required by professional bodies for coaching credentialing purposes. Yet in most helping professions, psychological and professional coaching bodies require ongoing reflective learning by way of supervision.

As I said in Chapter Eight, we are still on the journey of understanding what may be required to best support coaches, leaders and those who work within organisational CAS. I strongly believe that reflecting with others, by way of professional supervision, should be an industry standard to develop the capacity, maturity and reflexivity required to deliver team coaching.

Regardless of the industry standards, I will continue to offer professional supervision and teach peer supervision as I believe the wider system as a whole - the coach, their client, the team, the client system, the organisation, the coaching industry and the ecosystem we live in, all benefit from us reflecting together. It has been an absolute pleasure supervising Helen while tending her own "apple tree orchard" (Theory Break 11.2). She too has given and will continue to give the fruits of her labour to those who can benefit from it.

Helen is now providing individual and team coaching, and facilitating team coaching training to support other budding team coaches. To maintain and keep building her capacity and maturity, she continues to actively engage in peer and professional supervision. The systems Helen works in are all interdependent on Helen's ability to continue her reflective practice and bring best practices to her clients in her various modes of delivery. I am confident that Helen will continue to appreciate the importance of supervision to her practice, whether or not it is a requirement of industry bodies she subscribes to.

---

## THEORY BREAK 11.3: REFLECTION AND REFLEXIVITY

Reflection is process of looking at the past and what you were thinking, feeling and doing. It is about stepping back and considering what went well and what you might do differently next time.

Reflexivity (Cunliffe, 2009) goes deeper by noticing patterns and wider influences in the way we think, feel and do things. It involves deep understanding of "self," including: Our biases, what has shaped our philosophies, and psychological underpinnings in the way we relate to others.

It is about noticing, questioning and developing potential new ways to think, feel and do things.

---

## Other Support

**Author Helen Zink**
**Written in the voice of Rachael, speaking on behalf of all Helen's Other Support networks, professional peers, family and friends**
I will continue the theme of my discussion in Chapter Eight. I ended that chapter by saying that Helen's Other Support network is never more than

a phone call away, and the main benefit of our support is we know Helen better than anyone.

Since leaving her work with Green Apple Co and the Team, Helen and I continue to talk regularly and meet up for a chat over a coffee or cocktail. The subject matter of our conversations has not changed. We still talk about clients and our business ideas, and bounce ideas off each other.

However, I have noticed a difference in way we talk. Helen seems more confident and more emotionally balanced when she talks about her current clients and work. When the Team in this case and Michael come up in conversation, she is able to find some humour in events that unfolded.

I think everyone in Helen's professional and personal networks, including her family and friends, as well as me, will continue to hold important roles in her system. Referring to Helen's energy diagrams, Figure 7.10 and Figure 7.11, we are an important source of energy input. Our on-tap, often very direct personal feedback and insight ultimately impacts her coaching practice and interactions with clients. As those closest to Helen, we are here whenever she needs us.

## Chapter Eleven summary

**Author Helen Zink**
**Written in the voice of Helen as Coach**
The five system elements describe their respective futures in similar ways in this chapter, in that all intend to apply insight and learning from this case to their new circumstances. The Team's primary focus is maintaining momentum in the context of changing team membership. Michael will apply his new leadership approach in the context of his new role in a new system. Sally will ensure that the Function and Organisation are involved in the Team's future development work. I am applying the many lessons I learnt with new teams I am working with, and those within my Supervision and Other Support network continue to be there for me. Tammy also argues that supervision should be compulsory with the coaching industry, to ensure coaches have the level of capacity and maturity they require when working with complex clients, and I agree. Without supervision, I would not be here now, doing what I do and writing this book.

Although there is a lot of similarity in the future plans outlined, there are some intriguing differences as well. The Team talk about continuing their development journey with the support of an external coach, which is what they are familiar with. Yet Sally, in the Function and Organisation section, is adamant that an internal coach will be used.

Another difference relates to Michael. He describes his intention to apply his new leadership approach with his New Team and gives the impression he is confident in doing that himself. The use of a team coach is mentioned as just a possibility, and he does not mention any support he might need for himself. My experience is that leaders benefit from ongoing support to maintain new habits. I strongly suggest Michael works with formal one-to-one and team coaches to help preserve habits he wants to keep, and support him while he works through new complexities, he will do doubt encounter in his new role.

Like Chapter Ten, comparing different perspectives provides another level of insight – some similarities and some differences – meta-reflection. And to recap Chapter One (Theory Break 1.4), no one perspective is correct or better than another.

It will be interesting to see whether future plans described in this chapter play out as we all plan and hope. It will also be fascinating to observe the impact of the environment and interactions within CASs on best-laid plans. We will need to wait for Year Four, "the sequel," to find out!

# References

Bachkirova, T. (2016). The self of the coach: Conceptualization, issues, and opportunities for practitioner development. *Consulting Psychology Journal: Practice and Research*, 68(2), 143–156. https://doi.org/10.1037/cpb0000055.

Clutterbuck, D. (2022). *The challenge of the incoming team leader.* Retrieved from https://www.coachingandmentoringinternational.org.

Cunliffe. A. (2009). Reflexivity, learning and reflexive practice. In S. Armstrong & C. Fukami (Eds). *The Sage handbook of management, learning, education and development.* Los Angeles: Sage. https://doi.org/10.5465/amle.2010.48661199.

European Mentoring and Coaching Council (2020). *EMCC global team coaching accreditation standards framework.* Retrieved from https://emccglobal.org/accreditation/tcqa.

Hawkins, P. (2019). Systemic team coaching. In D. Clutterbuck, J. Gannon, S. Hayes, I. Iordanou, K. Lowe & D. MacKie (Eds), *The practitioner's handbook of team coaching.* Oxon: Routledge. https://doi.org/10.4324/9781351130554-4.

Hawkins, P. (2021). *Leadership team coaching: Developing collective transformational leadership.* 4th edition. London: Kogan Page. https://doi.org/10.1111/peps.12006_5.

Hawkins, P. (2022). *Leadership team coaching in practice: Case studies on creating highly effective teams.* 3rd edition. London: Kogan Page.

Hawkins, P. & Turner, E. (2020). *Systemic coaching: Developing value beyond the individual.* London & New York: Routledge. https://doi.org/10.4324/9780429452031.

International Coaching Federation (2020b). *ICF team coaching competencies: moving beyond one-to-one coaching.* Retrieved from https://coachfederation.org/team-coaching-competencies.

O'Connor, S. & Cavanagh, M. (2013). The coaching ripple effect: The effects of developmental coaching on wellbeing across organisational networks. *Psychology of Well-Being: Theory, Research and Practice.* 3:2. https://doi.org/10.1186/2211-1522-3-2.

# Conclusion

**12**

*Helen Zink*

---

### HOW TO READ CHAPTER TWELVE

I am Helen, the Coach in this story, and this is how this chapter fits
into the overall book.

   This chapter, which I narrate, wraps up the entire book by
summarising key take-outs for you to mull over and apply to your own
circumstances. The equivalent in a movie would be the "epilogue."
This chapter does not mark the end of the development story for the
five main characters this book is based on, just the end of their collective story.

---

I could not resist Michael's invitation to be "part of the experiment" that
ultimately became the content of this book. Given the chance, I would do
the same again.

   This book is the story of a Team, and their development and coaching
journey over three years, told from five different system perspectives. Just
like the movie *Babel* (González Iñárritu, 2006), the story is multidimensional,
complex (Theory Break 1.2) and filled with cognitive bias (Theory Break 1.3).
All five voices contributing to this book have tried to describe experiences in a
way that provides useful insight for readers.

   Learning took place at three levels (refer to Figure 1.3):

- In the moment – level one learning.
- Soon afterwards as insight became evident – level two learning.

DOI: 10.4324/9781003367789-15

- Now, sometime later, as we have the opportunity to reflect on the amazing journey again while writing this book – level three learning.

There was a lot of learning, and no one could have anticipated how challenging, crazy and messy, yet rewarding and transformational the "experiment" and this case would be for all involved.

## Approach

Section A described the coaching approach used in this case as eclectic in that it did not follow a particular STC methodology. At the same time the approach was not particularly unusual, in that main interventions involved regular team development sessions and one-to-one coaching of team members and Michael (although mostly informal in execution).

Environmental conditions in the system were extremely challenging, including several structure changes, significant system and processes changes, "hailstorm(s)", team member changes, and ongoing impacts of "leaf spot." These environmental factors continually tested the Team, Michael, and me as Coach as we all navigated through the journey, building significant resilience and learning along the way.

The experimental nature of my internal role in Year One exaggerated many of the challenges and traps that can occur in STC (Hawkins, 2021, 2022). It is important to remember that team coaching was not a planned development intervention/approach for the Team at the beginning of the journey. Rather, it was something I brought into the system as the Coach in this case.

## Team growth

Despite the incidental way the development approach was selected, and the many challenges the Team faced throughout the three-year time frame, progress was evident, with improved HPT assessment and engagement scores in Years Two and Three. As described in Section B, the Team, Leader, Function and Organisation, and I also observed improved behaviour, collaboration, delegation, teamwork and more effective leadership styles. As Jane articulated, "We became a more effective and a much closer, tight-knit team. We shared leadership, we challenged each other, we knew each other better, we had each other's backs, and we had a lot of laughs! And another key thing – we all invested in the teams reporting to us more, so the benefits of our work flowed widely through the organisation."

## Systemic growth

The Team clearly gained by investing in development and Section B describes benefits reaching a much wider audience too – all five system elements grew as part of the experiment. Each chapter in Section B includes a long list of good, challenging and learnt aspects from each perspective. Michael and I, in particular, emphasise personal as well as professional growth by being part of this.

The benefits and impacts of the journey impacted other parts of the system, illustrating the coaching ripple effect (O'Connor & Cavanagh, 2013), and the entire CAS grew and matured. This experiment really was a holistic and transformational experience.

## Comparing perspectives – similarities

In Section C, learning and insight from the five perspectives in Section B was combined and compared to identify similarities and differences. This provided another level of insight – meta-reflection. Key similarities include:

### Strategy enablement and change management

- Ensure there is alignment between organisation-wide strategy and the Team's development goals and interventions.
- Use an integrated change management approach if change is significant, including formal sponsorship, measurement framework, progress reporting and risk management.

### Team development and coaching

- If a team does not seem "ready," start anyway, and tailor content to their maturity level.
- Adapt the HPT model to meet the needs of the team and environment.
- Team dynamics, investment in connection and psychological safety are all connected.
- Regular team development sessions are valuable, and proactively balance structure versus flexibility to maximise learning.
- One-to-one coaching of team members helps embed change.
- Expect bumps in the journey, it will not be a smooth ride.

- Team development and coaching supports both team and individual resilience.
- Elicit support from stakeholders and involve them throughout the journey.
- Growth in the team may expose other gaps in the system.
- Team coaching creates a ripple effect.
- Invest in good endings.

## Leadership development

- The leader's leadership style needs to align with the strategic direction of the team.
- There is no correct leadership style – it depends on the circumstances.
- One-to-one coaching of the leader helps embed change.
- Take care with relationship boundaries between leader and coach.
- Leadership style can change, an old dog can learn new tricks.

## Coaching in general

- There are pros and cons of internal versus external coaching.
- Coach character and style needs to align with needs of the team and environment.
- Coach role clarity and continuous multi-stakeholder contracting is vital.
- Experiment with co-coaching.
- The coach learns and develops along with the system.

## Coach support

- Ensure the coach has all the support they need.
- Both professional one-to-one and group supervision are important, particularly in complex situations, such as STC (Hawkins, 2021, 2022).
- Everyone involved in group supervision benefits.
- Informal support networks are valuable too.

While there was good alignment across all five perspectives on the points above, there were differences in priorities (refer to Table 9.1). The Team highlighted collective resilience. Michael emphasised leader as coach supporting EQ; the Function and Organisation emphasised their own involvement; and I, as Coach, prioritised holistic ongoing development.

Supervision and Other Support acknowledged their critical role in my development "village."

## Comparing perspectives – differences

There were some areas where misalignment between perspectives was more significant, which created tension within the system. Interestingly, as Chapter Ten shows, most differences were known by one/some parties at the time, but there were delays in addressing issues, and some were never addressed at all.

The key point here relates to the impact of choices within a CAS. Just one alternative choice made by one party, whether big or seemingly small, may have a significant impact and change the entire system and outcomes for all involved – just like a small choice in the movie *Sliding Doors* (Howitt, 1998).

## The future

All five system elements talk about their respective futures in Section C, and how they intend to apply experiences from this case to their work, life, and development journeys beyond Year Three.

All agree their journeys are not over, and the Team's primary focus is maintaining development momentum. Michael is concerned with applying his new leadership approach in a new role. Sally talks about ensuring that Green Apple Co is more involved going forward. I apply all I have learnt with new teams I work with, along with continued assistance from my Supervision and Other Support networks.

## Collective development journey

As mentioned above, the Team were not the only party to develop during this journey. All involved experienced significant professional and personal growth, and the entire system benefitted.

Figure 12.1 summarises changes experienced by each of the five system elements this book covers. The Team, Michael, Consulting Services and Green Apple Co and I all show an upward trend in development indicators. The requirement for Supervision and Other Support declined as I grew, which is also a positive outcome. (Note survey results and maturity assessments contained in Figure 12.1 are self-assessed by each system element and do not reflect 360 views of all stakeholders).

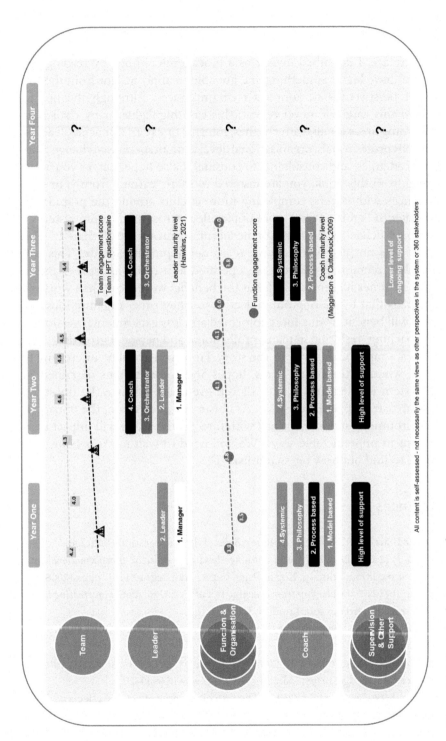

Figure 12.1: System changes over four years

## The end or the beginning?

In the Preface, I described myself as a pracademic. I hope by reading this book you have learnt something and are able to apply insight from the five different perspectives to your own circumstances. Although the unique events in this case will never repeat, this case highlights many challenges and learning areas for all team coaches, internal or external coaches, leaders, teams, HR professionals, organisational development specialists, change managers, academics, and consultants to consider. I also hope that, as you apply learning from this book, you are inspired to share learning from your own experiences with others, completing more circuits around the pracademic cycle (refer to Figure (i)) and more ripple effect across many more systems.

I quote Michael, as he sums up the learning journey we all shared: "This journey was not just a standalone team development exercise. This was a complete reengineer of how we operated as a team, as leaders and as people. At times it seemed hard, but the benefits were more than worth it. My hope is that by sharing our collective journey, other organisations and leaders will benefit from a more informed and less experimental version of team coaching, resulting in team, professional and personal growth."

"It is a wrap" for this part of the story. However, it will be interesting to observe whether the future plans, hopes and commitments described by each system element in Chapter Eleven eventuate – hence the questions marks in Year Four in Figure 12.1. As illustrated in this case, the impact of the environment and interactions within respective CASs will impact best-laid plans in unpredictable ways. We will need to wait for Year Four, "the sequel," to find out how big that impact is!

## References

González Iñárritu, A. (Director). (2006). *Babel* [Film]. Paramount Vantage.

Hawkins, P. (2021). *Leadership team coaching: developing collective transformational leadership*. 4th edition. London: Kogan Page. https://doi.org/10.1111/peps.12006_5.

Hawkins, P. (2022). *Leadership team coaching in practice: Case studies on creating highly effective teams*. 3rd edition. London: Kogan Page.

Howitt, P. (Director). (1998). *Sliding Doors* [Film]. Intermedia Films, Mirage Enterprises, Miramax.

Megginson, D. & Clutterbuck, D. (2009). *Further techniques for coaching and mentoring*. London: Routledge. https://doi.org/10.4324/9780080949420.

O'Connor, S. & Cavanagh, M. (2013). The coaching ripple effect: the effects of developmental coaching on wellbeing across organisational networks. *Psychology of Well-Being: Theory, Research and Practice*. 3:2. https://doi.org/10.1186/2211-1522-3-2.

# Index

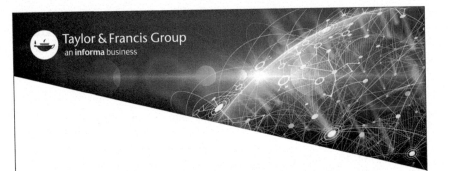